THE BOOK IN MOVEMENT

ILLUMINATIONS: CULTURAL FORMATIONS OF THE AMERICAS SERIES

John Beverley and Sara Castro-Klarén, Editors

THE
BOOK
IN
MOVEMENT

AUTONOMOUS POLITICS &
THE LETTERED CITY UNDERGROUND

MAGALÍ RABASA

UNIVERSITY OF PITTSBURGH PRESS

Published by the University of Pittsburgh Press, Pittsburgh, Pa., 15260
Copyright © 2019, University of Pittsburgh Press
All rights reserved
Manufactured in the United States of America
Printed on acid-free paper
10 9 8 7 6 5 4 3 2 1

ISBN 13: 978-0-8229-6587-9
ISBN 10: 0-8229-6587-9

Cataloging-in-Publication data is available from the Library of Congress

Cover design: Joel W. Coggins

**PARA CHEMA
Y
PARA OFELIA**

CONTENTS

ACKNOWLEDGMENTS

THIS BOOK is the product of over a decade of conversations and collective work with colleagues, family, friends, and compañerxs across the Americas. I began the project from my home just as a massive student protest movement was unfolding across the state of California. And as I was completing the last phase of my fieldwork, another rebellion erupted across the United States, and the home I returned to in Oakland was transformed by its energy. These local experiments with autonomy and resistance were not merely the backdrop for my studies and my writing; rather, they contributed directly to the ideas that appear in this book, in large part because they expanded the map of movement that unfolds in these pages by opening new dialogues and relations. As I write this, it is hard not to be filled with pessimism by the current state of affairs, but the collective action and energy of the people and places that appear in this book are a potent and continual expression of hope that energizes our present and futures.

While it would be impossible to name every person and place, I want to express my profound gratitude to all those who influenced and supported this project. I'd like to begin by thanking the many writers, presses, and collectives who so generously and openly shared their stories, experiences, and homes with me. In Mexico City, where this project really began in 2009, I especially want to thank all of my compañerxs in Jóvenes en Resistencia Alternativa and Bajo Tierra Ediciones, and especially my dear friends Mina and Gizella, for opening the collective, its history, and its futures to me. I also want to thank Mariana, Guiomar, and John for many years of conversation, encouragement, and friendship. In La Paz and El Alto, I thank Abraham, Waldo, Luis, Dunia, Oki, Marcelo, Pedro, Raúl, Claudia, Susan, and Nancy, and in Cochabamba, Alejandro. In Santiago, a hearty thank you to Lucia, Mario, Suijen, Gaby, and Pablo for opening their projects and sharing their stories with me. In Buenos Aires, my project was turned inside out and remade in ways I could never have imagined. For this, I first and foremost thank toda la flia de la FLIA, and especially Simón, Diego, Eze, Ale, Pablo, Jerónimo, Gaby, Germán, Geraldine, Matías, Daniela, Pablo, Marol, Florencia, and the compañeras of Radio FLIA/ La Pez en Bicicleta. La Cazona, La Gomera, El Pacha, La Libre, and El Asunto provided vibrant spaces for many of the projects and conversations that appear here. Many thanks to Claudia for her compañerismo and to Laura for her assistance with transcription. I am deeply grateful to Hernán for sharing the city with me and to Mabel and Pablo for their warmth and hospitality.

In Oakland, my compas in Radio Autonomía—Kayla, Ale, Profe, Nata, Pulga, Plebe, Luna, and La ChicaBoom—helped give new meaning to many of the questions and dreams that propel this book, and I thank you for your compañerismo on the air and in the streets. Many thanks to my friends and compas elsewhere with whom I have shared countless conversations and who have offered sharp feedback on many ideas and drafts, especially Dan Nemser, Mari Spira, Elisa Oceguera, Sampada Aranke, Liz Mason-Deese, Michal Osterweil, Ali Bektash, and Melissa Forbis. Thank you to Michelle, Chris, Jieun, Peter, and Nate for sharing in the experiment of making books together.

I've been a part of various intellectual and academic communities that allowed me to imagine and develop the questions and ideas that appear in this book. I truly don't think that this project, with its somewhat unconventional form, would have been possible anywhere but the doctoral program that was my institutional home at the University of California, Davis: the Cultural Studies Graduate Group. This program is, in many ways, a small pocket of resistance within the academy. The Estudios Culturales en las Américas research cluster I cofounded with Nick Sánchez and Robert McKee Irwin provided an essential space for thinking about my (non)discipline in a Latinx and Latin American perspective. Many thanks to all those friends and colleagues who gave such richness and rigor to my experience at UC Davis: Ingrid Lagos, Megan Bayles, Sampada Aranke, Sharada Balachandran-Orihuela, Abbie Boggs, Valerie Feldman, Michelle Yates, Elisa Oceguera, Ben D'Harlingue, Michelle Stewart, Chris Kortright, Nicholas Sánchez, Jake Culbertson, Emily Davidson, Isabel Porras, Tania Lizarazo, Julia Alejandra Morales Fontanilla, Diana Pardo Pedraza, and especially my radical cohort—CSLF—Terry Park, Elise Chatelain, Sara Bernstein, and Tallie Ben Daniel. The spectacular faculty at UC Davis offered me essential guidance and support in this project. Many thanks to Chuck Walker, Michael Lazzara, Parama Roy, Colin Milburn, Caren Kaplan, Eric Smoodin, Sergio de la Mora, and Angie Chabram. I thank Robert McKee Irwin for bringing me into the program and field of cultural studies and for his thoughtful and creative mentorship and friendship, throughout and beyond this project. Finally, this book would never have taken shape without my advisor, Marisol de la Cadena, who encouraged me and challenged me like nobody else ever has. She pushed me to find my place in ethnography, and it was her insistence that my project was not only in the stack of books on my desk but also crucially in the streets and workshops that led me to the many relations that appear in the pages of this book.

My path to this project began with the exceptional mentorship I received as an undergraduate at the University of Oregon, and I thank Analisa Taylor, Stephanie Wood, Carlos Aguirre, and Jesús Díaz-Caballero for their early, and ongoing, encouragement. Many thanks to my Social Science Research Council International Dissertation Research Fellowship cohort for helping me work through the first phase of writing, in particular Lisa Ubelaker and Steven Samford. I am grateful to my colleagues at the University of Kansas for their support in my first years as a faculty member, especially Santa Arias, Jorge Pérez, Stuart Day, David Roediger, Betsy Esch, Joo Ok Kim, Chris Perreira, Joshua Miner, Cécile Accilien, and Rachel Vaughn. And many thanks to my colleagues at Lewis and Clark College for making Portland my home and for providing the space and energy to see this project through.

In the final stages of preparing this book, many provided essential support, labor, and feedback. I am grateful to my friend and compañera Nancy Piñeiro for her work in translating and editing my writing so that it could travel more broadly. I thank Kate Wackett for her invaluable assistance in the final stages of revisions. I am tremendously grateful for Nate Freiburger's careful and thoughtful reading of multiple drafts of this book in its many versions. I thank the members of the FLIA for their comments and feedback on the zine version of this project that I circulated in 2016. And for their interest in and commitments to making this book multiple, through its translation and publication in the South, I thank Alejandro Schmied, Ezequiel Gatto, and Andrés Bracony. Many thanks to John Beverley and Sara Castro-Klarén for their early interest in and support of my book, and to my editor, Josh Shanholtzer, for his guidance and efforts in making these pages a book. I am very grateful to Juan Poblete for his insightful comments and to an anonymous reviewer for their thoughtful reflections and suggestions on my book and its potential.

My family has a special place in this project, which has roots in my experiences growing up but also in the things we share in our everyday life. Allison, thank you for the persistent support you've provided, even from great distances. My Midwest family I thank for making Kansas a home for us as I worked through the early stages of transforming this project into a book. My siblings—Baruch, Maya, Pablo, Santiago, and Ismael—thank you for helping me ground this work through daily reminders of how our many different paths can also be one. Bart, thank you for making Prince Street home to what is now a family obsession with the material life of books. My mother, Catherine, has not only been a source of inspiration for how to lead a balanced and creative life but has also provided endless material and emotional support for me in the multiple facets of my life as a mother and a scholar. And I thank her, too, for never hesitating to hit the streets to accompany movements and protests on the ground in the Bay Area as I followed and supported them from afar. As my teacher, colleague, friend, comrade, and interlocutor, my father is one of my most present and persistent cothinkers. I thank him for introducing me to those otros mundos for which Chiapas is just one name. Ofelia, mi corazón, this book is for you, because you make me see the world today and beyond with fresh eyes and a heart filled with joy and hope. More than anything, I thank Nate Freiburger, my partner, my compañero, and the thoughtful reader of every page I write, for his limitless support, patience, and love, and for making our rad little family together.

Research for this project was supported by funding from the UC Davis Chicana/Latina Research Center, the Tinker Graduate Research Award, the UC-MEXUS Dissertation Research Grant, the Advanced Graduate Research Fellowship from the Pacific Rim Research Program of the University of California, the Social Science Research Council International Dissertation Research Fellowship, the UC President's Graduate Fellowship in the Humanities, and the University of Kansas New Faculty General Research Fund, and the Faculty Development Fund at Lewis and Clark College.

Chapter 2 is derived in part from "Movement in Print: Migrations and Political Articulations in Grassroots Publishing" (2017), published in *Journal of Latin American Cultural Studies* 26, no. 1: 31–50, available online at https://doi.org/10.1080/13569325.2016.1272445. Part of chapter 3 appeared in "Notes on 'Organic IP' and Underground Publishing: Alternative Book Worlds in Latin America" (2014), published in *Anthropology Today* 30, no. 5: 20–23, available online at https://doi.org/10.1111/1467-8322.12133.

MAGALÍ RABASA

THE BOOK IN MOVEMENT

THE ORGANIC BOOK IN THE CONTINENT IN MOVEMENT

IT WAS still light out, late in the afternoon, and the line stretched down the block. Hundreds of young people, mostly teenagers from neighborhoods in the peripheries of the city, had traveled by some combination of foot, bus, and subway to make their way to the Colonia Roma in the center of Mexico City for a hip-hop show. The entrance to the venue, a steel roll-up door no wider than any other storefront on the block, was crowded with people waiting to pay their hundred pesos to get in the door. A "laboratorio de culturas subterráneas" (laboratory of underground cultures),[1] the Multiforo Alicia is a legendary venue for the underground Mexican rock and punk scene with an overtly radical political identity.[2] It borrows its name from *Alice in Wonderland* and adopted the Cheshire Cat as its logo. As I was pushed through the entrance and up the narrow stairs to the main auditorium, it almost felt like an inverted trip up the rabbit hole, and my senses were immediately scrambled as I made the abrupt transition from daylight to darkness, with little more illumination than the black lights picking up the graffiti-style mural covering an entire wall. For the next three hours, the space pulsed with the energy of the hundreds of bodies packed into the hot space—hands in the air (many holding camera phones), as the young fans recited the lyrics they had committed to memory of each and every song and spoken word piece. The organizers ensured the show wrapped up early so that the crowd would be able to get home before the subway stopped running at midnight. As I made my way back out to the street, I paused at the merchandise stand, where the most popular item being sold was not the usual CD or T-shirt, but rather a book.

The cover of the small book, *ImaRginación* by Aldo Villegas (also known as Bocafloja), features a well-known graffiti piece attributed to Banksy, "Kid Cowboy Brick Wall," on a weathered gray-green background.[3] Considered one of the forerunners of underground hip-hop in Mexico, Bocafloja has earned a broad international following through his collaborations with artists across the Americas. I had met Bocafloja in Chiapas the year before during the tour promoting his independently produced album *El manual de la otredad* (The Manual of Otherness). In the "Intro" to the album, he announces that this "manual de la otredad en este tiempo posmoderno" (manual of otherness in these postmodern times) reflects a "debate personal conmigo mismo" (personal debate with myself; Bocafloja 2007).[4] The rest of the album, like much of his discography, is laden with references to radical intellectuals from the Global South, so it came as no surprise to me when he told me of his plans to publish a manuscript. But I had no idea then that his book would eventually entangle me in the networks of writers, presses, and autonomous movements that would become the focus of this book.[5] I open with this story because I first dove into the underground worlds of books through the networks opened up to me by Bocafloja's book in Mexico City. In the four years that followed, I traveled further and further south, following a map that appeared to me as I moved across the continent—a map made of books.

The Book in Movement is about the print book in the networks of autonomous movements that zigzag across Latin America today. It follows the production and distribution practices of underground political publishing networks that accompany these current movements as they create and disseminate a new body of political theory articulated by and with the generation politicized at the turn of the twenty-first century. An integral part of the autonomous movements' conceptual production is their dialogical connection with experiences and struggles beyond their own local realities. As the ideas generated from the movements travel in unprecedented ways, multidimensional networks are multiplying across the continent. But in a historical moment constantly described with abstract concepts like *globalized* and *networked*, important questions arise about the concrete dimensions of such connectedness. This is why *The Book in Movement* asks the following questions: what is the stuff—the materiality—of these networks? What are the durable tools and technologies that make these connections persist, enabling the politics to expand and reproduce? To explore these questions, I focus on a specific material practice in the autonomous networks: the print book.

"SOMOS VOCEROS DE NUESTRA PROPIA EXISTENCIA"

The summer after *ImaRginación* was published, I was back in Mexico City where I met the publishers of the book: an anticapitalist youth collective that had recently started a small press.[6] I was intrigued by the apparent anachronism of the production of print books, not only in the context of such a digitally oriented medium like hip-hop but also in the young activist scene that the publishers are a part of. The collective is made up of young people who, like me, were politicized at the turn of the twenty-first century and cite the Zapatista uprising in Chiapas and the broader transnational alterglobalization movement as formative influences.[7] Indeed, as Argentine militant theorist Verónica Gago writes, "la insurgencia Zapatista . . . marca a toda una generación militante a escala planetaria" (2017a, 1; the Zapatista insurgence . . . frames an entire generation of activists at the planetary scale [2017b, 4]). The Zapatistas, like other autonomous movements, make strategic use of the internet and other digital technologies not just as propaganda tools but as fundamental axes of their anticapitalist praxis.

I use the term "autonomous" to refer to movements that, distinct from their leftist revolutionary antecedents, are not defined by any ostensive category, like class, party, or identity. Rather, these popular movements and experiments with autonomous politics are defined by their practices, including self-organization, horizontalism, cooperativism, and mutual aid. In this way, the twenty-first century movements, which as many have said are everywhere,[8] are characterized by their shift away from programmatic and top-down approaches to political organizing and privilege dialogue and communication as their basic modes while working from the everyday to build prefigurative politics.[9] While there is a significant body of scholarship dedicated to analyzing the new Latin American movements, this North-South attention has replicated the kind of intellectual imperialism that the region's scholars so poignantly denounce. Gago writes:

> Y justo cuando América Latina devenía una suerte de escena de vanguardia de la insurgencia, parecía quedar minorizada su producción conceptual, que no se podía ver sino como siempre tutelada. Como si no pudiese pensarse lo que aquí sucede más que como un aderezo experiencial para una adecuación bibliográfica que sigue el ritmo de 'modas' o teorías dominantes. (2017a, 2)

> And precisely when Latin America was becoming a sort of vanguard scene of insurgency, its conceptual production remained marginalized and was only ever seen as in need of tutelage. As if what happens here in Latin America could not be understood as anything more than the experiential dressing for a bibliographical adaptation that follows the rhythm of "fashions" or dominant theories (2017b, 5).

What she signals here is the failure or, worse yet, refusal of academics to recognize and value the wealth of intellectual production being generated *from* Latin America. This not only perpetuates the dynamics of intellectual imperialism and "asymmetrical ignorance" (Chakrabarty 2000) that fields like postcolonial, subaltern, and decolonial studies so compellingly critique but also the troubling binary between thought and action. The movements that have brought global attention to Latin America have done so, in large part, because of their tremendously innovative and creative use of media in self-representation.

Medios libres (independent or free media) is the name given to the diverse and decentralized networks of media producers who participate in and accompany the autonomous movements. This phenomenon became most visible, starting in the late 1990s, through the open online platform known as Indymedia, which grew into countless locally coordinated webpages—Indymedia Chiapas, Indymedia Seattle, IndyBay, Indymedia Athens, and so on—that anyone could freely access and contribute to with text, video, photography, or audio. The abundance of online media has been crucial for autonomous movements, including Zapatismo, as it has enabled the creation of direct channels of communication with the world. In doing so, the movements also contest the silence and misinformation imposed and perpetuated by the "mainstream" or "commercial" media, often described as a *cerco informativo/ mediático* (media/information siege or barrier). Digital and cybernetic technology is what allows communiqués and news to spread rapidly around the planet, as was the case with the Ejército Zapatista de Liberación Nacional's (EZLN) "Declaración de la Selva Lacandona" (Declaration of the Lacandon Jungle) on January 1, 1994.[10] But despite the vital place of *medios libres* in Zapatismo and the alterglobalization movements, there has long been a tension between the efficacy and reach of online media and the importance of face-to-face relations for building political networks *desde abajo* (from below).

In *Toma los medios, sé los medios, haz los medios* (Take the media, be the media, make the media), the Centro de Medios Libres (2013, 9) in Mexico asserts:

> Para romper un cerco informativo el problema no son las máquinas sino las personas que las echan a andar. La comunicación la hacen personas de carne y hueso, pero vivimos en una época de amor a las máquinas que nos impide comunicarnos. Hemos olvidado el sabor de las conversaciones a pie de parque, de escalera o de caminata, y creemos que tal o cual máquina logrará que tengamos comunicaciones eficientes. Lo importante es la parte humana, las nuevas relaciones sociales y las redes de comunicación de calle, pero ya no miramos ahí.

To break with the information siege, the problem is not the machines, but the people who make them work. Communications are made by flesh and bones people, but we live in an era of love of machines that impedes us from communicating with each other. We've forgotten the taste of conversations in the park, in the stairs, or on a walk, and we think that this or that machine will make it so we can have efficient communications. What is important is the human aspect, the new social relations and the street networks of communications, but we don't look there anymore.

The "seduction of machines," they caution, has created too great an emphasis on the *tools* of communication, eclipsing the vitality of the *social relations* that drive and shape them. The shift away from each other and toward machines, as they say, is a tension that must be recognized and interrogated critically. This book represents an attempt to work constructively from that tension. It is about how an object—the print book—makes and is made of relations.

As the title suggests, *The Book in Movement* is about a particular kind of book: it's about a book that is *in movement*, a book that is being recrafted and transformed as part of an emerging alternative political-economic praxis. I develop this idea of the *book in movement* by combining two sets of ideas. The first comes from historian of science Adrian Johns, whose groundbreaking 1998 work *The Nature of the Book* represents a new approach to thinking about how books are made and what they do. By offering a "new historical understanding of print" (Johns 1998, 28), he calls into question the apparent stability of the book as cultural artifact—as well as modern approaches to understanding print culture—by zooming in on the objects themselves. In this sense, I borrow from Johns a view of the print book as fluid, an object in movement. Johns's work on the history of the book represents a significant pivot in the way that this object is approached, most significantly through his compelling presentation of an alternative to Elizabeth Eisenstein's widely accepted notion of print culture as characterized by an inherent fixity. He writes, "We may consider fixity not as an *inherent* quality, but as a *transitive* one. . . . We may adopt the principle that fixity exists only inasmuch as it is recognized and acted upon by people—and not otherwise. . . . This approach allows us to recover the construction of different print cultures in particular historical circumstances" (Johns 1998, 20–21). As he goes on to assert, this approach places the social and the cultural at the center of our analysis of print. This is, of course, of tremendous significance for studies like my own that shift attention away from the centers of Euro-American cultural production to more marginal sites.

The second key set of ideas represents a rupture with the common language of "social movements." In my research I follow several books by Uruguayan militant and journalist Raúl Zibechi. Following decades of militancy in his home country and his exile in Spain, over the past two decades, he has accompanied new social movements across the Americas, documenting and analyzing new modes of rebellion in the twenty-first century. Through his panoramic perspective and his on-the-ground practice as a journalist, he proposes the language of "societies in movement." With this shift in language, he suggests a way of thinking less in terms of bounded movements as entities that can be easily named and identified and more in terms of the "societal movement." He borrows this idea from Bolivian philosopher Luis Tapia as a means of accounting for the varied and continually shifting forms of collective action and alternative social relations that emerge not only through formal organizations but also through quotidian processes of cooperation and dialogue.[11] Zibechi's and Tapia's ideas help us to think about spaces like Bolivia, where the popular rebellions since 2000 are difficult to describe in any singular terms. And with the broader idea of the continent in movement, Zibechi also helps us think about the region as a whole as experiencing movement, recognizing that the map that is emerging from below is not one of discrete social movements but rather of expanding webs of dialogue, influence, and coordination through which actors in Mexico, for example, become *articulated* with others in Argentina, or Chile, or Bolivia. Following Stuart Hall, I use the concept of *articulation* in the sense of a connection that is not fixed nor permanent, where the elements being connected are made and remade by their relations. In an interview, Hall explained, "An articulation is thus a connection that *can* make a unity of two different elements, under certain conditions. It is a linkage which is not necessary, determined, or absolute for all time. You have to ask under what conditions can a connection be forged or made. So the so-called unity of a discourse is really the articulation of different, distinct elements which can be rearticulated in different ways because they have no necessary 'belongingness'" (S. Hall 1996c, 142–43). The books I examine, like the relations that make them, are products and processes of such articulation. Maps, in this sense, are not spatial representations of a Euclidean cartography but rather a name I give to the appearance of multidimensional connections that span across territories.

The Book in Movement is about what books are and what books do in *the continent in movement*. But of all the things and people and processes that exist in this context, why focus on the print book specifically? This project began with a curiosity: why would young people be taking up the historic craft of printing and book production as part of an autonomous political praxis in the technologically advanced age of the early twenty-first century? What does the print book *do* in the networks of movements in an increasingly interconnected continent? And how does it relate to other media? The things people make when they come together face-to-face can be both tools and objectives in

FIGURE I.1. Mural, La Paz, 2011.

themselves—they have meaning not only as products but also as processes of social and material relations. Print books differ from other kinds of media in that their production almost always requires the participation of a collective of actors. Even today, it is extremely rare to find a book that has been written, designed, printed, and bound by a single person, whereas pamphlets, blogs, zines, documentaries, even music albums can easily be seen as the product of an individual producer when the components of their production are black-boxed, as they almost always are. While many writers and artists will state that their ideas or works are the result of collective processes and acknowledge the influence of others that they have worked with, in the case of print books, the collective and social character of the process is more than just symbolic.

Recognizing the convergence of people, machines, and materials in book production, Johns writes that "a printed book can be seen as a nexus conjoining a wide range of worlds of work" (1998, 3). Following Johns, I develop a transdisciplinary approach that combines object-oriented ethnographic methods with textual analysis to explore the varied arrangements of actors (both human and nonhuman) and ideas that the book articulates. In this approach, much of the conventional vocabulary used to describe and talk about books becomes inadequate. Terms such as "author," "authorship," and "knowledge," as well as "intellectual property," "intellectual" and "manual labor," "production," "distribution," and "reception," among others, are either transformed or lose their analytical utility. These terms anchor each of my chapters, as I place them into dialogue with the concepts proposed by the books I examine.

Throughout the book, I combine ethnographic narratives describing the *practices* through which the writers, presses, and movements make and circulate their books with theoretical analysis of the *concepts* these publications disseminate. In doing so, I argue that as a unique cultural artifact, the print book is double: it is the materialization of an alternative political-economic praxis that its pages—which is to say, its content—also propose. The book in movement is organic to the political practices it describes. It is a book made of the very practices that it transmits through its text. Like these practices, it is continually changing as it moves between people and places. It grows as it moves; it becomes something more while remaining the same. For these reasons, the concept I propose and develop in this book is that of the *organic book*. Like many of the concepts that emerge from autonomous politics and travel through the books, the organic book is a *concept-practice*: it can be thought of in substantive as well as processual terms. But rather than further introduce this concept abstractly, I first want to show it in practice.

THE ORGANIC BOOK

In 1995, within just months of each other, two books were published from within two prisons in the city of La Paz, Bolivia: *Forma valor y forma comunidad* (Value form and community form) by Álvaro García Linera and ¡A desordenar! *Por una historia abierta de la lucha social* (To disorder! For an open history of social struggle) by Raquel Gutiérrez Aguilar. The authors were both members of the Ejército Guerrillero Tupaj Katari (EGTK), a majority Aymara military and political organization that operated clandestinely in the 1980s in the *altiplano* of Bolivia. In 1992 García Linera and Gutiérrez Aguilar were detained and subsequently tortured for their political activity. The couple met in Mexico in the early 1980s, when they were both students at the National Autonomous University of Mexico (UNAM), and later traveled back to García Linera's home country, Bolivia, where they helped found the EGTK with Felipe Quispe.[12]

The two books could not be more different in their tone and approach, but they were intimately connected by not only the personal ties between their authors and their presence in the pages of each others' books but also in the conditions from which they emerged. The authors were not released for nearly two more years, after a total of five years of incarceration without any formal trial or sentencing. The first book came out of the men's prison at Chonchocoro, a dense and intensive study of Marx's *Capital* interpreted alongside chronicles of indigenous experiences from the colonial period.[13] The second was produced within the walls of the Obrajes women's prison, a combination

FIGURE I.2. Bookseller's boxes, La Paz, 2011.

of call to action and "narración autobiográfica y autocrítica" (autobiographical, self-critical narrative; Gutiérrez Aguilar 2006, 15).

Both books were created as responses to the grueling and painful tedium of indefinite detention: they were conceived as tools to support the authors in their battles to survive the brutal conditions of their incarceration, as well as tools that could contribute to the broader political struggles they were connected to outside the prison walls. Both books emerged from a need to make sense of what the authors were living while analyzing the broader historical-political contexts they came from and to which they hoped to contribute. Both were produced through the collective effort of many people: those who fought alongside the authors in the urban guerrilla, the communities they engaged with, the prisoners they lived alongside, the comrades who supported them materially and politically from outside, and the other writers, thinkers, and communities whose ideas they dialogue with in the pages of the books. These books were both the result of decades of political organizing *and* the starting point for future endeavors, and both would go on to be reedited multiple times, acquiring new life as each new edition traveled its own course.

The books that Gutiérrez Aguilar and García Linera wrote from prison are significant for many reasons. The first is that they reflect a watershed moment for radical politics in Latin America: a transition between the earlier vanguardist tradition of the revolutionary parties and armed insurgencies of the 1960s to 1980s and the new autonomous, horizontal politics of which the Zapatistas were perhaps the earliest expression. Gutiérrez Aguilar, herself from Mexico, describes the enormous joy and excitement she felt when she learned about the Zapatista uprising in 1994 while incarcerated in Bolivia. The exercise of writing her book from prison was, as she puts it, a product of thinking from that conjunction: "Esta reflexión está escrita . . . buscando tender un puente entre dos tradiciones de lucha; quiere ser una especie de traducción entre ambas" (This reflection is written . . . as an attempt to bridge two different traditions of struggle; it wants to be a kind of translation between them; Gutiérrez Aguilar 2006, 12).

The second reason is that they fall into a long history of carceral writing by political prisoners. While there are too many experiences to enumerate here, the trajectory I want to highlight connects the urban prisons in La Paz where Gutiérrez Aguilar and García Linera were incarcerated and tortured in the early 1990s to the prison in Turi, Italy, where Marxist political philosopher Antonio Gramsci famously penned his *Prison Notebooks* in the decade leading up to his death at the age of forty-six. Like the writings of so many political prisoners, they were all composed clandestinely, with varying degrees of encryption. They were able to be created and published through the efforts of networks of friends, comrades, and family members who provided vital support to the prisoners. But most of all, they are all books that exemplify one of Gramsci's most poignant assertions: that ideas emerge from *organic intellectual practice.*

Among Gramsci's most influential ideas is his differentiation between what he calls "traditional" and "organic" intellectuals. Whereas traditional intellectuals are situated as independent from other social groupings, organic intellectuals are identified with the interests of the class or group they think with and from. He explains the distinction as rooted in the place, not of ideas and thought, but of *practice*: "The mode of being of the new intellectual can no longer consist in eloquence, which is an exterior and momentary mover of feelings and passions, but in active participation in practical life, as constructor, organiser, 'permanent persuader' and not just a simple orator" (Gramsci 1971, 10). The *organicità*, or organic quality, of the intellectual practice connects materiality and ideation. Organic intellectuals are products and generators of the shared material conditions of collectivities of actors—in Gramsci's terms, a class. The contrast that Gramsci develops between traditional and organic intellectuals can also be understood in terms of the discussion of the term "organic" provided by Raymond Williams in *Keywords*. He explains that in the sixteenth century, the word "organicall" first appeared in descriptions of tools and engines as the opposite of "mechanicall" (Williams 1983, 227). He describes later usages of the term "organic," including "organic community" (versus the organized modern state) and "organic solidarity" (versus mechanical solidarity; Williams 1983, 228–29). In the varying senses of the term, Williams makes clear that a common element is the idea that what organic describes is a "kind of relationship" (1983, 229). Fellow Birmingham School theorist Stuart Hall's development of the concept makes evident the centrality of relationality to the concept of organic.

One of the most creative and insightful interpreters of Gramscian thought, Stuart Hall develops the notion of *organic ideology*: "Gramsci is never only concerned with the philosophical core of an ideology; he always addresses organic ideologies, which are organic because they touch practical, everyday, common sense and they 'organize human masses and create the terrain on which men move, acquire consciousness of their position, struggle, etc.'" (1996b, 431). Organic intellectuals—and the ideas they develop—are permanently engaged in the political practice they theorize, narrate, and relate. Gramsci's attention to materiality in intellectual and ideological practice is not unique—feminist theorists, for example, have also emphasized the embodied and material dimensions of critical thought—but his contributions to Marxist theory are so powerful precisely because of the ways he rejects reductionist approaches. As Hall so clearly conveys, Gramsci's work is best approached not as theory but as method, as a practical perspective—this is the crux of the Gramscian philosophy of praxis.

As I conceptualize the organic book, I am thinking with Gramsci and other praxis-oriented political theorists for whom there is no division between materiality and ideas. The organic book in this sense is a concept that is also an object that is also a practice. It defies categorization as its form and meaning are continually shifting. The organic book is a political-material object made of relations—it is never alone, and it is always connected to other books, other objects, other spaces, other actors. While Walter Benjamin and others have rightly insisted on the need to "insert [the book] into the context of living social relations," which are "determined by production relations" (1998, 87), I suggest that the organic book *is* a living social relation that unsettles the production relations of its time.

As I stated before, the organic book is a particular kind of book—an improper book that doesn't necessarily act like commercial, academic, elite, private, or other proper books. By the "proper book" I mean the object that Johns describes as the modern book (1998, 1), which is characterized by certain features and assumptions about the individualism ascribed to its authorship, the consistency of its content across copies and editions, its legal apparatus, its commercial value, and so on. These assumed characteristics—about the social, political, technical, and economic qualities of the book—as I will show, are thrown into question when we begin to examine the organic book. Significantly, I want to show how the organic book is *not* simply another version of the modern book, understanding the modern book to be that which is always also the colonial book, as modernity and coloniality are inseparable from the view of the colonized (Quijano 1999; Mignolo 2005; Lugones 2008). The classificatory schemes of the "coloniality of power" (Quijano 1999) work alongside those generated by the "author function" (Foucault 1998) and together define the "modern book."

The definition of the modern book is almost singularly focused on the question of authorship and utilizes the double function that authorship plays: as description for that which is authored and designation of particular attributes to both author and authored work (Foucault 1998, 210). Authorship becomes the primary attribute of the work through the way it creates an equivalence between author and text and in the work this equivalence performs in terms of classification. Concerns about authorship—particularly when taken as the central dimension of the modern book—carry the consequence of directing attention to relatively few dynamics of the book as a whole. These dynamics are those of appropriation (ownership), authority (valorization stemming from the identity of the individualized writer), and psychologization (the relation of the elements of the text or book reduced to the psychological character of its individual author). These are the very dynamics thrown into flux by the organic book.

The organic book is not a modification of the modern book but rather a book that challenges (or has the potential to challenge) the very notion of Eurocentric modernity through its interaction with *collectively imagined and executed* anticapitalist, antistate, anti-authoritarian, antipatriarchal, and anticolonial practices. I want to stress the *potential* because what is at play is, of course, not a wholly or purely transformed or even transformative object but rather one that represents *an attempt* to foster a different kind of encounter that critically acknowledges the relational privileges that have historically been bound to the object of the book. In this sense, the organic book is an autonomous object that emerges not from institutional dynamics and structures (nor a singular individual author) but rather from collective practices of experimentation and becoming. As I explore in greater depth in chapters 1 and 2, as an effect of such continuous and contingent processes and desires, the autonomy of the organic book is never complete—it is always in a state of production and reproduction. The organic book transforms what a book is and does both materially and politically as it emerges from the very practices it describes. As an organic object, it is sometimes unclear where one book begins and another ends. It is both a product and a process: not a fixed object but a "machine" that moves and exists in connection to other machines (Bratich 2007; Deleuze and Guattari 1987; Kirschenbaum 2008). As such, the organic book could be described as rhizomatic, to borrow from Gilles Deleuze and Félix Guattari—it is infinitely connected and can only be understood through its movement and the relations it makes. And these relations, like the organic object they accompany, are laden with tensions and contradictions. The task of *The Book in Movement* is to make a map—a description of spaces and forms of articulation—of the organic book by following the ruptures and connections that its production and circulation make visible.[14]

THE LETTERED CITY UNDERGROUND

The organic book is not in itself new. It has roots in early twentieth-century anarchist traditions in Latin America, where a political-intellectual project autonomous from the parties—and in tension with the university—emerged as a challenge to the hegemony of state knowledge regimes (Rama 1984). As Ángel Rama explains, anarchist thought at the turn of the century emphasized "la necesidad de una educación popular . . . que abarcara todos los aspectos de la vida y no sólo los políticos, en una cosmovisión nueva: las relaciones de trabajo, la vida familiar, los derechos de la mujer de los que sería primer proponente, la solidaridad con los trabajadores, la lucha contra el alcoholismo y también contra los curas, la alfabetización de niños y adultos, etc." (1984, 161–62; the need for a popular education . . . that was holistic, and went beyond politics: including labor relations, family life, the rights of women [of which the anarchists were forerunners in their defense], the struggle against alcoholism, anticlericalism, child and adult literacy, etc. [1996, 118]). The insistence on conceiving intellectual and political activity as inextricably linked to a more holistic concept of life is a hallmark of anarchism, and the methods developed for the publication and dissemination of anarchist texts connected the various facets of social, political, cultural, economic, and material life Rama alludes to.[15] The organic book, in this sense, is a materialization of that anarchist ethic. While there were impressive circuits of communication and influence connecting anarchist tendencies across the continent a hundred years ago, a defining characteristic of the organic book today in the *continent in movement* is the contemporary experience of autonomous politics as rhizomatically networked. The networked form that I explore in this project is a constitutive quality of the organic book today and is the unique product of the merging of the historic craft of printing, as a powerful practice and medium of articulation (in the sense of both expression and connection), and the new cybernetic and digital technologies that expand the speed, scale, and accessibility of communications.[16] In this sense, the print book today is an old medium being made new.

In a context of increased, and indeed extreme, concentration of publishing in the hands of multinational conglomerates, there has also been an explosion of alternatives, albeit small, to the capitalist model of publishing.[17] Craig Epplin (2014, 19) describes the contours of "late book culture" in Latin America, and specifically Argentina, as shaped by the same "technologies that make the operations of late capitalism possible," making "nearly all literature today . . . electronic in some sense." This includes the full spectrum of book culture, from the bestsellers by Grupo Santillana to the artisanal editions by *cartonera* presses. With my conceptualization of the organic book, I focus on a specific renewal or reinvention of the print book that is a direct product of the new modes of grassroots mobilization and networking that characterize autonomous politics in the twenty-first century. Like other scholars examining contemporary independent publishing in Latin America (Astutti and Contreras 2001; Vanoli 2010; Epplin 2014; de Diego 2014), I consider how the conjunction of old and new tools has several significant impacts for the book form by enabling greater decentralization of the production and circulation process. Three elements are particularly important to examining how the book is recrafted as a tool of autonomous political-economic praxis in the twenty-first century. First, the widespread use of personal computers and digital technologies has expanded access to publishing. Second, alternative presses increasingly adopt noncommercial licensing tools, encouraging the free circulation of texts. And third, the internet allows presses to rapidly exchange texts across vast territorial distances.

As I started to track the repeated publication of certain titles and authors, a loose and shifting network of small presses began to appear before me, connected in part by a set of common characteristics (or perhaps better stated, common ethics or principles): (1) a commitment to producing low-cost books; (2) an autonomous political perspective (vis-à-vis the state, the academy, and capital); (3) a praxis of *autogestión*; (4) a commitment to collective forms of organization; (5) use of public space in the circulation of books; and (6) engagement in local and transnational political networks of presses, writers, and movements.[18] In combination, these principles suggest an antagonistic relationship to capitalism and the commodification of books, as well as a strategic use of grassroots forms of articulation. More broadly, this dynamic mirrors the autonomous politics of the movements that the texts and the presses engage. What distinguishes the organic book from other books is the way that the characteristics and principles listed above are visible not only in its content but also, significantly, in the object itself and the ways it moves in the world. These are the principles that came to guide my selection of the books and presses I sought out in my fieldwork, as I moved through the many undergrounds of what Ángel Rama named *la ciudad letrada* (the lettered city).

Rama develops this concept through his historical analysis of the unique nexus of urbanization, print culture, and colonial and neocolonial state power. By examining the place of the *letrados*—"men of letters," the lettered elite tied to the state institutions—Rama argues that writing and print culture have been central to the production and maintenance of (colonial) state power in the continent. While the boundaries defining inclusion in the lettered city have become progressively blurred, the hierarchies of knowledge and power that Rama examines remain visible today. And as Rama discusses in "La ciudad revolucionada," the final chapter of his groundbreaking work *La ciudad letrada*, in the twentieth century the lettered city began to experience a "revolution" through, among other factors, the growth of popular education initiatives and the greater visibility of underground knowledge practices.[19] The organic book is a contemporary expression of that underground and the alternative socioeconomic relations it fosters translocally. So while Rama's concept works to make visible the modes of domination maintained and extended by the written word—and its primary vehicle, the book—in rethinking the lettered city in the twenty-first century, I seek to expand on what he proposes in that final chapter. By looking at the contemporary underground of both political theory and book publishing, I show the ways that the organic book represents something like a "revolution in the revolution," in which the persistent, if at times disguised, mechanisms of neocolonial domination and exclusion are challenged anew through the political *and* material transformation of the object of the book itself.

Rama's concept of the lettered city is focused rather generally on "Latin America's great cities," but it is important to recognize the significant differences between the distinct urban and national contexts. In my research, I have sought to account for the heterogeneous contemporary formations of the lettered city as I zoom in on not only a diversity of cities (Mexico City, La Paz, Buenos Aires, Santiago de Chile) but also the connections and tensions that emerge between them. The rhizomatic networks of the organic book are a site where we can detect a disruption of the coloniality of power and knowledge and the ordering of the lettered city: this double object (as the materialization of the praxis its content proposes) articulates the epistemological, the economic, and the social in a concept-practice. And while the organic book is most certainly not a phenomenon exclusive to Latin America, the historic and contemporary dynamics of the continent make its existence and potential especially visible.

The organic book is the product of "the insurrection of subjugated knowledges" in which "intellectual others" disrupt the modern colonial flow of knowledge that characterizes Rama's lettered city (Aparicio and Blaser 2008, 71–72). As Aparicio and Blaser (2008, 72–73) argue, such knowledge practices are "contaminating" the lettered city through "successive small changes" that "are noteworthy because of their eventual aggregate significance in the reconfiguration of power/knowledge." While they focus on knowledge practices, I am especially interested in the *materiality* of those practices as it manifests in the production and circulation of the organic book. What is at stake then is not simply a *redeployment* of the oppressive tools of the lettered city for liberatory ends—the "master's tools" Audre Lorde famously cautioned against—but rather a *reconfiguration* of the tools of power/knowledge produced by collaborative and often conflictive encounters between what Aparicio and Blaser (2008, 83) name "insurrectional and modern knowledge-practices." Just as they recognize that the changes we are witnessing are "small," I want to acknowledge too the extremely marginal place of the organic book: it occupies the *underground* of not only the lettered city but also the "revolutionized" lettered city and represents an "alternative to the alternative," as one publisher said to me.

PROVINCIALIZING THE HISTORY OF THE BOOK

The Book in Movement takes up Roger Chartier's (1992) now well-rehearsed query "Do books make revolutions?" shifting the view away from Europe to a context virtually invisible in book studies and especially contemporary book studies: Latin America. My study of the materiality of autonomous politics in twenty-first-century Latin America is an explicit attempt to make visible the ways that marginal groups subvert the universalisms and Eurocentrism endemic to dominant practices of knowledge production. In his now classic 2000 book, subaltern studies theorist Dipesh Chakrabarty makes a call to "provincialize Europe" as a means of countering the "asymmetric ignorance" that governs the production and flow of knowledge between "Europe" and the rest of the world. For Chakrabarty "Europe" is not a geographic location but rather a political, cultural, economic, social, and above all, epistemological referent: it is how he names the Eurocentrism that pervades not only Europe proper but the world. With his call to "provincialize Europe," Chakrabarty argues for a reorientation of history and theory that does not rely on "Europe" (or "the West" or "the North"). As I focus on a very particular object, the book, I dialogue with the rich conversations occurring in what is traditionally called the "history of the book" while recognizing the rampant Eurocentrism of this field.

I want to *provincialize* the history of the book through a twofold intervention. First, by introducing a contemporary Latin American perspective to the field, my aim is to bring greater visibility to the particularities of print culture as it exists outside of the academic and commercial publishing circuits, which most certainly take "Europe" as their point of reference (literally and figuratively). Latin American literary studies has long been concerned with the colonial roots—and persistent legacy—of print culture in the continent, and much has been written about the book in the colonial period and the

FIGURE I.3. Archive, Buenos Aires, 2011.

period of nation-building that followed independence. And while there is a rich literature emerging on new media in the region, the print book in the late twentieth and early twenty-first century has received limited attention. In this sense, I am interested in something akin to the "de-europeanizing" move that Benedict Anderson (1983) proposes in his study of nationalism, by emphasizing the significance of Latin America for contemporary book studies. With my particular interest in networks of alternative book production and circulation, I contribute a transnational approach to a small but growing body of scholarship on the recent history of publishing in Latin America. This includes studies of the Argentine context by Epplin (2014) and de Diego (2014), the Chilean context by Subercaseaux (2000) and Griffin (2016), and the Mexican context by Salazar Embarcadero (2011). These nationally focused studies emphasize the interplay between the heightened centralization and commercialization of publishing by transnational conglomerates and the rapid increase in alternative and independent publishing in the late twentieth and early twenty-first centuries. This body of scholarship also includes recent work by Marcy Schwartz (2011, 2014, 2016, 2018) on book culture in Latin American cities, in which she examines the social uses of the book through a focus on the movement of this object in urban space. Like Schwartz (2014, 421), I am interested in the "cartographies of . . . books that are not only part of larger landscapes of power, but also often resist or escape these power dynamics." With my transnational and transdisciplinary approach, I combine insights about the knowledge practices of recent social movements with analysis of the production and circulation practices of small presses. In doing so, I propose that what is at stake in the ways that knowledge (and significantly book) production is being reimagined is the formation of a different "lettered city," characterized by both an expansion of capitalist regimes and growing popular contestation to such models.

My second point of intervention as I work to provincialize the history of the book is more methodological. I am interested in shifting away from the disciplinarily situated historical and literary approaches that dominate the "history of the book" to develop a transdisciplinary perspective, which Jonathan Rose (2003) and others have called for under the umbrella of "book studies." Such approaches call into question textual stability and the fixity of print by paying particular attention to how the book works as a process while attending to its physicality and materiality (Howsam 2006). As Johns (1998, 61) asserts, assessing the significance of a book cannot be limited to analyzing its text—there are extensive webs of interconnected yet discrete domains, or in his words, "worlds of work," that must also be considered to account for the significance of the book. Johns proposes the notion of a "topography" (61) of the places of print as a way to assess the various articulated domains of the book. What emerges from such a topographical exercise is a multidimensional map not only of objects and materials but also of relations. I extend the insights of these interdisciplinary approaches by exploring what an *ethnography* of the print book can do for our understanding of the relations that are making—and that are made by—the continent in movement.[20] To this end, I draw on recent scholarship in anthropology and science and technology studies, and especially object-oriented ethnography, which offers valuable ideas for thinking about materials, relations, and networks of heterogeneous actors (human and nonhuman) through a focus on processes and materiality.[21]

In these ways, *The Book in Movement* is situated at the nexus of cultural studies and anthropology, bringing a view of and from Latin America today to the interdisciplinary field of book studies. In doing so, it endeavors to develop a political history of the present, through the examination of a specific cultural-historical conjuncture (Grossberg 2006; S. Hall 1992). While it may seem obvious, studies of the current moment are somewhat rare in book studies. As Craig Epplin (2014, 11) argues, the well established *history of the book* has given way to obsessions about the *future of the book*, with scholars largely overlooking the *present of the book*. Like Epplin I am concerned with the "constant formation of that present" (11) as I navigate the underground spaces of the book's production and circulation in Latin America today.

CAMINAR PREGUNTANDO

Before starting this project, in a short period of time I encountered a number of the same titles in bookstores and book fairs in different countries: Colombia, Peru, Mexico, and Bolivia. But each time, in each place, the books looked different. They had different covers, different textures, different prices, different weights. They were all produced by different presses: small, local publishers that for the most part could be described as "independent" or "alternative." My initial thought was, why not just ship the books from one country to another? Why go through the trouble of republishing a book that is already in print in another place? As I scoured the internet to learn more about the various presses (and others like them that I learned existed across the continent) and started to have conversations with participants in these projects, I began to understand that the answer was quite simple: it's far too expensive for small-scale presses to ship a heavy and cumbersome product like a book internationally. And while commercial and academic publishing is concentrated in a few major cities (Mexico City, Buenos Aires), a great deal of books sold in Latin America are produced in or through Spain or Spanish publishing conglomerates—an unsurprising yet nevertheless unsettling reflection of the persistent neocolonial dynamics that continue to shape cultural production in the continent today. But as I intuited then and later came to understand in greater depth, the economics of highly centralized commercial publishing and distribution is completely distinct from the calculations and metrics of utility that govern small-scale alternative book production.

It became apparent to me that any exploration of this radical publishing phenomenon would have to be transnational, so I began to lay the groundwork for what I thought would be a "multi-sited" ethnography (Marcus 1995) of the book in the continent in movement. While this project could certainly have included most if not all of the countries of Spanish-speaking Latin America, I chose to focus on three countries, Mexico, Bolivia, and Argentina, and specifically their capital cities, as they appeared to me as the most significant spaces not only of alternative publishing but also of autonomous politics. I organized my fieldwork to begin in the site most familiar to me, Mexico City, continued on to La Paz, and ended in the site I had never before visited, Buenos Aires. As it turned out, the very networks I was researching became the basis for my fieldwork, as contacts in Mexico connected me with people in Bolivia and Argentina and vice versa. By the time I arrived in Argentina, nearly a year into my fieldwork, I had a much better sense of who and what I would work with there. Along the way, I was put in contact with a press in Santiago de Chile and made several short trips to conduct interviews and participate in activities that press organized. In this way, Santiago became an improvised secondary research site, and because my visits coincided with the massive student protests of 2011, it proved to be a rich site for thinking through questions of autonomy, education, and alternative media.

The Book in Movement is about books—and the relations they make and that make them—but it is also about my relationship to the books and my experiences with them: the ways I am affected, moved, drawn, challenged, and compelled by them. I am not an outside observer of the practices and processes I describe. In each of my field sites, the form and level of my participation varied. In addition to the dozens of formal interviews I conducted, I participated in a wide range of public activities, including book presentations, book fairs, workshops, forums, seminars, protests, and performances. At each site I also participated in the day-to-day activities of the presses and their networks. In Mexico City I conducted my fieldwork while working in a collective, participating as an active member of the popular education and publishing committees. In La Paz I worked most closely with one press, though in a much more peripheral capacity, helping develop a communications platform for the project. I also participated as a volunteer at the first El Alto Book Fair, held in early 2011. In Buenos Aires I joined the organizing assembly for an itinerant book fair, which put me in contact with dozens of writers and presses. And in Santiago de Chile I worked with the organizers of the first Latin American Popular Book Fair. My experiences in each city brought me into contact with books and presses I otherwise would never have found. As such, while my everyday research followed the activities of certain groups—the ones I had most direct access to—I chose to develop my analysis of those projects and books that presented the richest questions about the political and material life of the print book in relation to autonomous politics. Rather than solely focus on those books or projects that conform to the characteristics I had laid out earlier, in each of the chapters I focus on those that I had the opportunity to most closely and deeply examine or that posed significant challenges to the concepts and ideas I approached them from. In this sense, I have endeavored to develop my approach following the insights of cultural studies scholarship inspired by Stuart Hall that emphasizes a practice of *radical contextualism* (Grossberg 2006) and thinking *without guarantees*, while also maintaining an awareness of the dynamics that shape scholarship *about* rather than *from* Latin America (Restrepo 2014).

A CARTOGRAPHY OF SOCIETIES IN MOVEMENT

The continent in movement is dotted with popular rebellions large and small, identifiable as such and not. While indigenous peoples have no doubt been at the forefront of many of the movements across the continent—most visibly the majority indigenous Zapatistas in Chiapas, Mexico—this does not mean that these are ethnic or indigenous movements per se. Oaxacan intellectual and former advisor to the EZLN Gustavo Esteva explained the distinction in a column published in *La Jornada* in early 2014, marking the twentieth anniversary of the January 1, 1994 uprising:

Advirtieron desde el primer momento que no eran un movimiento indígena. Su iniciativa tiene otro alcance. Las demandas indígenas, tal como parece verlas el zapatismo, sólo pueden satisfacerse en una forma de sociedad en que tanto indígenas como no indígenas gocen de justicia, emancipación, y libertad. Por la naturaleza del problema, bien identificada por los zapatistas, los cambios que hacen falta son de alcance nacional e internacional y en ellos los pueblos indígenas se encuentran en el principal frente de batalla, aquí y en casi todas partes.

They announced from the very beginning that they were not an indigenous movement. Their initiative has a different reach. The indigenous demands, as Zapatismo appears to see them, can only be met in a kind of society where indigenous and non-indigenous people alike enjoy justice, emancipation and freedom. Because of the nature of the problem, which the Zapatistas have so clearly identified, the changes that are needed are both national and international in scale and in them the indigenous peoples are on the front lines, here and almost everywhere else.

"Autonomy" is a term that has legal applications in the context of indigenous struggles across the continent, but this is not the autonomy I speak of when I say "autonomous politics." My understanding of autonomy resonates with the definition proposed by Ana Dinerstein in her 2015 book *The Politics of Autonomy in Latin America*. She explains that "autonomous practices, i.e., struggles for self-determination, self-organisation, self-representation, self-management, and indigenous autonomy—are not new" (Dinerstein 2015, 1). But as she goes on to argue, since the 1980s autonomy has been recreated "against and beyond neoliberal globalisation . . . and is inextricably connected with hope" (1). Key to understanding the "new" modes of autonomy of recent decades is the relation to prefiguration: "Prefiguration . . . is *a process of learning hope*. Autonomy is the organisational tool of this process" (2; emphasis in original). For this reason, she defines autonomy as "the art of organising hope."

Autonomy, in this sense, is a practice of what Tapia (2008, 115) calls *política salvaje* (wild politics), which is unstable, temporary, contingent, and fluid: "La política salvaje es lo que no construye orden social y político, es decir, instituciones, jerarquías y divisiones del trabajo político. Es política en tanto son prácticas que tienen que ver con la dirección de la vida y el movimiento colectivo" (Wild politics is that which doesn't construct a social and political order—that is, institutions, hierarchies, and divisions in political labor. It is politics that are practical and that have to do with the direction of life and collective movement).[22] Wild politics, he says, exceed the "stable places of politics," principally the modern state in its construction as the privileged space of all things political, and occupy what he calls the "non-places of politics": the political "basement" or "underground" (Tapia 2008, 96). This relational description of the space of autonomous politics resonates with the Zapatistas' expression of *desde abajo* (from below). To be clear, this is not an expression of a class positioning but a relational category that is not bound to any identity.[23]

Each of the sites that I travel to in *The Book in Movement* has experienced a remarkable surge of political movement from below since the turn of the twenty-first century. Mexico has been irrevocably transformed by the Zapatista uprising, which began in 1994 and has successfully merged an indigenous struggle with broader anticapitalist and autonomous politics. The massive Bolivian rebellions that began with the Cochabamba Water Wars in 2000 and continue to this day have destabilized the neoliberal model imposed in the 1980s with an anticolonial and anti-imperialist praxis. In Argentina the economic crisis of 2001 brought with it a massive popular rebellion of unemployed workers and the working and middle class that has transformed the urban landscape. And in Chile the new generation of students born after the dictatorship has made visible a much broader societal movement to free Chile of the psychic and material effects of the violence of the Pinochet regime and the neoliberal experiment.

In each of these contexts, the first decades of the twenty-first century have brought profound transformation at the grassroots level, which in some sites has also taken hold in the realm of institutional and state politics through the rise—and, in some cases, fall—of "progressive" administrations. But as many have aptly noted, the institutionalization of populist politics (as in the contexts of Evo Morales's Bolivia or the Kirchners' Argentina, for example) has been marred by, among other issues, widespread repression and cooptation of grassroots movements, demonstrating the inability of the state to promote and enact autonomous political ethics. And in some contexts, such as Argentina, for example, the return of the far right to power, as in the 2015 election of Mauricio Macri, has in fact reignited the sense of urgency surrounding autonomous politics. The conditions and histories of each of these contexts are, of course, tremendously diverse, yet at the grassroots level, there is also commonality that is found amid and through that difference. *The Book in Movement* is not an ethnography of social movements. It is an ethnography of an object, the organic book, and the relations and ethics that it materializes. So rather than attempt the impossible task of outlining an exhaustive history of each of the contexts, I offer necessarily partial (as both incomplete and subjective) glimpses into why these sites are so significant to my understanding of the continent in movement.

Mexico—still in the grips of a war that resists definition and has claimed more than 150,000 lives in twelve years—has a unique place in this project, as much because of my personal ties as because of its recent history. Since 1994 the majority indigenous Zapatista movement based in the southeastern state of Chiapas has directly contributed to the formation of widespread, loosely articulated grassroots networks.[24] Today those networks include a diversity of actors that are building autonomy as a means of directly resisting the narco-state complex that perpetuates the seemingly endless—and explicitly capitalist—war: self-defense militias, student activists, sex worker unions, indigenous communities, socio-environmental defense movements, urban anarchists, and every imaginable form of alternative media producers.[25] It is impossible to adequately express the profound and far-reaching influence that Zapatismo has had on political praxis not only in Mexico but around the world.

As this project began to take shape, I frequently traveled to Mexico to participate in various *encuentros*, or gatherings, organized in Zapatista territory, while also spending periods of time in Mexico City. When I returned to Mexico City in 2010 to formally begin my fieldwork, I immediately joined the collective that had published Bocafloja's book, Jóvenes en Resistencia Alternativa (JRA), and had the opportunity to participate in the initial meetings of what would become the national Red de Resistencias Autónomas Anticapitalistas (Network of Autonomous Anticapitalist Resistances).[26] This network includes many collective actors for whom the articulatory initiatives led by the Zapatistas were so significant. But the Red is not a Zapatista project, and in many ways it emerges from the necessity to work even more autonomously—which is to say, without the EZLN as the initiator or organizing force. In my view, this is precisely what the EZLN has been calling for: the autonomous and (trans) local organization of projects and initiatives that emerge from and respond to the realities of those working on the ground, wherever they may be.

In the "Sexta declaración de la Selva Lacandona" (Sixth declaration of the Lacandon Jungle) released in 2005, the EZLN offered a retrospective and prospective analysis of its movement: "nuestra pequeña historia es que nos cansamos de la explotación que nos hacían los poderosos y pues nos organizamos para defendernos y para luchar por la justicia" (our small history was that we grew tired of exploitation by the powerful, and then we organized in order to defend ourselves and to fight for justice; original and translation, EZLN 2005).[27] In the Sixth Declaration, the Zapatistas narrate their own complex history—the struggles to negotiate with the government, the decision to focus on building autonomy on the ground, the encounters with other groups in struggle around Mexico, and the decision to open their movement to the world more and more. The dialogical aspect of the movement—the interactions and exchanges with others nationally and internationally, or even intergalactically, as they often say—is synthesized at the end of the first section of the "Sexta":

> Y lo primero que vimos es que nuestro corazón ya no es igual que antes, cuando empezamos nuestra lucha, sino que es más grande porque ya tocamos el corazón de mucha gente buena. Y también vimos que nuestro corazón está como más lastimado, que sea más herido. Y no es que está herido por el engaño que nos hicieron los malos gobiernos, sino porque cuando tocamos los corazones de otros pues tocamos también sus dolores. O sea que como que nos vimos en un espejo.

> And the first thing we saw was that our heart was not the same as before, when we began our struggle. It was larger, because now we had touched the hearts of many good people. And we also saw that our heart was more hurt, it was more wounded. And it was not wounded by the deceits of the bad governments, but because, when we touched the hearts of others, we also touched their sorrows. It was as if we were seeing ourselves in a mirror. (EZLN 2005)

And just as the EZLN expresses the ways they see and feel their own struggle in the struggle of others around the world, there are innumerable references (named and unnamed) to the significance and resonance of the Zapatista experience in the organic books coming out of the various societies in movement across the continent. As I traveled from site to site, Zapatismo moved with me, in my thinking, in the books I gathered, in the conversations I had along the way. On the map that unfolds in *The Book in Movement*, Zapatismo appears in many more places than just Chiapas.

In January 2011, as the plane landed just before dawn at the El Alto International Airport, perched high up in the clouds above the city of La Paz at more than four thousand meters above sea level, I knew I was entering a very different place than the Bolivia I had visited just three years earlier. Five years had passed since the election of South America's first indigenous president, Evo Morales, who referenced the Zapatista slogan *mandar obedeciendo* (lead by obeying) in his inaugural speech in 2006. In the weeks after Christmas Day, I had been closely following the news from Bolivia while wrapping up my fieldwork in Mexico City. The end of 2010 in Bolivia had been marked by the *gasolinazo* and subsequent protests, which some characterized as the first popular uprising against a leftist government in the region (Zibechi 2011a).[28] Subsequent protests addressed the scarcity of sugar, wages that did not correspond to cost of living, and what many perceived to be an increasing rift between popular sectors and social movements and the "people's president," who was brought into office as a result of more than five years of massive mobilization against the neoliberal and neocolonial governments that had dominated the political landscape nearly uninterrupted since independence. The Bolivia I arrived in to begin my fieldwork was at a turning point. The growing disillusionment with the supposedly anticolonial and anti-imperialist popular government had come to the fore; for many, the limits of the revolutionary potential of a state project were being revealed.[29] The production of autonomous knowledge and praxis gained even greater significance, and it was in this context that I delved into the networks of presses and militant intellectuals, including many who had worked alongside Morales and García Linera.

Seven months later, I packed my bags and made the trip to my next field site, Buenos Aires, stopping off in Santiago de Chile for a ten-day visit en route. I had never been to Chile or Argentina, so I was relying heavily on the contacts that my friends in Mexico and Bolivia had provided, connecting me with presses, writers, and comrades in both cities. When I planned my trip to Chile months earlier, the political landscape was relatively calm there. But when I arrived in mid-July 2011, things were quite different. In late June a series of multitudinous protests began to spread across the country, with hundreds of thousands of students taking to the streets in protest against the increasing privatization of the Chilean public education system. Universities, colleges, and schools of all kinds were occupied by students, who along with their teachers and families began to transform the occupations into processes of *autogestión* (self-organization/autonomous operation) of the schools, developing curriculum and participatory educational programming. The 2011 student movement was both an extension of and a rupture from the 2006 Pingüino revolution, the massive movement of high school students. In the prologue to the Chilean edition of *Dispersar el poder*, Zibechi (2011b, 9) asserts that the Pingüino revolution represented a new era for Chilean social movements because of their deployment of horizontal and participatory forms of organization. But whereas the 2006 movement was relatively limited in terms of the reforms it demanded, the 2011 movement developed a deeper analysis of the crisis of education and debt in Chile and brought attention to a broader societal movement that included calls for a constituent assembly (Chile is still governed by Pinochet's constitution). This was the Chile I stepped into, first in July and again in December 2011, to learn from a multigenerational collective press that bridges not only those two moments of recent rebellions in Chile but also the socialist revolution of Salvador Allende.

While Chile in 2011 was full of new hope and political effervescence, Argentina was in a more retrospective phase when I arrived in Buenos Aires. Ten years earlier, the country had been profoundly shaken by an economic crisis that had been building since the 1990s and culminated with the sudden eruption of millions of people taking to the streets on December 19 and 20, 2001, with the cry of "Que se vayan todos, que no quede ni uno solo" (They all must go, not one can stay), ultimately expelling the government.[30] In the aftermath of the initial rebellion, popular neighborhood assemblies emerged not only across Buenos Aires but around the country, with ordinary people occupying spaces as they came together to organize themselves collectively to meet their basic needs. Workers cooperatives flourished across the country, including hundreds of *empresas recuperadas* (recuperated businesses) first occupied and then managed by the workers themselves. So 2001 was the culmination of popular struggles that had been building for some time in Argentina, challenging the brutal effects of the neoliberal policies. And significantly, it ushered in a new era of popular mobilization, in which public space is a site of transversal articulation, where individuals and collectivities from a diversity of experiences and sectors meet. In the six months leading up to the ten-year anniversary, I attended many events dedicated to this theme, learning about the meaning of "2001" from the firsthand accounts of workers, community organizers, students, intellectuals, and families of all classes. But whereas most discussions focused on the idea of the anniversary, the newly formed assembly at the Cazona de Flores, a social center run by about a dozen different autonomous projects including the Colectivo Situaciones, proposed a different approach: not ten years *since* 2001, but rather ten years *of* 2001—that is, ten years of rebellion, organization, and transformation.

These groups, like others, were also paying particular attention to the cooptation of the popular uprising and subsequent movements by the Kirchner government, which came into power in 2003. The ten-year anniversary of 2001 also coincided with the one-year anniversary of the police raid on the Parque Indoamericano, a massive urban park that had been occupied by three thousand families, mostly Bolivian and Paraguayan immigrants, in which three people were killed, demonstrating the conjunction of land and housing conflicts, pervasive racism and xenophobia, and the increasingly violent state policies aimed at controlling and enclosing public space in Buenos Aires (Taller Hacer Ciudad 2011). The same group from the Cazona de Flores also organized events and published a book related to the Indoamericano, raising questions about the changing shape of the city, that were otherwise absent from the 2001 commemorations. This was the backdrop for my fieldwork in Buenos Aires: a moment of collective reflection and theorization on the possibilities and limitations of popular organization of political and economic alternatives and the meaning and practice of community.

By following actors and objects across different borders, this ethnography is neither comparative nor multisited but rather *networked*. The project is about the connections and relations that make the continent in movement, and in this way it is less about what happens in each of the discrete sites than it is about the ways they are connected. It is not about specific places or people but about an object: the book. People, places, things, and practices appear and reappear across the chapters. For these reason, the chapters are not organized around a set of case studies or sites but around the stages in the life of any book. Chapter 1, "Becoming the Book," analyzes the interplay of horizontality and dialogical knowledge practices in the process through which the idea to make a book comes about. Chapter 2, "The Workshop Book," explores the craft space of the book workshop, where books are assembled, printed, and bound as a site of *provisoriedad* (provisionality) and experimentation. Chapter 3, "The Unbounded Book," focuses on the ways that books are shared between presses and reedited in different contexts, following the transversal networks and intellectual property practices through which the organic book becomes unbounded. The final chapter, "The Networking Book," is an exploration of the distribution and circulation practices through which books reach potential readers, arguing that the marketing of the organic book is a practice of *encuentro* (encounter). Each chapter moves through various sites to explore how *concepts* from the organic books (horizontality, *provisoriedad*, transversality, *encuentro*, etc.) can be understood through the *practices* that perform them. In this sense, the major body of theory and the key concepts that inform my analysis of the presses and movements are drawn from the organic books themselves.

As the final chapter explores in greater depth, autonomous movements enact an ethic of *encuentro*: a concept-practice that places greater emphasis on face-to-face engagement and dialogue over any program of action. *Encuentro* is contingent and fluid—most of all, it is organic. A praxis of embodied, nonhierarchical politics, in the movements *encuentro* can take many forms: the EZLN's dialogical rhetorical strategies, the assembly organization model of the neighborhood groups in Argentina, or the transnational forums and gatherings where movements converge. But *encuentro* also occurs in ideas, in words, in stories, and in the objects and spaces through which they travel. The story of the organic book is a story of *encuentro*. It is the story of a continent articulated through movement.

ONE

BECOMING THE BOOK

No se trata de crear una estructura, un aparato, sino un espacio horizontal e igualitario, una suerte de plaza pública . . . donde fluya la palabra y la comunicación entre sujetos iguales.

It's not about creating a structure, an apparatus, but rather a horizontal and equal space, a kind of public plaza . . . where there is a flow of words and communication between equal subjects.

—RAÚL ZIBECHI, *LA MIRADA HORIZONTAL*

AN EARLY December stroll through the improvised stands that crowd Avenida República in central Santiago de Chile, with less than the equivalent of twenty dollars in my hand, yielded me a hefty stack of small books. Books with distinct textures and densities. With their colorful, dynamic designs, the covers of these inexpensive books share more aesthetically with the political graffiti that adorns the city than with the classic tomes that fill the stacks of the library at the national university. Less than a mile away from this popular Latin American book fair, the halls of the University of Chile seemed to mirror what these books describe. Plastered with wheatpasted posters and spray-painted slogans, the formality of the university as the authoritative site of institutional knowledge had been radically disrupted by the nationwide rebellion underway. The six-month occupation of the schools and universities of the country in 2011 transformed these formal institutions into temporary autonomous zones (Bey 1991) where students, teachers, and their families were building alternative spaces of education and community organizing. These zones are the most visible manifestation of this *sociedad en movimiento* (society in movement; Zibechi 2008b). Those occupying the universities connected with others outside the educational system who are similarly engaged in a reimagining of their work, education, healthcare, neighborhoods, and cities after decades of economic and political violence brought on by the Pinochet dictatorship. Back at the fair, a kind of palimpsest of revolutionary imaginaries emerged, with independently produced books lining the very block that housed three torture and detention centers during the dictatorship. The books tell stories of articulated resistance: stories of alternative political projects in Chile along with their counterparts across the continent that are also creating permanent experiments of imagining and creating another sociability against and beyond capitalism and its especially invasive form, neoliberalism.

Among the objects on display was an early book written by an invited speaker at the fair: Raúl Zibechi. *Dispersar el poder* (*Dispersing Power*) is a study of the historical events in El Alto that shook Bolivia in the first five years of the twenty-first century.[1] Yet it is not only a book concerning Bolivia: a scan of the short table of contents reveals that the book is made of other relations that connect Bolivia, Argentina, Chile, Mexico, and Uruguay. The book—like any book—is in movement as the reader flips through it: the cover and the pages turn, held together by the binding. But there are other kinds of movement that converge and interlock in everything that makes this object, politically and materially. This small book has had a large life since it was first published in 2006 by the Bolivian press Textos Rebeldes. It has been remade again and again, with each edition generating and being generated by different arrangements of relations and practices, as this chapter begins to describe. With its multiple editions and geographies, *Dispersar el poder* is an exercise in how to produce an object that is organic to the politics it describes. And as the single book that has been reedited in not only all four of my research sites but also my former home city of Oakland, it holds a unique and symbolic place in this project, and as such it appears and reappears in this and all of the following chapters.

This chapter closely examines the relations that make organic books through analysis of *Dispersar el poder* alongside two other books. *Pensar las autonomías: Alternativas de emancipación al capital y el estado* (*Thinking Autonomies: Alternatives for Emancipation from Capital and the State*) is a collection of original essays from across the continent, edited by Jóvenes en Resistencia Alternativa ("Youth in Alternative Resistance") and represents more than a decade of their work with movements and militant intellectuals. *Caleidoscopio de rebeldías* (Kaleidoscope of rebellions), written by Buenos Aires–based popular education practitioner Claudia Korol, explores and moves through the myriad spaces of collective thought and popular education in radical movements in Argentina and beyond.

FIGURE 1.1. Feria del libro popular latinoamericano, Santiago, 2011.

RELATIONAL SPACES OF THE BOOK

In *Dispersar el poder*, Zibechi (2006, 87–88) identifies one of the most crippling tendencies of "old" movements (which also exist today): "Durante más de un siglo los movimientos antisistémicos han forjado sus estructuras organizativas de forma simétrica al capital, a los estados, los ejércitos, y otras instituciones hegemónicas en el sistema que combaten" (For over a century, antisystemic movements have developed their organizational structures in parallel to capital, the state, the military, and other institutions of the system they fight; Zibechi 2010, 45). He asserts that in doing so, these movements effectively "assume the state form," even as they purport to struggle against "the state" and capital. In the first sentence of *Dispersar el poder*, Zibechi (2006, 25) establishes the historical-political perspective of the book, signaling a rupture with that "old" tendency: "El ciclo de luchas e insurrecciones que los pueblos que habitan Bolivia protagonizan desde el año 2000, es quizá la más profunda 'revolución en la revolución' desde el levantamiento zapatista de 1994" (The cycle of struggles and insurrections instigated by the Bolivian people in the year 2000 is the most profound "revolution within the revolution" since the Zapatista uprising of 1994; Zibechi 2010, 1). Why does Zibechi open by connecting these two distant movements, one in Mexico and the other in Bolivia? Zibechi is certainly not the first to make this connection. John Holloway, Raquel Gutiérrez Aguilar, and Gustavo Esteva are among the many militant intellectuals who have analyzed the connection between Chiapas and El Alto, noting the resonances between the Zapatista experiment with indigenous self-governance and the urban Aymara process of communitarian organization and rebellion. In both contexts, autonomy is the common horizon for the popular struggles premised on a rejection of the form of the racist, colonial, capitalist state and the relations it reproduces.

Autonomy (which may or may not be defined in relation to the state) takes many forms as it is enacted, and in this sense is more a practice than an ideology. As Colectivo Situaciones (2006, 227) writes: "La autonomía, entonces, más que doctrina, está viva cuando aparece como tendencia práctica, inscripta en la pluralidad, como orientación a desarrollos concretos que parten de las propias potencias, y de la decisión fundamental de no dejarse arrastrar por las exigencias mediadoras-expropiadoras del estado y del capital" (More than being a doctrine, autonomy is alive when it appears as a practical course of action, inscribed in plurality, as the orientation of concrete developments that emerge from particular forces, and the fundamental decision to refuse to be dragged along by the mediating-expropriating demands of the state and of capital). I highlight this definition, written by an Argentine militant research collective that has accompanied the Zapatistas and the Bolivian movements, because it defines "autonomy" as a situated concept-practice that can only be understood in terms of *doing* (as in collective action), rather than as an idea or theory to be applied. This emphasis on doing underscores the contingent and processual nature of autonomy as a political and social aspiration that is never complete. In this sense, it is more a "horizon of desire" (Gutiérrez Aguilar 2008b)—a becoming, and an "organizing of hope" (Dinerstein 2015)—rather than a fixed state.

A bit further into the introduction, Zibechi specifies that the significant connection between the Aymara process and Zapatismo is not only the shared desire for autonomy but specifically the construction of a different kind of power—which is not a static *poder-sobre* (power-over) but a dynamic *poder-hacer* (power-to).[2] This Zibechi calls "anti-state power," naming an alternative collective sociability that rejects the hierarchical and authoritarian relational dynamics generated by capitalism and neoliberalism. "Antistate" is just one expression of this alternative power-to—and that is the one Zibechi identifies in El Alto at the turn of the twenty-first century. While neoliberalism also could be said to wield a kind of antistate power in its attacks on the state and its consolidation of nonstate power, it is important to note that neoliberal attacks on the state are ones that simply target its redistributive dimension, and in that sense they do not seek the elimination of the state. As the darling economist of neoliberal doctrine, Friederich Hayek (1976), has written, the state is essential to liberal economic policy as an arbiter in transactions among private individuals. Indeed, he says that this juridico-legal role of the state could even be seen as a means of production, providing the legal framework for capital accumulation. In this sense, neoliberal discourse that presents itself as antistate is anything but that: it is a reform of state institutions to inhibit any redistribution that would counter a market fundamentalism that uses the state to engineer the market as social regulator and produce an order of unfettered capital accumulation. In the opening chapter of *Política Salvaje*, "Una deconstrucción punk del neoliberalismo" (A punk deconstruction of neoliberalism), Luis Tapia (2006, 22) notes the necessity of the state for neoliberal policy when he writes:

El neoliberalismo es un discurso y una práctica de disciplinamiento. En la medida en que se reduce o deja de existir el espacio político de ejercicio positivo de las libertades, y se nos obliga a actuar en el mercado, la tendencia a la subordinación a los poderes económicos es inevitable. En el mercado capitalista no se delibera porque en él no somos iguales. La política de ampliación del mercado como regulador social es una eliminación de sujetos políticos.

Neoliberalism is a disciplinary discourse and practice to the extent that the political space of a positive exercise of freedoms is reduced or ceases to exist. We are obligated to conduct ourselves in the market, and the tendency toward a subordination to the economically powerful is inevitable. In the capitalist market there is no deliberation because in it we are not equals. The politics of expanding the market as social regulator is an elimination of the political subject.

What Zibechi identifies as "anti-state" must also be understood as anticapitalist (in the sense of rejecting the market as the most appropriate social regulator) and anticolonial. The state in Bolivia (and elsewhere, of course) as a product of colonialism is an inherently racist, capitalist, and patriarchal structure and has been used to establish a social, economic, and political order that reflects and reproduces this.

If the "new" movements, these "societies in movement" (such as Zapatismo and the Bolivian cycles of popular mobilization), effectively reject the form of the state and capitalism, it is worth examining how the production of what we might call "knowledge"—that is, ideas, thought, theories, or narratives—related to these movements is part of this political, economic, and epistemic transformation. But the concept of knowledge is problematic in this context, precisely because it presumes that something is "known" and that the possessor of said "knowledge," the author, has the authority to do so.

As Roland Barthes, Michel Foucault, Roger Chartier, and others have reminded us, the role of the author is a modern invention which emerges in the seventeenth century and is directly tied to forms of proprietorship that accompanied the growing commodification of literature (M. Rose 1993, 1). While anonymity became attached to the objective truth of scientific discourses, literary discourses "came to be accepted only when endowed with the author function" (Foucault 1998, 213), which is about ownership of the discourse but also legal responsibility for it, drawing the act of penning ideas into the juridical realm. Relatedly, the author function also acts as a basis for identifying motivation and intent and in this sense imposes an idea of unity which Foucault and others rightly argue is problematic. The modern author that emerges in the seventeenth century has been the subject of significant critique, including from postcolonial theorists who have noted the difficulty of delinking the idea of authorship from the dynamics of power and colonization. The organic book is a contemporary expression of a similar complication of the role of the author, through practices that productively question the capitalist, colonial, and patriarchal dynamics that undergird modern authorship. This has to do not only with the attempts to recognize collective and dispersed modes of knowledge production but also those efforts related to the relinking of intellectual and technical labor—what Walter Benjamin identifies in "The Author as Producer."

In this address to the Institute for the Study of Fascism, Benjamin (1998, 95) calls for a reorientation of the political utility of intellectual production by connecting the actors and roles separated under capitalist production: "By experiencing his solidarity with the proletariat, the author as producer experiences, directly and simultaneously, his solidarity with certain other producers who, until then, meant little to him." In what amounts to a call to action, Benjamin identifies the problematic division of labor in intellectual production and insists that the "revolutionary struggle" requires that the author ally with the proletariat by intervening in production through a combination of technique and solidarity. This is precisely what the organic book materializes as object and practice. It can be said, then, since the very role of author is remobilized as a kind of "producer" in the spirit of Benjamin's proposal, with the organic book, authorial intent transgresses the division between manual and intellectual labor, as the authors (collective or individual) position themselves purposefully within the broader relations of production. The relational spaces and practices that constitute the organic book reconfigure this dynamic of authorial intent in the sense that the figure of the author is constituted by its relations to other actors in the process, thereby dispersing authorial intent from the single individual mind to the collective of actors who make up the organic book. Authorial intent becomes dispersed, similar to the way that anthropologist Edwin Hutchins (1995) has argued that cognition or thought has been mistakenly located in the brain and should be better conceptualized as deeply social: it is physically distributed through artifacts and people as they interact in a task that has been undertaken. Hutchins (1995) calls this "distributed cognition." What we think of as knowledge is not to be found in deep structures in the mind but is rather situated in a complex network of relations composing the world of cultural production.

Much as with the notion of the author, there is a fixity assumed in the category of knowledge, which is not necessarily attached to parallel concepts like thought or idea, which have a relational, provisional quality. And so, in this chapter, I use the term "knowledge" but recognize that it is an inadequate name for the diverse forms of thought, analysis, theorization, and narration that the various Spanish terms *pensamiento*, *conocimiento*, and *saberes* convey. While *pensamiento* refers to "thought," *conocimiento* and *saberes* translate as "knowledge," with the latter often equated with *sabiduría* or "wisdom." All of these terms are used in the books I examine here, though there is little consistency in how or where they appear as descriptors of such practices. But what is most significant for my analysis in this chapter is not the name we give to the ideas, stories, and theories that are collectively produced but rather the practices through which they become visible and shareable in the tools and objects of their expression—in this case, the heterogeneous materials of the organic book.

This chapter explores these central questions: What are the relations and practices that become the organic book? How does a focus on collectivity, dialogism, and horizontality reorient practices of thinking and communicating as relational and active rather than authoritative and fixed? I interrogate how the practices that make organic books similarly—or in parallel—disrupt or break with the colonial and capitalist relations that are endemic to state, academic, and otherwise insitutional knowledge production. As Ramón Grosfoguel (2013), following Enrique Dussel, has argued, colonial expansion generated particular forms of epistemic exclusion and destruction. These, in turn, were enforced through the mechanisms and relations of the lettered city. The practices of the organic book represent the struggle against the power of the lettered city, through the construction of other modes of knowledge. I explore the potential ruptures made visible by the organic book as moments of what John Holloway (2010a) calls "negation and other-doing." An Irish transplant to Mexico who has accompanied the Zapatista movement over the past twenty years, Holloway is one of the writers whose work circulates through organic books. "Negation and other-doing," he argues, involves a simultaneous rejection of one way of being or doing and the creation of another, and as such these processes are productive (Holloway 2010a).

In what follows, I examine the collective practices at play in three books, to see the movement and fluidity of *knowledge-as-doing* that become organic books. Much of the trouble with the concept of knowledge stems from its ties to the binary of thought and action. Many attempts have been made to overcome this binary opposition between thought and action, and they have their own extensive genealogy: Marx's philosophy of praxis, Foucault's notion of discourse, Bourdieu's habitus, Haraway's situated knowledges, among others. I do not recite the entire genealogy here, but I think it is important to recognize that there is a long and complex one and to illustrate that this binary of thought-action is a perennial problem in the social sciences and humanities.

Rather than invoke any one of these particular solutions to the problem of the thought-action binary, I follow recent scholarship in science and technology studies (STS) that starts from an understanding that "like other human activities, knowing is embedded in practices" (Law 2016, 19). Instead of seeking an abstract theoretical solution to the thought-action binary, I follow work in STS that focuses on knowledge practices. This is a shift in which "knowledge is not understood as a matter of reference, but as one of manipulation" (Mol 2002, 5). My concept of knowledge-as-doing focuses on the ethnographic specificity of knowledge practices distributed and enacted in the organic book. In the field of science and technology studies of medicine, "the knowledge incorporated in practices does not reside in subjects alone, but also in buildings, knives, dyes, desks . . . and in technologies like patient records" (Mol 2002, 48). Similarly, ethnographic focus on the knowledge incorporated in the practices related to the organic book uses knowledge-as-doing as a way of attending to knowledge embedded in practices and distributed through heterogenous materials.

The modes of knowledge-as-doing that I explore in this chapter might be called *autonomous knowledge practices*. The French activist group Bureau d'études/Université Tangente describes the process of autonomous knowledge in the following terms: "Autonomous knowledge can be constituted through the analysis of the way that complex machines function. . . . The deconstruction of complex machines and their 'decolonized' reconstruction can be carried out on all kinds of objects. . . . In the same way as you deconstruct a program, you can also deconstruct the internal functioning of a government or an administration, a firm or an industrial or financial group. On the basis of such a deconstruction, involving a precise identification of the operating principles of a given administration, or the links or networks between administrations, lobbies, businesses etc., you can define modes of action or intervention" (quoted in Casas-Cortés and Cobarrubias 2007, 119). The process of deconstruction can be seen in the production of organic books precisely through the tense, if not paradoxical, relation of many of the participants to the institutional spaces and practices their projects seek to "negate," in Holloway's (2010a) terms, as they create other modes of thinking, writing, and publishing but also more broadly of relating. The writers and editors whose books this chapter examines all have varying degreees of proximity to the spaces and structures of institutional knowledge production that their books seek to challenge. This proximity is what facilitates the explicit or implicit deconstruction of the dominant machines as part of the process of creating autonomous machines.

If we conceptualize the book not as an object that exists as a mere conduit of ideas but as a thing that makes and remakes relations and has material effects, then the book comes into view as "a little machine" (Deleuze and Guattari 1987). A "machinic assemblage," the book brings together the various elements that make it (materials, objects, actors, dynamics, ideas) into a fluid, ongoing process that is neither fixed nor predictable. It exists and functions in relation to other machines: the state machine, the capitalist machine, and the "communitarian social machine" (Zibechi 2006)—which disperses power and generates antistate relations. Zibechi (2006) defines antistate relations by describing their effects. In this sense, a key question his book poses is how movement (as an action) and movements (as collective actors) dismantle institutions—both state structures and modes of populist politics that reproduce dynamics of domination.

Interdisciplinary scholarship in book studies emphasizes the importance of examining the nexus of relations that compose a book or, as Johns (1998) puts it, how the book is a process that connects "a wide range of worlds of work" and cannot be thought of as simply a medium for the transmission of some discretely produced meaning. I am interested in the questions that are raised by an exploration of books as practices and relations rather than as static artifacts. When the book as an object is produced through the very political and material practices that its content describes, emergent social, economic, and political relations not only make the object but are also produced in the process as enactments of those very relations. In this chapter, I examine a defining characteristic of the organic book—its connection to autonomous knowledge practices which are horizontal, dialogical, and, above all, collective. Focusing on the processes through which ideas become books, I explore how the content of the text is produced and the project of making a book emerges.

This chapter follows the stories of how three organic books came into being: *Pensar las autonomías*, *Dispersar el poder*, and *Caleidoscopio de rebeldías*. All three books explore the question of how to engage ideas and practices that break with the colonial and capitalist dynamics of the state and its extension into everyday life. They each propose distinct concept-practices that are significant dimensions of the organic book: dispersion of power, autonomous praxis, and popular pedagogy. The processes and products of these three organic books are in many ways worlds apart, yet they reflect a sense of plurality and connectedness that is at the foundation of the well-known Zapatista ethos "a world where many worlds fit."

THINKING, WRITING, PRINTING AUTONOMIES

"El debate sobre la autonomía ha abierto un campo fértil de discusión sobre las alternativas sociales, políticas y productivas al capitalismo desde innumerables experiencias locales surgidas desde abajo" (the debate about autonomy has opened a fecund field of discussion about social, political, and productive alternatives to capitalism from countless local experiences that emerge from below; JRA 2011, 9). The introduction to *Pensar las autonomías* begins with this description of the space from which this book grows: "un campo fertil" (a fecund field) populated with "innumerables experiencias locales" (countless local experiences; JRA 2011, 9). This description is mirrored visually on the book's cover. The bold, stark black, white, and red design is softened by the hundreds of tiny words of varying sizes that are clustered together to form the delicately outlined letters: a-u-t-o-n-o-m-i-a-s. There are dozens of different words, they appear repeatedly, and some jump out to catch my eye more than others: *subversión* (subversion), *emancipación* (emancipation), ética (ethic), *poder* (power), *lucha* (struggle), *consejo* (council), *libertad* (freedom), *resistencia* (resistance), *clase* (class), *trabajo* (work). The layering of letters and words conveys a sense of interconnectedness and diversity—a disordered web of concepts and practices. Directly below the title, the names of the fourteen authors appear above the logos of the three groups responsible for the publication: Sísifo Ediciones, the printer; Bajo Tierra Ediciones, the publisher; and JRA, the editor.

Bajo Tierra began as the publishing project of JRA, a youth collective based in Mexico City, best described by their slogan: "¡autonomía! ¡autogestión! ¡horizontalidad!" (autonomy! autogestion! horizontality!).[3] When I first met them in 2009, the twenty or so members of the collective ranged from fifteen to forty-five years old, and though they joked that after nearly a decade of organizing, "algunos ya no somos tan jóvenes" (some aren't so young anymore; interview, Mexico City, 2010)[4] the name of the group suggests an understanding of "youth" as a relational category grounded in both a rebellious sensibility and a socially or economically marginalized position. And while the founders of the collective, who began organizing as university students, are now in their thirties, one of the organizing principles that guided the collective was the regular, open invitation to new members via social media, their word-of-mouth networks, and public events. JRA's work as a collective became most widely known in the mid-2000s through the massive music festivals they organized, as fundraisers for various autonomous projects, including the Zapatista autonomous communities. These annual events were the result of long-standing relationships between JRA and politically engaged musicians, including Panteón Rococó, La Maldita Vecindad, Los de Abajo, Salario Mínimo, and Bocafloja. The concerts connected them to a wide audience of youth across Mexico City, young people drawn by the musical acts performing as well as the political impulse behind the festivals—a generation of young people interpellated by the Zapatista struggle and attracted by the opportunity to show solidarity from their urban location. The concerts also connected JRA with a web of alternative cultural spaces across the city that became points of sale for tickets for the events: skate shops, punk shops, bookstores, cafés, social centers, infoshops, and so on. This same network of independent businesses and organizations would later serve as the blueprint for the local distribution strategy of Bajo Tierra's publications.

Another fundamental axis of JRA's public work as a collective is rooted in its ties to the public universities across Mexico City, where it has organized a series of initiatives since the mid-2000s, including Zapatista solidarity campaigns, conferences, fundraising efforts for mobilizations and protests (against the COP-16 UN Climate Change Conference, for example), anticapitalist and autonomous youth camps, and publication presentations. The connection between Bajo Tierra Ediciones and the universities is multifaceted: these institutions are obvious sites for promoting and distributing books, as students are a prime audience for the political texts being produced by Bajo Tierra. But the contacts that JRA developed in the universities also directly influenced the shape of its catalog of publications, as many of the same intellectuals and scholars who supported its initiatives on campus turned to Bajo Tierra to edit and publish their works. Raquel Gutiérrez Aguilar and John Holloway of the Benemérita Universidad Autónoma de Puebla both published books with Bajo Tierra, and others have participated in Bajo Tierra's book presentations as panelists.

Pensar las autonomías represents a kind of culmination of these more isolated expressions of the political-intellectual relationships JRA has built over the past decade. Both internally as well as in its public initiatives, JRA has built a working bibliography of texts and materials that it draws on in their ongoing theorization and practice of autonomy. And JRA has sought to connect its work as a youth collective with the writers whose works have the most resonance with its praxis. The project of *Pensar las autonomías* is the materialization of the conversations and exchanges that those relations have generated and reflects an autonomous knowledge practice. Over the course of about two years, JRA extended invitations to more than a dozen writers to contribute essays to what would become its first original anthology. All of Bajo Tierra's earlier books were either single-authored books or texts that had been previously published by other presses. With *Pensar las autonomías* JRA made public a less visible facet of its work—the internal collective processes of research, theorization, and writing. While no doubt connected to work that happens within the state institutions of the public universities, this is a book that connects intellectual "worlds of work" (Johns 1998) that find neither their point of origin nor conclusion in the academy. The volume articulates processes of political organization, collective theorization, militant research, and nonprofit-oriented or *autogestivo* production in a concrete object.

Autonomy is a concept that defies clear and simple definition—hence the impulse to dedicate an entire volume to "thinking" about it. It is precisely this quality that makes it such an apt descriptor for the "countless local experiences" that are at once dispersed and connected by their shared repudiation of the social and economic ordering of capitalism. In this sense, autonomy is understood as an oppositional practice that breaks with not only the logic of "the state" (as autonomy is often conceived)—and especially the "hegemonic dogma" of "liberal democracy" (JRA 2011, 9)—but also of capitalism, a more far-reaching system that cuts across territories and borders. In the introduction to *Pensar las autonomías*, JRA (JRA 2011, 9) describes autonomy as "an experiment of social reorganization," drawing from the ways the term is used by different collective actors: "quienes luchan, se organizan, resisten, crean y construyen estos experimentos de reorganización social desde abajo, aluden a la palabra autonomía para nombrar estas prácticas" (those who struggle, organize themselves, resist, create and construct those experiments of social reorganization from below, allude to the word autonomy to name those practices). The emphasis is on the *practices* of autonomy, rather than an *ideology*, and the essays compiled in this volume theorize this concept through the on-the-ground practices of *los de abajo* (those from below). As Claudio Albertani (2011, 54) writes in his contribution, "La autonomía no es una secta, una ideología o una agrupación política, sino un camino de lucha" (Autonomy is not a sect, an ideology or a political group, but a path of struggle). Albertani (2011, 54) goes on to identify what he considers the three major veins that historically anchor the "principio de autonomía" (principle of autonomy): (1) the anarchist tradition; (2) libertarian marxism; and (3) indigenous civilizations around the world. In Mexico the process that most obviously makes visible the intersection of these three, but which Albertani scarcely mentions, is Zapatismo.

The Zapatista experience is the thread that articulates the wide range of writers and perspectives that appear in *Pensar las autonomías*. Only half of the texts name Zapatismo, and the editors make no mention of it. Nevertheless, in Latin America and especially in Mexico, Zapatismo's conceptual and practical contributions have been so widespread and so profound that today they are a referent that can go unnamed and still be present. Zapatismo merges a concern with autonomy as a principle of governance with autonomy as a relational political position in all aspects of life, including collective knowledge practices. This expression of autonomy becomes articulated most overtly through a language of alterity—*la otra educación* (the other education), *los otros medios* (the other media), *la otra economía* (the other economy), *la otra geografía* (the other geography), and so on[5]—that, rather than attempt to clearly define the character or scope, simply marks a non-institutional (autonomous) position, leaving open the possibilities for what that can include. The otherness that is used to describe Zapatista autonomy is effective in the way it simultaneously defines and blurs—this multiple movement signals a break from something, a rupture or flight whose end is unknown.

The fifth essay in the book was written not in Mexico City but in the capital of the nearby state of Oaxaca, a prominent yet peripheral point on the political-intellectual map of Mexico. Gustavo Esteva, described in his biographical note as "an activist and deprofessionalized public intellectual," is one of the founders of the Universidad de la Tierra–Oaxaca, an autonomous learning center.[6] In the 1990s he served as an "advisor" to the Zapatistas in their negotiations with the federal government and was an active participant in the popular rebellion of 2006, which he and others have called the Oaxaca Commune (Esteva 2010). He opens his essay "Otra autonomía, otra democracia" (Other autonomy, other democracy) with a scene from the 1996 meeting of more than one hundred advisors invited to the Selva Lacandona to meet with Subcomandante Marcos and other Zapatista leaders. The debate about how to define autonomy was an obsession in the early years of the Zapatista rebellion because part of what was at stake at that moment was the consolidation of a legal framework for recognizing indigenous autonomy. Though at the time it felt like a betrayal, the 2001 gutting of the law meant to institutionalize the San Andrés Accords was in fact the catalyst for the profound reimagining of autonomy that ensued following the Zapatistas' retreat from any engagement with the government. Rather than continuing to look to the legal framework of the constitution and Congress for legally afforded autonomy, the Zapatistas turned their gaze inward—and radically outward[7]—and focused on building autonomy in practice. Esteva (2011, 122) writes: "De esa autonomía tratan estas notas, de la autonomía como proyecto político que da continuidad histórica a la antigua resistencia de los pueblos indios y la transforma en un empeño de liberación compartido con muchos otros grupos sociales" (These notes are about that autonomy—the autonomy that as a political project creates historic continuity with the earlier resistance of indigenous people and transforms it into a collective determination for liberation shared with many other social groups).

The writers whose texts are compiled in *Pensar las autonomías* represent a range of relationships to the institutional site of knowledge production of the university and academia. The book itself is partially a product of academia, in the sense that JRA's work in the universities helped them build their networks. Similarly, the writers who contributed texts are (to varying degrees) at least partially connected to academic institutions. Many of them earn their living as professors and researchers for major universities, others work in "alternative" education projects that rely on funding from various NGOs or foundations. They were all trained in formal universities, but their trajectories reflect moments of rupture with the strictures of those institutions and with the conventions of knowledge production that are endemic to state and academic institutions. As researchers, professors, and theorists they deterritorialize their practices as they engage in intellectual work that seeks to build horizontal and dialogical relations. Many are academics who seek to primarily form relations and networks outside the academy and in doing so aspire to make research a militant practice.[8] The texts they produce, in many cases, appear to be no different from any other academic publication: saddled with citation after citation, using often dense and inaccessible language and prose. But while the texts do not necessarily radically transform the form of academic writing, the relations that bring their ideas to the page are not confined to the space or dynamics of academic institutions—namely, the hierarchical construction of a class of authorities, experts, and theorists. These relations certainly include the movements—whose experiences are recounted in the essays—with whom the writers engage as interlocutors and participants, but they also include the alternative projects the writers choose to disseminate their work, like Bajo Tierra Ediciones. These writers all certainly have access to the commercial and academic publication circuits (which would likely produce bigger runs and broader distribution), but they often make the political decision to publish their works through other means, understanding this to be an important part of their process as militant or activist writers and intellectuals.

A unique book in the Bajo Tierra catalog, *Pensar las autonomías* is the first original publication that JRA composed as a collective. Unlike the single-authored books that it was the first to publish, for which Bajo Tierra/JRA was responsible for editing, design, printing, and distribution, with *Pensar las autonomías* JRA took on a more authorial role as the editor of the work. The collective was the architect of the book, deciding which writers to invite to participate, selecting the topics for their original contributions, organizing the essays, and composing a more extensive introduction than the brief prefaces it prepares for every one of its publications. In this book, the process of thinking autonomy through the analysis of concrete experiences of social movements becomes part of a more extensive practice of autonomy through alternative approaches to writing and publishing. As the collective makes evident in the introduction, *Pensar las autonomías* is conceived of as a space for collective "reflexión sobre la emancipación" (reflection about emancipation; JRA 2011, 12), and "la intención de este debate no es crear un nuevo paradigma, dogma o plan sobre el cambio social, sino abrir el pensamiento a numerosas posibilidades y potencias del camino de las autonomías, pero también de sus peligros, riesgos, contradicciones, incertidumbres y dudas" (the intention of this debate is not to create a new paradigm, dogma or plan of social change, but to open our thinking to numerous possibilities and forces of the path of autonomies, but also its dangers, risks, contradictions, uncertainties and doubts; JRA 2011, 12). The debate, as they call it, does not seek to define but rather to "open thinking" relationally in an ongoing process of "contestar y reformular" (questioning and reformulating; 12). *Pensar las autonomías* is an organic experiment of collective theorization about autonomy, one that is open-ended, processual, and incomplete.

DISPERSING POWER/DISPERSING AUTHORITY

In the prologue to the most recent edition of *Dispersar el poder*, Zibechi (2011b, 8) names the intervention he aspires to carry out with his writing: "la necesaria descolonización del pensamiento crítico, para liberarlo de su carga eurocéntrica, masculina, blanca, cientificista y con pretensiones de objetividad" (the necessary decolonization of critical thought, to free it of its Eurocentric, masculine, white, scientist, and objectivist charge). This statement resonates quite directly with what he describes in the first edition as an "epistemological earthquake" (Zibechi 2010, 83) produced by the emergence of new political subjects previously obscured by the subject-object relations of the colonial state. The dominance of statist relations and discourse is interrupted first by the movements the book describes and again in the composition of the book itself. Referring to the process of conceptualizing the text, Zibechi (2011b) notes that his challenge in El Alto—the site of Bolivia's most tumultuous and widespread popular mobilizations—was to "despejarme de lo que yo sabía" (estrange myself from what I knew). Noting the Eurocentrism that permeates political theory in Latin America, he makes a distinction between theory that emerges from philosophical concepts, "from books," and theory that emerges from "reality," from "the people that are doing things." Zibechi certainly develops his analysis in part through his readings of people far removed from the realities he describes—he cites Pierre Clastres, Gilles Deleuze, and Toni Negri, and many other influences go unnamed. But he doesn't give the theories he borrows "from books" more weight than the ideas he finds "on the ground," and in this sense he attempts to bring a wide range of thinkers into a more symmetrical conversation.[9] His suggestion is that theory that only exists in books is static and abstract; theory that comes from collective action is dynamic and grounded. I take Zibechi's distinction a step further to distinguish books from organic books, which are those objects that are made of the relations and antagonisms of the autonomous politics they describe.

Zibechi's analysis of the spatial construction of El Alto runs throughout *Dispersar el poder*, with one chapter exclusively dedicated to this theme: "La ciudad autoconstruida: dispersión y diferencia" (The self-constructed city: Dispersion and difference). El Alto, interestingly, does not adhere to the classic checkerboard grid-form of colonial cities in Latin America. The rectilinear pattern, which Ángel Rama (1984, 6) notes is a mechanism of colonial hierarchy and social order, is notably absent here, reflecting a city built by its inhabitants, rather than by some model imposed by an external force. In an inversion of the usual transfer of symbolic power into material forms, in El Alto the materiality of the urban landscape reflects the unique communitarian dynamics of a city that was born from a crisis in neocolonial rule—the rapid, mass migration of indigenous peasants caused by the violent imposition of neoliberal policy resulted in the sudden sprouting of an improvised city built and ordered by the very people who were populating it. El Alto, as it exists today, is the product of a relatively recent wave of mass migration. However, it is worth noting the historical significance of this city, as the site from which anticolonial rebel leaders Túpaj Katari and Bartolina Sisa maintained their siege of the city of La Paz for more than six months in 1781. Zibechi maintains that El Alto is a spatial reflection of the dispersion of power emblematic of the waves of mobilization across Latin America at the turn of the century. In his assessment, El Alto is unique because it is a dense and territorially bounded site of anti-neoliberal political practice. At once chaotic and ordered, leaderless and organized, spontaneous and routine: El Alto manifests the qualities that the networked form of recent movements—and, as I argue, their communication and knowledge practices—takes.

Dispersar el poder, as a material object, intriguingly becomes a space where other relations (nonstate, antistate, autonomous) are made and reproduced in the telling of the story and the composing of the book-object. The narrative structure, and the composition of the text itself, echoes the relations described in it: both the communitarian relations that bind the movements and the antagonistic relations that mobilize them. But these relations, significantly, are not simply the object of Zibechi's analysis—they are also the relations that are made in, around, and by his book. In the chapter on the urban spatiality of El Alto, for example, Zibechi's close reading of a report prepared by Rafael Undaburu for the United States Agency for International Development, "Evaluación de la ciudad de El Alto" (Evaluation of the city of El Alto; 2004), serves several functions in terms of visibilizing the antagonisms. First, it makes evident the contrast between the state's conception of power and organization and that of the communities that populate El Alto. He explains:

> Todo el estudio encargado por USAID está teñido por un fuerte ataque a la dispersión porque dificulta el control social, impide la creación de un panóptico urbano—político pero también social, cultural, y organizacional—que sea capaz de englobar amplias poblaciones bajo la misma mirada-mando. Dicho de otro modo, la fragmentación-dispersión implica relaciones cara a cara en las villas, que se articulan entre sí y con otras urbanizaciones en base a modos sumergidos en la cotidianeidad. (Zibechi 2006, 75–76)

> The entire study commissioned by USAID is tainted by the attack on dispersion because dispersion makes it hard to exert social control. It impedes the creation of an urban-political panoptic—political but also social, cultural, and organizational—that could encapsulate broad populations under the same umbrella of control. In other words, fragmentation or dispersion implies face-to-face relations in the villas, articulated among the people themselves and with other urbanizations based on forms developed in everyday life. (Zibechi 2010, 36)

As he states, what the USAID study identifies as the "fragmented" form of neighborhood organization in El Alto—and defines as an obstacle to development—is in fact a spatial dynamic that actively resists absorption or management by the state and that generates a different kind of community relations (Zibechi 2006, 74).

Second, Zibechi's reading of the USAID report underscores one of the central critiques he presents throughout the book regarding the methodologies and politics of Eurocentric knowledge production, which maintain and reproduce the subject-object dichotomy that endows the subject the power to speak, think, theorize, and know. Referring to the methodology of the USAID study, he writes, "los 'objetos,' o sea la población alteña, nunca tienen la palabra; mientras, los 'sujetos' de la investigación sólo consultaron una serie limitada de 'informantes clave' que nunca son mencionados por sus nombres ni citados directamente" (Zibechi 2006, 7; the "objects"—the population of El Alto—never get to speak, while the "subjects" of the investigation are limited to a group of "key informants" who are never mentioned by name or cited directly [Zibechi 2010, 33]). Certainly, a USAID report is a very specific kind of text, nothing like the kind of analysis Zibechi strives to produce. But his inclusion of this kind of state knowledge production demonstrates the complete disjuncture not only between the "subjects" and "objects" connected in the study but also between the very concepts of power and organization that each "side" of this relation employs.

The communitarian relations, what Zibechi describes as the "máquina social comunitaria" (communitarian social machine), appear in his descriptions of El Alto but also in the form of the narrative he produces. In the prologue, Raquel Gutiérrez Aguilar and the editor, Luis Gómez, write: "No intenta establecer definiciones, ni quiere estipular principios generales. Más bien, pregunta y duda mirando hacia lo nuevo, hacia la creatividad humana que desborda los conceptos previos vaciándolos y exhibiéndolos como límites del pensamiento. En ese movimiento, convierte al conocimiento en potencia de la propia lucha social" (He doesn't attempt to establish definitions, nor does he want to stipulate general principles. Rather, he asks questions and doubts looking toward the new, toward that human creativity that exceeds the prior concepts, emptying them and exposing them as limits of our thought. In that movement, he converts the knowledge into the strength of the social struggle itself; Gómez and Gutiérrez Aguilar 2006, 17). What they allude to here is the way that the arguments presented are not structured through the pairing of "real" events with theoretical concepts extracted from some other external source, meant to essentially confirm what we think we already know. Zibechi repeatedly refers to the protagonists of the stories told in the book in an effort to authorize his claims through the actors' own analysis. The final page of the introduction articulates the contributions of the many whose voices come through on every page, though this is not the usual acknowledgments section common to most books. In its form it might seem to be, but when read alongside the footnotes, prologues, epilogues, quotations, and references that give the book its unique texture, the names that fill this cluster of brief paragraphs call out to the reader, making her complicit in the collective process of imagining that the book makes visible. Accessibility, then, becomes a question not only related to consumption of the book but also to its composition as the plurality of actor-authors participate in its making.

The overwhelming majority of the theorists and thinkers cited are not external to the context and events the text describes. They are actors immediate and organic to the recent history that the text documents. Far from an essentializing gesture, this repertoire of action-thought corresponds to the approach Gómez and Gutiérrez Aguilar describe above: concepts are not applied, fixed, or defined—they emerge from and through the relations that make and tell the story. The militancy of the antistate movements that become the protagonists is also present in the research practices that compose the book. In resisting the conventions of research and writing, the book departs from the positivism and objectivity that stand as pillars of academia and journalism, respectively. The distinction between writer and press only became marked after the ideas were formed. Zibechi describes the weeks he spent in El Alto, accompanied by an editor from the Textos Rebeldes press, walking the streets of the city, talking with organizers, collectives, and intellectuals. While in many ways Zibechi's research practice resembles ethnographic fieldwork, it has a much brisker pace. He is a journalist by training—he says he spent weeks in El Alto, not the customary years an anthropologist might dedicate. But his writing (in this book in particular) does not fall neatly into one category or another. And while his presence in El Alto is much like that of any journalist, the difference is in the ways his work there becomes articulated to other sites, other actors, other practices. It is his frequent and vast movement across the continent combined with his engagements with those making, printing, and distributing his writing that give his work the organic quality that *Dispersar* makes so apparent.[10]

What is at stake in *Dispersar* is not the production of the "real" or "true" history or the definitive analysis produced by an outside observer but rather an interrogation into what Gómez and Gutiérrez Aguilar (2006, 18) call "las posibilidades de estabilización y permanencia—no de institucionalización y congelamiento—de la energía social desplegada y hasta hoy, incontenible, que *al producir la historia reciente* de Bolivia, de los Andes, viene al mismo tiempo transformándola" (the possibilities of stabilization and permanence—not of institutionalization and freezing—of the social energy that is being deployed and until now has been uncontainable, and the process of *producing the recent history* of Bolivia, of the Andes, simultaneously transforms it). Understanding recent events, and engaging in the ongoing production of history, becomes a militant exercise in examining the potential for these antistate relations to become more permanent—if always provisional—as the process of thinking, analyzing, debating, and writing itself transforms the history in progress. This is a hallmark of militant research (Juris 2008; Colectivo Situaciones 2007) be-cause, as John Holloway (2010b, 11) insists, "books [are] part of a historical moment, part of the flow of struggle." The effects they have are not consistent, as books made in the usual manner are more likely to grate against the flow of struggle, rather than run with it and for it (the aspiration of organic books). *Dispersar el poder*, in the process and practice of its composition, clearly aims to run with the flow of struggle, acting as a tool for advancing that historical moment beyond the local experiences it describes.

As I explore in greater depth in chapter 3, this particular book has had many lives, touching many sites of struggle as presses have picked up the text, reprinting their own versions of it across Latin America, the United States, and Europe. Various elements of the book-object are, of course, transformed in the process: design, materials, value, copyright, language. Interestingly, in distinct editions, there is a variety of paratexts that provides a sort of political translation of the main text to the local context of each publication. The added texts include new introductions, forewords, prologues, epilogues, translator's notes, publisher's notes, back cover texts, and featured reviews. Some are carried over from edition to edition, while others are unique to a single edition or disappear in others. The paratexts, which transform each edition of the book into both a local and translocal book, connect political conversations and practices across disperse sites.

The first edition, published in 2006 in La Paz, features a prologue written by Raquel Gutiérrez Aguilar and Luis Gómez, who like his coauthor is also from Mexico and lived in Bolivia for many years. The prologue, which has been included in most editions other than the English translation, suggests the dynamic of the book's plurality in its title: "Los múltiples significados del libro de Zibechi" (The multiple meanings of Zibechi's book). As the book moves and is rethought, reprinted, reread, it becomes multiple—it is continually remade as it comes into contact with different arrangements of experiences, practices, and actors. The epilogue by Colectivo Situaciones (2006, 226) from Buenos Aires comments, "La comunidad, contra todo sentido común, produce dispersión . . . dispersión del poder, guerra al estado" (Community, against all common sense, produces dispersion . . . dispersion of power, war on the state). Dispersion, which Colectivo Situaciones defined as a transversal connection, is in a sense what the book as a multiple and dynamic object produces, particularly when generated through practices that explicitly and implicitly reject statist forms of relations and knowledge. This concept of the production of community as the dispersion of power is key to understanding the significance of autonomous knowledge. Zibechi argues that dispersion of power is precisely the opposite of what the state, as the institutionalized place of politics, creates. This particular book makes its argument explicit not just through Zibechi's political analysis and description—stories of the Aymara uprisings that shook, and continue to shake, Bolivia politically, socially, epistemically. The argument is also manifested in the relations that make the book (the movements and activists and thinkers Zibechi works with across the continent), as they are made visible through the book.

KALEIDOSCOPIC KNOWLEDGE PRACTICE

The book *Caleidoscopio de rebeldías* was born in Buenos Aires in 2006, yet the experiences that compose it span back over more than twenty years and stretch across the continent from Mexico to Chile. The link across these temporal and spatial boundaries is the writer of the book: Claudia Korol. A founder of the magazine turned press América Libre (Free America) and the popular education collective Pañuelos en Rebeldía, Korol grounds her work as an activist, a writer, and an educator in a practice of solidarity. If a single word could describe *Caleidoscopio de rebeldías* it would be, no doubt, "solidarity." For Korol, solidarity is not a radicalization of philanthropy in the typical North to South model; it is the ethical commitment to recreate and reimagine social relations not mediated by the logic of the state and capital, which is to say, efficiency, profit, endless accumulation, and growth. The formation of new social relations is the practice of "vivir la solidaridad en lo cotidiano" (living solidarity in the everyday; Korol 2006, 19). What she calls "descolonización cultural" (cultural decolonization) is an ongoing process of "inventa[r] territorios de libertad y solidaridad sobre la base de la movilización político pedagógica de un pueblo que va sabiendo lo que sabe, y va aprendiendo a ser" (inventing territories of freedom and solidarity on the basis of political-pedagogical mobilization of a people who go on knowing what they know and learning how to be; 23). She defines "cultural decolonization" as processual, always incomplete, and aspiring toward collective liberation from "todas las formas de alienación" (all forms of alienation; 23). In other words, a struggle for autonomy through relations of solidarity. Solidarity, as a quotidian political practice that exceeds the designated spaces of politics (in the sense outlined by Tapia 2008), is the formation of fluid, shifting, multidimensional relations where resonances emerge—not taking the form of unconditional support, but rather as a commitment to encounter and dialogue, a *caminar preguntando* (walking while asking questions) together. *Caleidoscopio* is made of such resonances. It is a book made of the relations that connect disperse sites of popular struggles for autonomy.

The title of the book is a direct reference to how Korol sees and experiences movement in the continent: as ever-shifting and rearranging elements in motion together. The "kaleidoscope of rebellions" is another term for América Libre (Free America)—the name of the press. Like the artwork that adorns its cover, the book is composed like a kaleidoscope, moving in and out of different spaces, with connections across territories coming into focus and then fading back. As the narrative travels through her personal accounts and analysis, drifting from chronicles of specific movements into broader descriptions of the connections across the various movements, Korol juxtaposes her narration with that of her comrades in Chile, Argentina, Brazil, Mexico, Guatemala, and her voice becomes one among many. The book is divided into four sections: "Educación popular" (Popular education); "Crónicas de América Latina" (Chronicles of Latin America); "Guevariando la historia" (Guevarizing history); and "Crónicas breves" (Brief chronicles). The first section is a combination of brief essays and talks given by Korol at various *encuentros* and events in the early 2000s, including one presentation that consists entirely of questions which she posed as "provocaciones" (provocations) during the Foro Social de las Américas in Ecuador in 2004. Throughout the book, Korol's attachments to a language of socialism and Marxism are present, in some ways identifying her with a certain generation of Latin American intellectuals, though these terms appear in constant and productive tension with her feminist ethics, her commitments to autonomy, and her solidarity with indigenous struggles.

While her individual voice is centered throughout the book, her voice has no greater authority than the actors whose stories fill the pages, and she writes her own presence into the text alongside the protagonists of the movements, making visible the relations of solidarity that make up this book. Throughout, Korol (2006, 30) describes the movements, and in particular the unprecedented networks that connect them, as engaging in "resistencia al pensamiento único" (resistance to singular thought). This resistance to singular thought—evident in the diverse experiences that merge in the kaleidoscope—connects the political work of the movements with the question of how autonomous knowledge is produced, what form it takes, and for what purposes.

In Korol's experience, autonomous knowledge is the product of popular education and emancipatory pedagogy, which she describes as a process of "reflexión 'desde los movimientos populares,' desde su praxis, su memoria histórica, sus necesidades y los procesos en los que se va constituyendo un nuevo bloque histórico social que altera los lugares conocidos de los grupos sociales que los integran" (reflection "from the popular movements," from their praxis, their historical memory, their needs, and the processes through which a new historical social force alters the known spaces of the social groups that compose them; Korol 2006, 37). Radical education and pedagogy are the foundation of many twenty-first century movements in Latin America, and anchor the prefigurative character of their praxis. One of the key material tools of popular education is the organic book. Korol notes that the pedagogical quality of the movements takes many forms, ranging from alternative schooling systems (as in the case of the autonomous education of the Zapatistas in Mexico or the Movimento Sem Terra in Brazil) to political education efforts within productive projects (workers cooperatives, alternative media initiatives, community food systems, etc.).

On a Friday evening in late winter 2011, I made my way to Industrias Metalúrgicas y Plásticas Argentina (IMPA, Plastic and Metallurgic Industries of Argentina), a factory where aluminum packaging of all kinds is manufactured, from spray cans to toothpaste tubes to candy wrappers. The factory fills a large block along the train tracks in what is now one of Buenos Aires's most desirable areas. In May 1998 the workers of the factory organized themselves and occupied the factory, taking over its management. Since then, IMPA has thrived, like hundreds of other *empresas recuperadas* (recuperated companies) across Argentina, becoming much more than a factory.[11] In the twenty years it has been worker owned and operated, IMPA has expanded to include a community library, an autonomous school and university, a theater workshop, and a range of other spaces for the workers and others to come together. In addition to the projects officially housed in IMPA, dozens of other groups use the expansive space of the factory for their own autonomous projects.

I made my first trip to IMPA to participate in one of the weekly workshops coordinated by the Pañuelos en Rebeldía Popular Education Team. I learned about Pañuelos en Rebeldía—Claudia Korol's project—from a comrade of mine, a young political science professor at the University of Buenos Aires and teacher at one of the Movimiento Popular La Dignidad's *bachilleratos populares* (popular adult schools). My friend had studied in the Masters Program in Popular Education that Korol once coordinated at the Universidad de las Madres de la Plaza de Mayo and encouraged me to attend the workshop at IMPA to connect with the team members. As I recount the connections that led me to this workshop, what emerges is a map of precisely the kinds of relations between collectives and individuals that are made visible in Korol's book. The now institutionalized (and highly controversial, in part due to its implication in various corruption scandals) Fundación Madres de la Plaza de Mayo connects an older generation of activists with a worker-owned factory through a popular education project that has contributed to the formation of alternative schools like those of the Movimiento Popular La Dignidad. The relations that make up this map go on and on, extending far beyond the city limits of Buenos Aires or even the national borders of Argentina.

I entered IMPA through a massive steel sliding door, climbing a ramp next to a loading dock. Though my destination was a popular education workshop and I could hear the echoes of drums from the theater inside, it was immediately evident that I was entering a factory. Miscellaneous equipment was lined up against one wall, and at the end of the entrance I could see boxes of materials. Just past the ramp, I reached a large open space; in the center a small group of people was gathered in a circle of folding chairs, waiting for the workshop to begin. A young woman confirmed that I was in the right place and said that we'd be starting shortly. The workshop happens weekly, and while I had been concerned that I would be the only newcomer, it was obvious that this was not the case. In many ways, the physical space we occupied within IMPA reflected the relational dynamics of the group: open, unbounded, porous, contingent, shifting. When someone asked about Korol, we were told that she was out of town. It then seemed clear that even if she had been present, she wouldn't necessarily have been the leader of the workshop—despite being the group's most senior member and founder.

This particular session was focused on the experiences of members of Pañuelos en Rebeldía at the Florestán Fernández Popular Education Center: a school of the Movimento Sem Terra (MST) in Brazil open to participants from across Latin America. Several of the facilitators had participated in a four-month cycle at the school, and after the screening of a documentary about it, a conversation was opened about the process of living and attending the rural school, the pedagogical structure of the MST, and the relationship of Pañuelos en Rebeldía to the MST and other participants at the school. The comments shared by those who had attended the school were far from romantic—there was no idealizing the experience or the structure and logic of the MST school. They described a discomfort they felt with the disjuncture between the rhetoric of emancipatory pedagogy and the traditional vertical structure of many of the classes. Several participants confessed to feeling surprised at the degree of discomfort they felt—both politically in their reactions to the pedagogical orientation of the school and personally in their own difficulties of adjusting to a context so removed from their (relative) privilege as residents of a major cosmopolitan city. I found these moments of candid reflection surprising, and they gave the workshop—and my overall impression of Pañuelos en Rebeldía—a richness in terms of the expression of a complicated relationship to their counterparts in other parts of the continent. The MST center is not held up as a model but rather as a particular approach appropriate to the context and realities of that particular movement. The experiences of Pañuelos en Rebeldía with the MST are precisely the kinds of moments where concepts are tested and other ideas emerge.

Korol's book, published by América Libre—a radical press that operates alongside Pañuelos en Rebeldía—was printed at the print shop of the Fundación Madres de la Plaza de Mayo. The press, which is an extension of the magazine, later separated itself from Las Madres due to what members describe as a need for greater autonomy. These relations—between Pañuelos en Rebeldía and IMPA, the MST, Las Madres, and other organizations—are both the material basis of their knowledge practices and the process through which their political ideas emerge. This is to say that these relations with the organized, productive projects of various movements, including IMPA's factory space, MST's education center, Las Madres's university and print shop, are necessary to the material production of not only the tools (books) that Pañuelos produces but also to the very ideas that fill the pages of the books and are the product of the workshops. The resultant books are enactments of the complexity of the relations that make them and of a political meaning that exceeds what is contained in the words on the page.

What each of the projects that intersect in this book posit, in distinct terms, is a subversion of the division of political labor. At IMPA workers all earn equal wages, regardless of their specific job. In the MST, cooperativism aims to make all participants in the movement equal agents in political and productive labor. In the Universidad de Las Madres, alternative education is conceived of as a means to bridge generations in the production of counterhegemonic knowledge. Each of these experiences is wrought with contradictions, and these fissures between rhetoric and reality are magnified as the movements come into contact with one another. The position of "intellectuals" and de facto leaders within these movements is a particularly salient site to interrogate these disjunctures, and Korol dedicates much of her analysis to this question.

Caleidoscopio de rebeldías is not the story of a single movement, nor is it the product of a single writer's thought. Each chapter moves us from one site to another, through different moments and spaces of struggles for emancipation. The words that fill the pages are, in many instances, Korol's. In other instances the words are explicitly attributed to other participants in the movements. But regardless of whose voice the ideas are expressed through, Korol makes explicit efforts to qualify everything in the book as the product of a collective process. She, and others she cites, may be seen or identified as "intellectuals" in their respective movements, but what they communicate are "saberes construidos en la resistencia" (knowledges produced in the resistance; Korol 2006, 15). Emancipatory pedagogy and popular education are the tools Korol promotes for collective, autonomous knowledge practices. Ideas and concepts formulated in this way are necessarily infused with the complexity of that collective practice: "La labor pedagógica de los oprimidos obliga a interpretar al mundo tal cual es, en sus dimensiones macro y micro, objetivas y subjetivas, en sus interrelaciones. Toda tentativa de simplificación otorga ventajas a quienes han hecho del conocimiento una de las armas poderosas en las que sostienen y reproducen su poder" (The pedagogic labor of the oppressed forces us to interpret the world as it is, in its macro and micro, objective and subjective dimensions, in its interrelations. All attempts to simplify it grants an advantage to those who have made knowledge one of the most powerful weapons in their maintenance and reproduction of power; Korol 2006, 28). This is to say that the process of rendering the tangled nature of reality—and better yet, of politics—simple, tidy, and familiar only serves to reproduce the "common sense" through which the state and other institutions of power maintain their dominance. For Korol the subversion of this "bourgeois common sense" is the subversion of what Zibechi calls "state relations" and what we might think of more broadly as institutional or static relations. Collective knowledge practices emerge from a commitment to engaging with the complexities, contradictions, and difficulties of everyday praxis. Conceived of in this way, the relations that are both the medium for and the subject of these knowledge practices are dynamic relations. The isolated intellectual is incapable of enacting autonomous knowledge because autonomous knowledge *is* the enactment of autonomous relations. Key to this idea is the fact that autonomous knowledge here is always collective. Drawing on Gramsci, Korol signals the dangers of the intellectuals of any movement becoming separated from the day-to-day practices and existence of the movements. The usual sites of intellectual labor—NGOs, the academy, and other state institutions—are intentionally divorced from the everyday, and their hierarchical and static order depends on this separation for legitimacy. But as Korol (2006, 36) notes, citing Gramsci, "El error del intelectual consiste en creer que se puede saber sin comprender y especialmente sin sentir y ser apasionado" (the error of the intellectual consists in thinking that one can know and comprehend without feeling and being passionate). An intellectual with concrete experience, collective commitments, and passion is a different kind of intellectual—potentially an organic intellectual.

But my interest here lies not in outlining the conditions for the emergence of organic intellectuals but rather in exploring the autonomous knowledge practices at work—the stuff of organic books. And I argue that the only way to see autonomous knowledge is through objects and the relations that produce them. For Korol (2006, 53) autonomous popular education is "acción cultural por la libertad." The making of books is a process that brings together many of the elements that she outlines as fundamental to popular education as the praxis of liberation, including a transformation of the relationship between practice and theory; a reclaiming of the quotidian as the site of popular struggle; and the recuperation of a communal sociability (Korol 2006, 38–40). The book, as the concrete tool through which experience is compiled and theorized, has multiple functions: on the one hand it's the medium for the broader circulation of ideas, and on the other hand its very production is itself a process for collective reflection and theorization of political praxis.

So, why a book? Why not a magazine? An article? A website? Books, by their very nature, require a conjunction of different kinds of work for their production. While one of the key ideas that Korol emphasizes is the importance of translating face-to-face experiences and oral culture into written language, she also argues that a book is the most useful form this written material can take. This has to do, of course, with the greater durability and permanence of the book-object versus other print forms and the commitment that both publishers and readers invest in this particular form. Perhaps more significantly, for Korol the actual process of composing a book is a process of theoretical production. Making a book is another instance of a collective knowledge practice, in the sense that the collective work of producing this object is a process of meaning-making—the political and theoretical ideas contained in the book do not end with the writing of the text. The text is the collection of words that can be contained in a notebook, a computer file, a stack of sheets of paper, or—potentially—a book. But a text has no essential material form. And we can only interact with a text through the form it takes as some kind of document—some of which require more or less labor to produce. In connecting many kinds of work, the bookmaking process is collective, and the book-object itself is steeped with political meaning as a result of all the relations involved in its production.

BECOMING BOOK: MOVEMENTS, WRITERS, PRESSES

The details of the three books examined in this chapter are vastly different, and this particularity of knowledge practices—all examples of knowledge-as-doing—is precisely what makes them organic books. I have not attempted to trace constant elements to compare three cases side by side; rather, I have looked at the particular processes that each book and its stories manifest. In doing so, my interest lies in elucidating how the organic book—in the ways it is conceived—contributes theoretically and politically to the broader practice of autonomous politics. The movements depart from dogmatic and vanguardist approaches to politics, wherein certain subjects propose answers and programs for transforming society. The new movements, and especially the autonomous movements that are the subjects of these books, emerge through doing "wild politics" (Tapia 2008)—a politics uncontained by either institutions or existing concepts, a politics only made visible by the relations that are formed in the process of doing. Organic books—as the objects organic to these politics—are best understood through the relations that make up, and are made by, these practices. What defines an organic book is not a set of consistent criteria. Rather, an organic book can only be defined by its practices: how it is made, what it does, and how it works. The three stories explored in this chapter express distinct yet overlapping collective knowledge practices and follow how these practices become books. The titles alone express the different contents: *Pensar las autonomías* is about the process of disrupting dominant thought through the praxis of autonomy; *Dispersar el poder* is about the formation of antistate power; and *Caleidoscopio de rebeldías* is about connections forged across diverse territories in pedagogical experiments.

Pensar las autonomías bears the names of more than a dozen writers on its cover, alongside dozens of concepts that are explored in the essays: struggle, ethics, antagonism, emancipation, class, work, capital, power, disobedience, rebellion, movement, community, collectivity, resistance, and others. This edited volume is literally made of the relations that articulate the collective editor—Jóvenes en Resistencia Alternativa—with autonomous and anticapitalist politics and struggles across the continent. That an urban youth collective is the editor and compiler of this volume is significant—urban youth certainly are not the typical authority of knowledge (more commonly the university professor, state intellectual, or NGO researcher) that assumes this kind of networking role. Autonomy, defined by the editors as the disordering and continual reorganizing of the social from below, is the construction of collective forces and of possibilities. This provisional concept stands in contrast to the logic of the state—and this book stands in contrast to the logic of dominant knowledge production.

For *Dispersar el poder*, I examined how the composition of the text itself mirrors the spatial dynamics that gave way to the unique reorganization of power in the popular mobilizations in El Alto. We saw the operations of the *máquina comunitaria dispersadora* (communitarian dispersion machine) in the unique urban terrain of El Alto and in the production of knowledge about and from it. In understanding the practice of community to be the production of dispersion, antistate knowledge emerges as the product of the fluid, nonhierarchical, contingent relations. The "decolonization of thought" that Zibechi references is exposed in concrete terms through the production of knowledge (and the tools of the circulation of knowledge—books) that does not rely on authoritative institutions or concepts.

Caleidoscopio de rebeldías takes the metaphor of its title as the organizing mechanism for its contents: movements come in and out of focus, change shape, and become fragmented and reconstituted as they interact with one another. The kaleidoscope becomes the symbol for solidarity—the definition of radical relations Korol proposes. Resonances emerge, not repetition nor reproduction, and this occurs as much in the analysis and the chronicles Korol compiles as in the spaces of popular education and anticapitalist praxis where she and her books move. The kaleidoscope of knowledge practices is the embodiment of the resistance to singular thought that popular education and emancipatory pedagogy posit as their guiding principle. And when those knowledge practices take the form of specific tools—books—a second process of collective theorization and political work emerges. As a member of one press commented, "estar en una editorial es una posibilidad de militar" (being part of a press is one possibility for militant activity; interview, Buenos Aires, 2011). The collective processes through which organic books emerge are spaces where "words and communication flow" dialogically, recalling Zibechi's (2000) description of the *mirada horizontal* (horizontal gaze) of Zapatismo in the epigraph that opens this chapter. This dialogism and horizontality are what make the organic book possible, what allow it to come into being.

I have explored the idea of knowledge-as-doing in the mode of autonomous knowledge practices, asking how they are enacted and what kinds of relations, materials, and actions both compose them and which they articulate. Arguing that autonomous knowledge (the stuff of organic books) is better seen through relations and practices than in terms of the referents of knowledge, I have examined specific moments in the initial composition of these organic books and the formation of the political ideas that fill them. By describing the overlap between the relations through which ideas are generated and the relations through which they become books, I have endeavored to show some of the material and political effects of these knowledge practices, which are characteristic of the organic book. While subsequent chapters specifically address the material labors of crafting, reediting, and distributing organic books, this chapter has considered how such books come to be—through what kinds of relations and practices. In the next chapter, I move my analysis into a crucial space of book production—the printing workshop—to focus on the economic and technical practices which connect the site of book printing and assembly to the autonomous politics of the movements that produce them. In doing so, I explore how the political commitment to producing low-cost books generates experimental practices.

TWO

THE WORKSHOP BOOK

Los costos de los libros son bajos. Cuanto mejor sea un libro más barato debería ser. Un precio alto no debe ser un premio sino un castigo. Los precios nos apartan de la lectura, los precios desprecian a los lectores. Si a los que tienen el poder de fijarlos no les importa otra cosa que el dinero, estamos obligados a que no nos importe otra cosa que la cultura. . . .

¡Editemos libros genéricos que contrarresten el negocio editorial!

The costs of books are low. The better the book, the cheaper it should be. A high price should be a punishment, not a reward. Prices distance us from reading, the prices deride the readers. If those who have the power to set the prices of books don't care about anything other than profit, then we have no choice but to care about nothing other than culture. . . .

Let's publish generic books that oppose the publishing business!

—GUILLERMO DE PÓSFAY, *LA FURIA DEL LIBRO (GENÉRICO)*

JUST THIRTY-SIX pages long and composed of short essays, poems and micronarratives, *La furia del libro (genérico)* (The fury of the [generic] book; 2005) is a manifesto penned and published by Guillermo De Pósfay, one of the most prolific writers and publishers in the underground literary scene in Argentina today. In this small chapbook bound with a simple matte black cover bearing the image of a fist shaped like South America, De Pósfay calls for the making of "generic books"—inexpensive but high quality books—as an alternative to the books produced by profit-driven commercial publishers. These generic books, he says, when made affordably and sold at cost, are able to reach more readers who are in turn nourished and empowered by them. Books in this sense are not seen as simply another cultural commodity to be consumed by the individual reader but as a necessary component of social transformation. The manifesto is admittedly romantic in its characterization of the power of books, but what it asserts about the economics of publishing is compelling: as a kind of non-commodity—or at least an *alter*-commodity—the value of the generic book is entirely dependent on its accessibility and its utility. Generic books, De Pósfay suggests, can do things that other (commercial) books can't, and their impact reaches beyond the individual consumer. De Pósfay's generic book resonates with my central concept: the organic book. Much like Antonio Gramsci's concept of the organic intellectual—who, distinct from the "traditional" intellectual, is identified with the interests of the class or group she or he thinks for and with—this kind of book is organic to the politics and contexts it engages, describes, and theorizes. And like the generic book, it is neither academic nor commercial, neither elite nor private. But just how are generic or organic books made? What does a production process look like when the use-value of books (what De Pósfay counts as "culture") is prioritized over their potential exchange-value, or profitability?

In this chapter, I move through different spaces where such books are made, shifting between two interconnected—but in many ways distant—cities: La Paz and Buenos Aires. Over the past two decades, along with the rural migration within Bolivia to urban centers like El Alto (Rodgers, Beall, and Kanbur 2012) migration to Argentina has also exploded, further entangling these two countries economically, culturally, and politically (Cerrutti and Parrado 2015).[1] Often named the "poorest" country in South America (and home to the largest indigenous population proportional to its overall population), Bolivia stands in sharp contrast to its southern neighbor, and especially to that country's capital city, often called the "Paris" of Latin America. While Bolivia often falls off the map of the book industry in Latin America, Buenos Aires is a city internationally recognized for its unique relationship to this cultural object—it is a hub of Latin American publishing, and in 2011 UNESCO named it the "World Book Capital." The "lettered city" that Ángel Rama analyzes in his eponymous groundbreaking work looks quite different in these two countries. A neocolonial center-periphery dynamic between Argentina (especially the capital) and Bolivia produces the kind of asymmetric ignorance that Dipesh Chakrabarty (2000) refers to when he calls for "provincializing Europe." "Europe" (here much more than a territorially bound space), he explains, is the unnamed referent in all histories, with a one-way dynamic of recognition and intertextuality with the rest of the world (Chakrabarty 2000, 28). This asymmetry can also be seen as an effect of the enduring "coloniality of knowledge" theorized by Aníbal Quijano (2000). Here, Buenos Aires stands in for "Europe": Argentine books fill the bookstores in La Paz, but there is practically no circulation of knowledge in the other direction—Bolivian books are scarce in the city that ranks internationally as having one of the highest rates of bookstores per capita. Yet if we shift our attention away from the usual spaces of book culture, the commercial and academic presses and the bookstores that sell their products, other circuits begin to appear. And these networks are distinct not just because of the kinds of products that move through them but because of the practices that make them.

As I move between these two very different cities, I consider how books are made in spaces marginal to the commercial, academic, and even so-called independent or alternative book industries. In both sites, I look beyond the realm occupied by well-known alternative presses (like Plural in La Paz and Tinta Limón in Buenos Aires) and the recuperated worker-run commercial print shops of Buenos Aires (like Chilavert, for example) to explore smaller, less visible spaces where political books are made. How does their distance (intentional or circumstantial) from larger-scale printing and publishing operations create the possibility for reimagining the book while prioritizing affordability, collaboration, and creativity? In this chapter, I explore what I call the "book workshop"—be it the print shop or any other places where books are crafted—to understand how organic books are produced through experimentation with different technical, economic, social, and political practices. I understand experimentation to refer to any process that involves the formulation of a question and the assembly of improbable elements; experiments always have the possibility of failure. Discussing the notion of "collective experiments," Bruno Latour (2011, 2) argues, "today . . . the laboratory has extended its walls to the whole planet." With the shifts "from science to research, from objects to projects, from implementation to experimentation" (12), Latour makes the claim that we are all engaged in collective experiments. Experimentation is therefore fundamentally based on a departure from the implementation or an application of models—it is the development of questions and material practices for their ongoing interrogation by those engaged in the experiments. This, I argue, is precisely what is at play in the crafting of organic books: they *can* fail, and this, rather than being perceived as a problem, is expected, for results emerge only from experimenting. In fact, it could be said that the organic book workshops are continually failing, as their efforts to develop anticapitalist approaches to book production always fall short of full autonomy from the very structures they critique. They simultaneously reject and rely on certain structures and modes of production, but their ongoing experimentation with different ways of producing books is propelled by the horizon—rather than doctrine—of autonomy.

In examining how books are designed, printed, assembled and bound, I borrow C. Wright Mills's definition of craft as the practice of the freedom to experiment, exploring the book workshop as a space of craft work as opposed to industrial production. Craftsmanship, in this sense, is best understood as a "formgiving activity," as Marx defined it in the *Grundrisse*, suggesting that the making of things in this way contributes to the development of individuals and social relations. This is significant because craft-as-experimentation in the production of durable, concrete artifacts exemplifies how manual labor *is* an intellectual enterprise (Crawford 2009; Sennett 2008). In *Lines: A Brief History* (2007), Tim Ingold discusses the impact that the technology of print had on creating the division between the labor of *inscription* (the composition of ideas and words—the work of the author) and that of *impression* (the manual or mechanical printing of a pre-composed text—the work of the printer). Citing Raymond Williams, Ingold (2007, 127) explains that this distinction took root in late eighteenth century England: "If the author is a literary artist, the printer is a typographic artisan," with the latter (the craftsman) considered a "manual labourer without intellectual, imaginative, or creative purpose." The workshops where I follow the making of organic books challenge this division of labor and the technological determinism implicit to it. To be sure, this is not a new intervention. As Nicholas Thoburn (2016, 17) discusses, radical publishing has long relied on the printer as "something of a nexus." Citing Régis Debray's essay on the media forms of socialism, Thoburn describes this nexus as the "pivot" of socialism, in which the printer functions as a "worker intellectual or an intellectual worker" (17). While it could be said that the organic book reactivates the printer as worker intellectual, it is also important to note that it does so while blurring the boundaries of the various kinds of work involved in bookmaking. As this chapter demonstrates, the printer is not only a printer, just as the previous chapter detailed transformations in the position of the author.

As I will show, for the crafters of organic books, neither the technology of the book nor the tools used to create them determine the way these objects are made. Rather, it is *provisoriedad continua* (continuous provisionality, or constant improvisation) that defines their craft as an ongoing process of experimentation. In the founding text of the autonomous social center La Cazona de Flores penned by the Argentine militant research group Colectivo Situaciones, *provisoriedad* is explained in this way: "Se trata de forjar un nodo de prácticas (una institución) 'por un tiempito,' capaz de alentar nuevos cruces y de hacer variar los roles, con apropiaciones y sin propiedades, con tiempo para el descanso y recursos contra las fijaciones" (It's a question of forging a node of practices [an institution] "for a little while," capable of encouraging new crossings and of making the roles vary, with appropriations and without properties, with time for rest and resources against fixity; Colectivo Situaciones 2010).[2] Provisionality as a political principle can be understood as a means of making the partial and the temporary—whether intended or not—generative of new possibilities.

The inherent inefficiency of continuous provisionality and experimentation is fundamental to the process of producing objects outside a logic of profit and competition. This process allows the emergence of what feminist political economists J. K. Gibson-Graham call "new economic imaginaries" that go beyond the "capitalocentrism" of work and production. By "capitalocentrism" they mean "the unquestioned dominance of capitalism" and the ways it functions in our economic *and* social thinking and practice (Gibson-Graham 2006, 4). The practices that make possible the sort of noncapitalist imaginaries they refer to are those that are not defined through their relation (oppositional or otherwise) to capitalism. This transgression is precisely what John Holloway (2010a, 21) refers to with the idea of creating "cracks" in capitalism: "a crack is the perfectly ordinary creation of a space or moment in which we assert a different type of doing." This idea of creating cracks is based on the distinction he establishes between two types of activity: doing versus labor. This opposition is grounded in Marx's analysis of abstract and concrete labor, where the former refers to the alienated labor that produces exchange-value and the latter refers to the "life-giving activity" that produces use-value (Holloway 2010a, 89). If, as Holloway asserts in his twelfth thesis, "the abstraction of doing into labour is the weaving of capitalism" (87), then the revolt of doing against labor, where productive activity is reclaimed as useful by the doer, is fundamental to the ongoing process of "cracking capitalism."

The organic book offers a view into the specificity of what it means to crack *print* capitalism. While the print book's cultural value and "sacred" quality (L. Miller 2007, 19) has long defined it as a distinct kind of commodity, it has never been removed from the logic of commerce. As Febvre and Martin (1997, 109) sustain in *The Coming of the Book*, "From its earliest days printing existed as an industry, governed by the same rules as any other industry; the book was a piece of merchandise which men produced before anything else to earn a living, even when they were . . . scholars and humanists at the same time." The suggestion here is that there is an inherent conflict between the intellectual and the humanistic on one hand and the commercial and the industrial on the other. And while this has undoubtedly produced economic dynamics unique to book production and consumption, Ted Striphas (2009, 6) argues that the idea that books "belong at a significant remove from the realm of economic necessity is one of the most entrenched myths of contemporary book culture." Books, as Thoburn (2016, 41) also maintains, do not "transcend the realms of capital." What organic books and other modes of alternative book culture make visible, however, are the ways that this cultural product is the site of ongoing and renewed practices of autonomy.

As I explained in chapter 1, for the twenty-first-century movements, autonomy appears not as a doctrine or a stable practice but as a diversity of modes of resistance to domination by the "mediating-expropriating demands of the state and of capital" (Colectivo Situaciones 2006, 227). There are always tensions and contradictions within any autonomous practice, and rather than be ignored or obscured, this lack of "purity" is activated as a political ethic. In her study of the relationship between *cartonera* presses and corporate transnational publishing, Lucy Bell (2017, 58) discusses the complexity of resistance to institutional and commercial demands: "in spite of the impossibility of complete independence . . . the 'capture' (be it state or corporate) is challenged to a certain extent through the channeling of dissent into alternative practices." What she suggests (and I share her argument) is that the contribution of such approaches to publishing is not an alternative *model* of publishing but rather a sustained—if limited—challenge to the dominant model of publishing. One of Bell's central arguments is that the growth of the transnational publishing market has in fact "paradoxically fueled the emergence of independent craft publishers" (54). Bell examines craft publishing within the *cartonera* movement, which began in 2003 in Buenos Aires and is characterized by the production of handmade books of photocopied A4 pages stapled into a hand-painted cover made of recycled cardboard purchased from cardboard collectors, or *cartoneros* (Barilaro 2009, 47).[3] Like Tinta Limón, Colectivo Situaciones, and countless other political and artistic projects (Giunta 2009), the first of the *cartonera* presses, Eloísa Cartonera, emerged from the political turbulence and effervescence of the aftermath of the 2001 economic crisis in Argentina and grew from a collaboration between writer Washington Cucurto and artist Javier Barilaro (Barilaro 2009, 46). They describe the project as being born "on one of those furious days when people filled the streets to protest and fight back" (Eloísa Cartonera 2009, 62). Like the producers of the organic book, the *cartonera* presses transgress the division of labor that characterizes contemporary publishing, in part through their adoption of nonhierarchical forms of organization. In this way, both the *cartonera* book and the organic book are produced through practices that are, in part, construed as acts of refusal, expressions of a kind of "¡Ya basta!"—refusal to be absorbed into commercial markets, refusal to operate within an individualistic logic, and refusal to be driven by profit rather than usefulness. Refusal, of course, does not in itself imply autonomy from those structures and dynamics, but it does generate other possibilities for doing things differently.

But refusal does not simply emerge from a conscious decision to create another way of doing and being in the world. In the twenty-first century, autonomous modes of production organized under the ethos of *autogestión* are often the product of crises, in which work, production, and the social relations that drive them unravel, forcing people to pursue alternatives. As Mabel Thwaites Rey (2010, 187) notes in her contribution to *Pensar las autonomías*, in the case of Argentina, "estas prácticas autogestivas crecieron como consecuencia de una crisis profunda" (these autogestive practices grew as the consequence of a profound crisis). In Argentina, and indeed elsewhere, the very precarity and contingency that neoliberalism imposes on communities and economies can be mobilized in the creation of possibilities for experimentation in collective practices of production.

The organic book workshop—as a space dedicated to *doing* together and making products whose value is measured by their *usefulness*—is a site for the creation of the kinds of alternatives that Holloway (2010a) calls "cracks." In what follows, I combine close examination of the materiality of the books themselves with analysis of technical, economic, political, and social practices at play in the workshops. In doing so, I revisit a question posed by Adrian Johns (1998) in *The Nature of the Book*: how does the social character of the print shop affect its products? I want to push this question further to consider the ways that these products—the books themselves—are not just symbolic reflections but actual materializations of the social, political, and economic relations at play in the workshops and their broader contexts. The craft and experimentation that occurs in these spaces yield books that embody ways of thinking about and organizing work beyond "capitalocentrism" and that function more as mutable social objects than as fixed commodities.

"PERO AQUÍ TENEMOS NUESTRA IDIOSINCRASIA EN COMO HACEMOS LAS COSAS"

In the first edition of Raúl Zibechi's *Dispersar el poder* (Dispersing Power), released by the Bolivian press Textos Rebeldes in 2006, the clean design of the cover—a collage of clear brown and yellow text, a bright blue background, and a vivid photo of a crowd of Bolivian workers—quickly contrasts with the book's interior.[4] The newsprint pages that carry the text—referred to in the industry as "the guts" or "los interiores" (the insides)—seem to indicate that this book is made to be used, to be read and marked up and shared, rather than collected and skimmed and displayed. The first technical flaw appears on the second page of the text: a footnote that has been left unfinished, the sentence ending abruptly with "puede verse en" (see in). I read this as evidence of a book composed hastily but perhaps more out of urgency than carelessness. Two dozen pages later, the first handwritten corrections appear in the text. These marks are the work of Hugo,[5] the founder of a small, family-run print shop at the top of one of La Paz's notoriously steep, narrow streets, and the workshop, I would come to learn, responsible for designing, printing, and binding the overwhelming majority of the books produced locally by presses that identify themselves as "political" or "militant." While they no doubt jar the reader, as the lines of the handwritten letters clash with the uniformity of the Times New Roman font, these marks are more than a mere blemish on the pages. They make visible the presence of another actor in the life of any book, not the author or the editor but the printer—a figure so vital to the production

FIGURE 2.1. Workshop, La Paz, 2011.

of a book-object but who usually becomes an unremarked absence in the final product.

A glance around Hugo's shop makes clear that he will print just about anything—the walls of his compact workshop are plastered with everything from proofs of political book covers to rock posters to calendars bearing the logos of butcher shops and images of half-naked models. But along one wall of the shop, a glass case is filled with books that tell of a very different kind of work that happens here. Titles dating back more than ten years line the shelves, and the logos and names of a dozen or so presses mark the spines. Alongside the Textos Rebeldes titles, I see books by some of the most prolific radical theorists in Bolivia: Silvia Rivera Cusicanqui (Editorial La Mirada Salvaje, El Colectivo 2, Taller de Historia Oral Andina), Alison Spedding (Editorial Mama Huaco), Pablo Mamani Ramirez (Willka, Centro Andino de Estudios Estratégicos), and the Grupo Comuna (Muela del Diablo). This small library creates a sort of map of the political relationships that Hugo has developed over the years as the print shop of choice for La Paz's radical and militant presses. This family-run shop has many elements of a small commercial business. There is an owner who is the life of the business, ever present and ceaselessly and tirelessly working. There are several waged employees, all of whom have specific tasks that they focus on. The shop has the basic equipment found in any commercial print shop: offset press, guillotine cutter, and binding and folding machines. The shop offers competitive rates in relation to the other dozen or so print shops that line the same street. And much of the material that it produces—calendars, posters, brochures, pamphlets—could be produced in any one of those shops. Yet in my conversations with the printer, he makes evident his personal and political commitments to the work of the political presses, like the Textos Rebeldes collective, that bring their books to be printed here. This commitment to making quality books accessible, paired with decades of experience in the printing trade, means that Hugo aspires to find every conceivable way to lower the cost of the books while weighing the balance of aesthetic quality with political utility. The printer works with the publishers and authors, experimenting with elements including design, layout, paper quality, and volume, to determine the most cost-efficient ways to produce a quality book. For example, rather than purchase the more expensive *papel ahuesado* (off-white or ivory paper)—preferred over white paper because it is more aesthetically pleasing and easier on the eyes—Hugo has found that by purchasing plain white paper and staining it himself, he can achieve the same effect at a fraction of the cost.

By producing books so inexpensively for these small presses, Hugo manifests his political commitments, creating the possibility for a different kind of book production while intervening in—or at least retreating from—both the commercial book market and the piracy market. The sort of interstitial space that Hugo occupies in the world of print in La Paz, producing pirate-priced books *and* commercial materials, is the result of the experience he has accumulated through years of experimentation with the tools of his trade: paper, ink, machines, digital technology. And this is part of the answer he gives me when I ask why some titles published by Plural Editores (considered the most well-known and widely circulating publisher of political and academic texts in Bolivia) are printed by Hugo. I tell him that I was surprised to see him listed as the printer in several Plural titles I own, since I know that they have their own print shop. But Plural, he explains, is unable to reach the uniquely low costs that Hugo achieves in his shop despite having this valuable infrastructure in-house. Perhaps their print shop is too caught up in the usual way of making books, too distant from the real work of craft defined by a freedom to experiment. Plural is, without a doubt, the most established independent publisher of political books in La Paz, yet its books are forced to compete locally with the countless books made by Hugo for the dozens of small presses that he considers his *compañerxs* (comrades). In the few serious bookstores in the city, the Bolivian-produced titles on the shelves stand out for their affordability, and Plural is clearly working to align itself more closely with books made by Hugo than the exorbitantly priced imports from Spain, Mexico, or Argentina.

The printer explains that the "commercial" jobs he does—for businesses, for government agencies, for NGOs, all of whom are charged standard market prices—are a key component of his strategy of making political books cheap and accessible. The experimentation he engages in as he works to make such books more affordable is therefore clearly tied to his political commitments. The books that need to be circulated widely—and thus compel him to experiment with ways of reducing costs—are the ones being produced by his comrades at the militant presses. To be sure, these books don't necessarily look "cheap" (at least not at first glance), since Hugo's keen attention to the details of design allow inexpensive materials to be disguised by an appealing aesthetic. In the Textos Rebeldes edition of *Dispersar el poder*, one of Hugo's greatest strengths as a print shop comes through on every page: the skills and experience to maintain the lowest possible cost for books made by militant presses. In this particular book, the handwritten corrections show a commitment to producing a quality text that is complete and readable but a reluctance to spend the extra time and incur the added costs needed for creating new negatives to correct small errors. The sharp cover design almost masks the inexpensive newsprint that lies within it. And priced at just nineteen bolivianos in bookstores in La Paz (compared to fifty-five to eighty bolivianos for a similarly sized book printed by the most prominent leftist press in La Paz), the accessibility of this book is outstanding. In a conversation about his practice, Hugo tells me that "lo que vendemos aquí son imágenes" (what we sell here are images; interview, La Paz, 2011). But given the technical imperfection of his products, this idea of making and selling images isn't simply about appearances and aesthetics. As I see it, the "images" he makes are also reflections of the relationships and political commitments that underpin his work. The image of the relations that produced a book like *Dispersar el poder* (and that is reflected in the form of the object) is of a nonhierarchical collective process connecting authors, editors, and printers in an effort to disseminate ideas in a practical manner. One of the key concepts Zibechi develops in *Dispersar el poder* is that of the "dispersing social machine," made up of a dense network of relations that are fluid, nonhierarchical, and contingent. The image Hugo crafts in his workshop (which I interpret quite literally to refer to something concrete and tangible like a photograph rather than a reflection) is, in a sense, analogous to the kind of networks Zibechi describes in his study of the rebellions that shook El Alto in the first years of the twenty-first century.

The tension between correctness and functionality is what Richard Sennett argues relinks the quality of the "practical" with "practice" in craft production. This is more than apparent in Hugo's books, and this tension is made manifest in another aspect of the production process: the legal registration of the publications. The first line on the legal page or copyright page—an element of a book often overlooked by the usual reader—tells us that one thousand copies were printed of the first edition. The next line lists the *depósito legal* (DL, legal deposit)—a requirement for publications of this kind in Bolivia, which requires the printer to file a simple form with the state for each book they produce along with five copies which are eventually cataloged at the national libraries. When I asked if the DL paperwork is ever denied, the printer quickly explained that no, the DL number is issued on the spot and simply creates a record and an archive of Bolivian-made books. Below the DL appear the names of the author and the editor, the design and photography credits, and the contact information for Hugo. Conspicuously absent is the telltale © of a copyright.

Far from being an explicitly radical gesture, the absence of the copyright symbol has more to do with a sort of commonsense disregard for what is considered as unnecessary branding, bureaucracy, and proprietorship. Here again functionality overrides correctness: any concern over the potential pirating of material produced in his shop is addressed through a practical approach. The printer explains his view on the matter: "es opción del autor de ir y hacerlo—tú tienes el derecho de registrar tu autoría. Pero aquí tenemos nuestra idiosincracia en como hacemos las cosas. . . . Siempre del libro que produces sacan fotocopias así es más barato. . . . La fotocopia de un libro cuesta 15 bolivianos. Ya nosotros tratamos de alcanzar a 15 bolivianos para que no fotocopien, entonces el cliente lo ve. Esa es la idea" (The author has the option of going to complete it—you have the right to go and register your authorship. But here we have our idiosyncrasy in how we do things. . . . Any book you produce people will make photocopies of it because it's cheaper. . . . The photocopy of a book costs fifteen bolivianos. So we try to get as close as possible to fifteen bolivianos so that they won't photocopy it, and the client sees that. That's the idea; interview, La Paz, 2011). Hugo's response to the demand for cheap copies of texts and the realities of widespread piracy (in both its sophisticated and more crude forms) strikes me as at once obvious and genius: make books cheap enough that the incentive to photocopy or pirate them disappears, or at the very least, is called into question. In Hugo's approach to dealing with the threat of piracy, the relation of bookmaking to book buying is renegotiated, with a dynamism and mutability that mirrors the very kinds of alternative relations that a book like *Dispersar el poder* describes. By being produced so inexpensively, prioritizing low cost over profit, the book resists becoming a commodity produced to compete with other commodities in the generation of profit. Its creation is, of course, dependent on a variety of capitalist tools and structures (industrial machinery produced by large corporations, mass produced paper and ink, licensed software, etc.), but the product is designed to move through and promote a different economic ethic. The books made here are produced as inexpensively as possible, to be sold at close to cost. They are "generic books" of the sort De Pósfay describes in his manifesto, but there is nothing generic about the process through which they are made—Hugo's workshop is a very personal space. When his *compañerxs* bring their projects to his shop, a creative process unfolds to produce the book in a way that will be most useful to them.

A major difference between the printer himself and the authors and editors of the books he crafts lies in the ways these various actors identify themselves politically. While Hugo does not consider himself a militant or even really a political person, the *compañerxs* who bring their projects to his workshop most certainly do identify as such. Yet the way that he works—offering lower rates to the small presses by experimenting with tools and materials to achieve lower production costs—makes him part of a broader political sphere that the books themselves help create. The books that come out of his shop occupy a space between those produced by the independent publishers and the pirated editions that flood the markets of both La Paz and nearby El Alto. Crafted through small-scale, highly personalized, and often flawed production and offered at extremely affordable prices, Hugo's books resist subsumption into either the category of commercial books or of handcrafted artisan books. These are books that come close to the category of non-commodities, as their use-value is prioritized over their exchange-value. These are practical books: they are made of, and themselves make, practices. But the practices themselves, like the products they generate, are not stable.

Hugo's practice is not an alternative *model* of book production; it is an ongoing experiment with provisional practices aimed at reducing cost and increasing accessibility. In this sense, he contributes to what one of his authors, Luis Tapia, calls the *política salvaje* (wild politics) of Bolivia, one of the key concepts I presented in the introduction. The practices of wild politics are unstable, temporary, contingent, and fluid. Rather than replace one model with another, wild politics disorganize, unsettle, and *desordenan* (disorder) that which is established—for example, the social relations and economic principles that underlie commercial, profit-oriented production.[6] Tapia states that one effect of this unsettling is a decommodification of social relations, which he says make wild politics implicitly anticapitalist because these forms of collective action negate the logic of exchange-value as an organizing principle (2008, 124). Wild politics are the domain of Zibechi's dispersing social machine. The products and tools of such politics—in this case the books—share these qualities, embodying the processes they emerge from. In some cases, these processes are literally inscribed on the products themselves, as I found in the books made in another organic book workshop over a thousand miles south of La Paz.

"UNA ESPECIE DE ESCUELA EDITORIAL"

Months after I left La Paz with my collection of books from Hugo's print shop stuffed in my suitcase, I came across a book that had a similar weight and texture when I held it in my hands at a book fair in Buenos Aires, a local edition of a title I had acquired in Mexico City the year before: *Autonomías indígenas en América Latina* by Francisco López Bárcenas.[7] I decided to buy it for comparison. But before getting back to my home library, where I'd be able to examine them side by side, this particular book spent some time traveling with me, and it did so comfortably. Fewer than one hundred pages make up this diminutive paperback that measures just shy of four by six inches. In my mind, its proportions are most immediately comparable to the multiple passports that have enabled my movement across the continent. And this little book moved with me just as easily. As I moved around the city, I slipped it in and out of my coat pocket frequently, and the short chapters lent themselves to the kind of interrupted reading on public transportation that is, for many, a part of daily life in Buenos Aires.[8] The paperback cover is sturdy with a glossy lamination. Four booklets, each stapled together, have been affixed to the spine with a strong adhesive. Though not hand-stitched, this book will hold up much better than many of the expensive commercially produced paperbacks I've acquired that crack easily, their loose pages spilling out. The booklet form ensures that no pages will be lost. This reassured me as I firmly gripped the little book, turning pages all the way back, hastily stashing it in my shoulder bag as my subway stop approached. I get the sense that this book was made to be used like this. Made to travel, made to pass through many hands, made to spend weeks at the bottom of a backpack—retrieved from time to time when little pockets of time allow for quick reading sessions. It's as brief as a pamphlet but much sturdier, and I couldn't ever imagine throwing it away. It has a real spine, complete with author and title, and the images that adorn the cover are bold. Despite its size, it is, without a doubt, a book.

The cover bears a simple black and white design, with just the first two words of the title popping out in bright red ink. Save for a slim black border, it is filled with a photograph. The image shows a circle of young men, dressed in ponchos and woven headbands, lifting heavy wooden sticks that meet in the air, their mouths agape in a collective cry. In the background, a crowd looks on, filling a major avenue in front of a colonial-style government palace. It looks to me to be an image of a Mapuche protest from Chile, but I have no way of verifying this, since no photography credits or captions appear anywhere. While I'd love to have my hypothesis confirmed (or debunked), I'm left thinking that it doesn't really matter where this photograph was taken or who took it. I open the book, flipping past the first page, where I've made a note of where and when and for how much I acquired the book. These details are important to me because they are part of the story of how these pages, words, and images came to be bound together, landing in my hands. I make it a point to include these notes in each book I acquire. These details help me recall the space where I encountered the book and the people I may have interacted with there. The next page bears the title and author, printed in block letters. The combination of the kind of ink, the printer, and the type of paper make the letters appear to be slightly uneven, far from the technical perfection one might expect in commercially produced books. The striations that interrupt the black ink tell me that this book was not printed on an offset machine but a photocopier of some sort. The paper on which the ink rests is similarly imperfect—a heavy variety of newsprint, slightly grayish in color, with traces of light brown fibers still visible. This paper is obviously a cheaper alternative to the clean white or off-white bond used for books. But beyond its aesthetic differences, it serves the same purpose: it is sturdy to the touch and holds the ink without bleeding through from one side of the page to the other. The "guts" of the book, this low-cost paper is one of the main factors in determining the price of the book. And at twelve pesos (just under three dollars), this particular book is more than affordable.

Turning the title page, I see that its reverse bears the usual technical information about the book's origins, as most do. I read through, line by line: title, author, press, edition number, publication date, press location, but no sign of the little © of a copyright. The only mention of any rights, reserved or otherwise, comes in the last line: "La reproducción parcial o total de este libro está completamente permitida y fomentada" (The partial or full reproduction of this book is completely permitted and encouraged). The publishers of this book are not interested in controlling, in any way, the movement of the text. They not only permit but actually encourage that it be reprinted elsewhere. Who are they? How was this book made? Why do they make books? And why do they make books like this one? The rest of the page briefly answers some of these questions, with a paragraph describing their collective process: "Como cooperativa de trabajo autónoma e independiente proponemos nuevas relaciones laborales, donde la ganancia equitativa, la horizontalidad, el aprendizaje constante de nuevas tareas, la imaginación y la reflexión sean principios en nuestro laburo cotidiano. Para cualquier propuesta, crítica, e información, o bien si te interesa formar parte de este proyecto, podés escribirnos a . . ." (As an autonomous and independent workers' cooperative we propose new labor relations, where equal pay, horizontality, the constant learning of new skills, imagination and reflection are principles of our daily *laburo*.[9] If you have any proposals, criticism, or questions, or you want to be a part of this project, you can write to us at . . .). Those ten short lines of text say a great deal about where this object came from, making it clear that this book was not made in the usual way—this is to say, the commercial approach to book production characterized by a Taylorist production model, uniformity and consistency, intellectual property restrictions, and editorial control. This book and others made by this press are the product of an undeniably inefficient process, yet one that yields accessible products.

When I arrive at the workshop to meet the members of the cooperative, we gather in the center room, a space cluttered with boxes and varied tools, most noticeable among them two old-fashioned iron standing screw presses. The long, battered wooden table at the center of the room is covered with tidy stacks of paper, some are prefolded, others lay flat. Between the papers I see thread, a few needles, some glue, two old staplers. Perched on old chairs and stools of varying degrees of stability are five members of the cooperative and me. Roaming around us, moving between the three rooms of the print shop, is a toddler who occasionally topples over onto the cushion of her diaper. In her tiny hands she clutches bits of paper, scraps recovered from the floor.

I set my recorder on the table, grateful for the miniature tripod that keeps the microphone slightly elevated above the wooden surface. To one side, booklets are being folded, making a slick sound each time a ruler is run along what will become the spine. On the other side, the stapler is repeatedly slammed down, piercing the booklets and jolting everything on the table. In front of me, another set of booklets are being slowly and carefully hand-stitched, with no sound at all. The members of the collective have agreed to spend their afternoon talking with me, but this doesn't mean work stops. To the contrary, it continues at its usual pace in a workspace where conversation and slow, deliberate learning is prioritized over any sense of commercial efficiency.

As they take turns filling in bits about the story of the press, a gourd filled with yerba mate is passed around, marking the scene as typical of Buenos Aires. Yet two of the most vocal participants in our conversation speak with distinct accents that reveal their status as transplants to the Argentine capital: one from Mexico City, the other from Bogotá. The young Colombian describes his sense of how they work:

> Lo que funciona mucho aquí es lo que yo considero una especie de escuela editorial. Como que yo acá estoy aprendiendo a diagramar, diseñar, con programas que no trabajaba antes. Funciona la escuela: mientras se va haciendo se va aprendiendo. En un futuro me sentiría capaz de hacer un libro. Me siento capacitado. . . . No hay egoísmo en los conocimientos, desde hacer un libro a otras cosas. Acá la idea es que todos hagan todos los trabajos . . . que no haya un diseñador. Lo que estamos haciendo ahorita es compaginar y abrochar el papel—lo puede hacer el que diagrama en el computador. Todo

se cuenta como horas trabajadas, eso hace que sea mucho más interesante la cooperativa. No es que diagramar vale el doble que doblar papel—es una hora trabajada.

What really occurs here is what I consider to be a kind of school of publishing. I'm here learning to do layout, design, with programs I didn't work with before. The school works: while we are doing we are learning. In the future I think I'll feel capable of making a book myself. I feel well prepared. There isn't selfishness about knowledge here, be it about making a book or about other things. The idea here is that everyone does all the jobs . . . that there's not just one designer. What we're doing right now is collating and stapling—and this is something the person that does layout on the computer could do. Everything counts as hours worked, and that makes this cooperative much more interesting. It's not the case that doing the layout is worth twice as much as folding paper—it's all an hour worked. (Interview, Buenos Aires, 2011)

The cooperative rejects the usual division of labor whereby members of a project or a business are each specialized in their respective areas of work. Here, in contrast, there is no fixity to the roles that each member can play—in fact, they insist on rotating through the various roles and functions, valuing all work equally. In doing so, they certainly create a less efficient workplace and method of production—but efficiency is not their objective. What is at play in their approach to cooperativism is an underlying ethic of mutual aid that is at once material and political, economic and pedagogical. With their refusal of an unequal division of labor and efficiency as an operating logic, like other crafters of organic books, they also reject the division between manual and intellectual labor. More than a business, this is, as they say, "a kind of school of publishing," but it is a school with no teachers, no textbooks, no models for how and what to learn. The pedagogy is provisional, the lessons practical experiments. But it also is a self-sustaining economic project where work is done collectively and cooperatively and where an anticapitalist ethic exists in constant tension with the capitalist structures that surround it.

Over the past two decades, Argentina has become a sort of hotspot of cooperatives and recuperated businesses of all sorts, with groups of workers expelling their bosses and occupying their workplaces.[10] These range from artisan bakeries to ceramics factories to large hotels, and to the passerby many are indistinguishable from normal businesses with conventional hierarchical management and organization. This explosion of worker-run businesses has been accompanied by a range of institutional categories and legalities aimed at recognizing and regulating this sort of operation. But the members of this cooperative are quick to distinguish themselves from the highly bureaucratized form that characterizes their large-scale counterparts, as in the cooperative factories. They are a cooperative by practice, not by design. They explain to me that they do not function as a formally constituted cooperative: "Estamos fuera del cooperativismo legal. No es una cooperativa legal, sino porque nos juntamos a hacer algo. Y repartimos las ganancias. Viene del principio más real, que es cooperar" (We exist outside of the legal form of cooperativism. This isn't a legal cooperative, rather it's a cooperative because we come together to make something. And we share the earnings. . . . It comes from the more concrete principle, which is to cooperate; interview, Buenos Aires, 2011). Here the emphasis is on the *practice* rather than the *idea*; their work is conceived of more in terms of the verb, "to cooperate," rather than the noun, "a cooperative." Marcelo Vieta (2010, 3) analyzes this distinction through the concept of "new cooperativism," which he describes as "experiments" with mutual aid that emerge "out of immediate social, cultural, or economic needs rather than from pre-existing cooperativist sentiments." Rooted in action and practices rather than in principles and models, the new cooperativism Vieta describes is, as he says citing J. K. Gibson-Graham, an experiment with living "beyond capitalocentrism," though in many cases the ideological dimensions of these projects are not explicitly pronounced. What is particular about the organic book workshop as a space of new cooperativism is the fact that the politics that motivate and inspire their cooperative are in fact quite visible, as they spill off the pages of the product they craft collectively.

At one end of the central main room, a narrow doorway connects to an open and sparsely furnished room where just three computers are set up atop simple wooden tables, with an old printer at one end. At the other end of the workshop, a small room is filled with a risograph machine, a photocopier, and a printer. One wall is covered with proofs of book covers—some handmade silkscreen designs on recycled cardstock, others full-color designs printed on an offset press. Yet an offset press—generally the anchor of a print shop—is noticeably absent. They explain that the color book covers are the only piece of the books not produced in-house; they are printed on an offset at a different print shop in the neighborhood. The book pages themselves are printed on-site on either the photocopier or the risograph. Often figured as enemies of the book for their place in the making of cheap pirated reproductions, here these machines are resignified as key tools of the trade of craft book production. Opposite the wall of book covers is a large cabinet filled with books. As I quickly scan the contents, I'm immediately struck by the variety of colors and dimensions of the books that occupy the shelves. There are at least a dozen different books with the seal of their press on the cover. Several other titles are printed in-house but aren't edited by them. And dozens of others are titles from other presses across Argentina that they have done exchanges with to increase the circulation of their materials. Despite the material diversity of the books on the shelves, after a quick scan two main themes standout from the titles produced and distributed by this autonomous "school of publishing": pedagogy and autonomy.

As I examine the machines and tools alongside the stock of books, I begin to understand more about *how* they make books, and more importantly *why*. Over the past decade, the work of this collective evolved as they slowly developed their shared relationship to print culture and eventually the book-object. Initially, they acquired a photocopier to make flyers, pamphlets, handbills, and the like for student organizations, autonomous cultural centers, and various political and cultural initiatives that flourished in the post-2001 Argentine context. From that new experience with printing and basic design came the desire to make a book. With no prior experience, the collective immersed itself in an experiment of independent publishing and distribution and cooperative labor and self-management that has lasted well over a decade, becoming the primary work of the participants. They share a commitment to the object of the book as opposed to other more ephemeral forms of print culture or political and cultural expression. One collective member puts it this way: "Yo hago lo que hago por el objeto del libro en sí. Es una cosa que te alimenta, no como el pan o la cerveza, cigarrillos, están todo bien, te alimentan, pero no duran" (I do what I do because of the object of the book itself. It's a thing that nourishes you, not like bread or beer or cigarettes, which are all good—they nourish you—but they don't last; interview, Buenos Aires, 2011).

Across the three rooms, this workshop holds all the tools and equipment necessary to make a book. And, indeed, hundreds are made here each month. The design and layout happens on the three old computers. The proofs are printed on the laser printers, and the pages are then duplicated on the risograph machine. The glossy color covers are sent out for printing at a nearby printshop. All of the cutting, stitching, binding, and pressing happens in the middle room—the social and productive hub of the shop, where members of the collective sit together around the long table, collating, stapling, stitching, gluing, pressing while sharing mate and conversation with each other and the other *compañerxs* that pass through daily. Most small presses will do runs of five hundred to one thousand books at a time, as the materials and time required in typical offset printing making smaller runs too inefficient. Here, where printing happens on a risograph machine, runs can be as small as they want. And they explain to me that, in fact, while they used to make five hundred copies of a single title at once, in recent years they've shifted their strategy to be able to maintain a more diverse stock of titles, ensuring the continuous production and distribution of the books they've collectively determined should be available to their audience and community—the readers who move through the alternative cultural spaces where their books circulate.

The unlikely effects of having "less professional" equipment are, as it turns out, major advantages for the political objectives of the collective. Without having to commit to the investments that offset printing require, they are able to make smaller runs of more books, maintaining an exciting and diverse stock of books, avoiding the constant battle of any press between the desire to sell out of a book (to be able to make more books) and the desire to have a full and varied catalog in print. And maintaining that diverse catalog—which is a kind of living archive of their ongoing work as a collective—is fundamental to their broader political desires. As one collective member remarks, "es tener una herramienta para difundir . . . lo que es importante. Lees un libro y te dice lo que tú quieres decir bien bonito. Nunca habrías encontrado esas palabras, las encuentras. . . . También se trata de la conciencia de la cooperativa también. Y después a través de los libros que publicamos, se multiplica hacia fuera" (it's about having a tool to disseminate ideas . . . that you think are important. You read a book and it says what you want to say in a beautiful way. You never would have found those words, and there you find them. . . . It's also about the consciousness of the cooperative. And then, through the books we publish, that is multiplied and projected outward; interview, Buenos Aires, 2011). The practices that they experiment with are theorized in the texts that make up their books. Like the shelves I browsed in their workshop, their 2015 catalog, which can be found online on a file-sharing platform, includes a wide range of editions of books about the very practices at play in their cooperative: mutual aid, solidarity, autonomy, popular education, communal and indigenous organization. And with the materials, cost, and paratexts that they design, they build on the ideas that the texts express. What they circulate are expressions, concepts, ways of knowing—and the form of the products they make reflects the relationship they strive to construct between production and consumption. This is not to suggest that there is a complete or pure relationship between the ideas they promote through the texts and the practices they enact in their cooperative, but rather to show the ways that intellectual and manual labor are reconnected through both the craft and content of their books.

Part of what I find most intriguing about this project is that the whole book—from concept to object for sale—is made in this small workshop. And the artisanal craft of making books by hand, as well as their project as a workers' cooperative, is in constant—and productive—tension with the political desire to see certain concepts circulate and to make certain books more accessible by producing them inexpensively and consistently. The way they work to make these objects is thus deeply connected to the political worlds and concepts that the books' pages carry. For this collective, it's clear that making books is indeed a craft with deep political implications: "El que trabaja haciendo libros trabaja haciendo cosas muy sofisticadas—el libro me parece una tecnología muy alta. Tiene que ver con el pensamiento y es trabajo con las manos, por eso me gusta mucho. . . . Es muy ¿cómo se dice? gratificante, como que te devuelve muchas cosas al hacerlo, es un placer. Por eso tratamos de no separar los trabajos y valorar lo que une lo intelectual con lo manual. Eso para mí es fundamental" (The person that works making books is working in the production of very sophisticated things—I think the book is a very high technology. It has to do with thought and it is work you do with your hands, that's why I like it so much. . . . It's really—what's the word?—gratifying, it gives a lot back to you as you make it, it's a pleasure. That's why we try not to separate the different tasks and to value that which connects manual work with intellectual work. That, for me, is fundamental; interview, Buenos Aires, 2011). In this workshop the practices of new cooperativism are combined with a technology—the book—that is particularly well suited to not just reflecting but actually embodying the social relations and dynamics that go into its production. The book, in its complexity, its durability, its cultural use-value, is capable of acting in ways that other products of cooperative production—be it the bread, beer, or cigarettes referenced earlier—and other forms of less durable print media cannot.[11]

Book production, as the members of this cooperative assert, is a particular kind of craft because of the ways that the subject and the object are assembled together. Adrian Johns (1998, 75) describes the printing house as a "strange hybrid of library, scriptorium, study, home, and workshop," noting that in the context of early modern London, the practices of these shops were considered of great "epistemological value." As a hybrid space, it could be said that the printing shop of the organic book yields "hybrid" products—understanding books to be much more than mere vehicles for the transmission of ideas. To an extent, the cooperative workshop I describe here seems to have more in common with the printing houses of seventeenth century London than contemporary publishing houses, characterized by an increasingly fragmented production process. Selection, composition, edition, design, printing, binding, and distribution all happen under the same roof. And all the members of the collective, at some point, rotate through all of these tasks, learning the skills necessary for their execution. Returning to Debray's concept, it is clear that the members of this collective are "intellectual workers" or "worker intellectuals" of the kind he describes in socialist printing. But they are definitively products of a different political moment from Debray's. While they identify as workers, their project is aimed at a reimagination of labor relations through a collective practice of pedagogy, as they state in all of their books.

In the space of this workshop, and the materials and contents of the books it produces, I see evidence of a reclaiming of *doing*. Making is connected to learning, and the process as well as the product are valued for the usefulness to the producer and the consumer alike. The use-value of the book lies not only in the utility of the finished product but in the very practices that compose it. The members of the cooperative, in recounting its history, tell a story of experimentation with print. What started as a side project reproducing ephemeral propaganda morphed into a publishing and distribution cooperative, with a pedagogical objective built into their labor practice. These "strange hybrids," like the printing houses of past centuries, become even more hybridized in the making of organic books—significantly, production and consumption are blurred. The materials they print become the textbooks of their school of publishing. In the next section, I examine another set of workshops in Buenos Aires to see how the experimental practice of crafting organic books takes up tools and occupies spaces in even less conventional ways.

"HASTA QUE UN DÍA EL SINDICATO ANARKOPACIFISTA DE ENCUADERNADORES TERMINÓ CON LA MONARQUÍA"

In the last weekend of November, I make my way to the tree-lined side street in Almagro that is home to La Tribu: an alternative radio station and cultural center that in the past five years has come to function as one hub of the "cultura libre" movement that has proliferated in Buenos Aires.[12] I've come to participate in the fourth annual Fábrica de Fallas (Bug Factory—in the sense of a computer bug or glitch), described as a "Festival de Cultura Libre y Copyleft" (Free Culture and Copyleft Festival).[13] In just a half block, I walk past the dozens of stands that are packed in—some housing vendors of various handcrafted goods, others workshop spaces where small crowds are huddled around tools for making things—a computer, a map, a mobile garden, art supplies—listening, learning, doing together. The entrance to La Tribu is always visible from a distance—a colorful mural adorns its three-story facade. Today, the entrance is especially visible because of the improvised swimming pool that has been creatively fashioned out of an old dumpster. A half dozen half-naked bodies fill it as festival participants seek relief from the sticky heat by submerging themselves in the water with cold beers in hand. Above them, massive speakers on a tiny balcony blast the live radio broadcast out onto the street.

One of the organizers of the Fábrica de Fallas describes the event as "una excusa, festiva a veces, más seria otras, para que alrededor, antes y después, suceda la política" (an excuse—sometimes festive, other times more serious—for politics to happen around it, before and after; Vázquez 2010, 160). The space is indeed very festive, but there is no doubt that something more is happening here—something "more serious." I'm reminded that looks can be deceiving as I approach the workshop I've come to attend and see that half of the equipment is set up on the hood and in the trunk of the old car parked behind the

FIGURE 2.2. Street workshop at Fábrica de Fallas, Buenos Aires, 2011.

stand. A long table set atop sawhorses of questionable stability has been transformed into a miniature mobile print shop. On one end are two old PC laptops (run almost exclusively on free software) and a laser printer. Several people are huddled around one of the computers, watching as a scruffy, shirtless young man gives a demo on basic layout using Scribus, a free software program, to design a book using one of the PDF files that a workshop participant brought on a USB pen drive. As he explains the steps to create the booklets that will eventually make up the book, double-sided prints come flying out of the printer. At the other end of the table, stacks of paper are being folded into tidy booklets, then stitched and glued and bound into books. Three people lean over the table, patiently guiding the needle and thread through the booklets, creating a crisscross design along the spine. A tub of white glue sits open, a paintbrush hanging out. At the edge of the table several completed books have been set out to dry, bound tightly by homemade vises fashioned out of particle board and wingnuts.

The telephone pole behind the stand has an arrow-shaped sign taped to it with upside-down letters that say "Autoedición" (Self-Publishing). A larger handmade sign taped to the car window reads "Taller permanente de armado de libros" (Permanent Workshop on Book Assembly). This more prominent sign, made by the workshop facilitators rather than the festival organizers, is a more accurate description of what is happening here—it isn't so much about publishing one's own work as it is about learning to craft books. And this is just one day of a permanent mobile book assembly workshop the facilitators continually move from place to place—book fairs, festivals, their own work spaces. It is a workshop in two senses: a class on how to make books *and* a studio where books are made. And it is not simply about one stage of the book production process, be it editing, layout, design, printing, or binding. Rather, it's about the assembly or composition of books in a more complete sense: from idea to object.

Several weeks later, making good on a long-standing invitation, I visit the studio of some of the organizers of this mobile workshop. I ring the bell on a quiet residential street tucked just behind the train tracks. A long narrow entryway leads to the back unit of the building, where three rooms connect around a small patio. Something about the combination of the piles of bikes, scattered cigarette butts, the smell of cumin, and the cases of empty beer bottles reminds me of the many squats and co-ops I've spent time in. And this is indeed a cooperative, I'm told by the two brothers I talk to in the kitchen while they prepare homemade hummus. It is a cooperatively run workshop, and in the historical tradition of the craftsman's workshop it is a combined living and work space. But this is not a private space. While I've arrived here responding to a personal invitation from some of the cooperative members I've been working with in the Feria de Libros Independiente y Alternativa (FLIA, Independent and Alternative Book Fair), countless others have passed through this space responding to the open invitation to "el público en general y en particular" (the general and specific public) to come learn hands-on about how to make books, from editing to design to printing to binding. Their website

FIGURE 2.3. Street workshop at Fábrica de Fallas, Buenos Aires, 2011.

explains that these open workshops are free and always open and insists that "está bueno que seamos muchxs y que estemos apretadxs" (it's good for there to be a lot of us and for us to be packed in here). And for those that can't make the trip to the workshop, a list of resources on book production appears on the same page. The website also explains that this is a space of "trabajo autogesti-vo" (self-organized work):

No nos parece menor el modo en el que se hacen las cosas por eso procuramos que a la hora de trabajar no haya órdenes ni jerarquías. Éstas no son más que un mal innecesario productor de las grandes desigualdades y catástrofes que sufre el mundo en que vivimos. Basándonos en el reparto igualitario de las ganancias y procurando cooperación en las distintas tareas que nuestro trabajo implica buscamos garantizarnos una cómoda propuesta laboral.

For us, the way things are done is significant, and this is why we want to ensure that in our work there be no orders nor hierarchies. These are an unnecessary evil that produces the major inequalities and catastrophes that our world suffers from. We seek to guarantee ourselves a comfortable work situation by grounding ourselves in the equal distribution of earnings and cooperation in the various tasks that our work demands. ("Acerca" 2018)

The walls are plastered with posters from book fairs, proofs of book covers, magazine cutouts, paintings. A large strip of recycled paper bears a hand-painted statement, a sort of inspirational slogan for the workshop: "hasta que un día el sindicato anarkopacifista de encuadernadores terminó con la monarquía" (until one day the union of anarcho-pacifist bookbinders brought an end to the monarchy).

As we move into another room, divided between two workstations, along one wall I see two computers and a printer. Along another wall, a long table lined with benches serves as a place to stitch booklets together, though I imagine it sometimes doubles as a dining table. In the next room, a tall, wide workbench sits in the middle of the room, strewn with glue, paint brushes, scissors, rulers, and more of the homemade vises I saw at the festival a few weeks back. A guillotine—the most valuable tool in the room—sits on a small table in one corner, across from a massive old iron bookbinding press. My eyes are quickly drawn to the other end of the room, where a shelf holds tidy stacks of cardboard rectangles of different sizes and dozens of spools of brightly colored ribbon create a rainbow where they hang from the wall. A cabinet alongside it holds a small stock of books made by the cooperative, with texts ranging from anthologies of poetry to essays on anarchism. Some of the titles have the sort of uniformity one would expect from a printed book, while others are made in a different fashion with covers of different colors and textures holding the pages together, a sort of merging of a more formal artisan bookbinding and the *cartonera* aesthetic.

A couple from Barcelona arrived a while before me, and they've been busy learning how to stitch the booklets together. We take the stack of booklets they've assembled to the main binding table, and together we learn how to assemble hardcover books. Over the next few hours, we slowly work through

FIGURE 2.4. Workshop, Buenos Aires, 2011.

the various stages of production, as our hosts teach us with a combination of patience, skill, and pure love of the craft. While we work on our books (which are not ours to take but will become part of the co-op's stock), the co-op members take turns working on a job they've been commissioned to complete: 150 copies of a paperback book for the Argentine Workers' Central Union. A much larger run of the book will be printed later at a commercial print shop, but because the editors needed copies urgently for an upcoming event, they commissioned this cooperative to handmake a smaller quantity. Runs of fewer than five hundred books are inefficient in a commercial printing context, but such large-scale print jobs take time. So when the union members found themselves pressed for time, urgently needing books for their event, they turned to this artisan bookbinding cooperative to do the job.

As my visit revealed, this workshop produces a wide range of books. One of the first that I acquired at a book fair months before visiting the workshop is a small paperback edition of *En el café* by the late nineteenth- and early twentieth-century Italian anarchist Errico Malatesta. The 144 pages of this compact book are bound by a shimmery silver cover made of a recycled TetraPak container that was likely filled with fruit juice in its first life. As it turns out, these sturdy containers, made of paperboard, polyethylene, and aluminum, make for excellent book covers because the combination of materials makes them extremely durable without being overly stiff. The front cover is decorated with a sheet of watercolor splatter-painted paper, and a long xeroxed band of green paper bears the title and author's name in a stylized, semi-abstract script. The particular book that I hold in my hands is unique—no other copy has the same combinations of colors hand-painted on its cover. The design of the cover tells me that my book was made by a person, and my experiences in this shop tell me that it was probably not the same person that made other copies of the same book. The social character of the shop, to recall Adrian Johns's (1998) question, clearly affects its products: the open, improvised, and experimental quality of this workshop as a space of learning that anyone can visit and participate in is reflected in its products. Uniformity is not a concern here—what matters is that books get bound, that more and more people learn the craft, and that the shop sustains itself.

Inside the book, the "copyright" page (where no copyright appears) reads:

> Este libro fue integramente elaborado con software libre. Ese software libre fue operado por seres humanos que viven, conviven, soportan y cometen humanidades. Las humanidades, por definición, son imperfectas, así que si encontrás un error en el libro te pedimos por favor que nos lo indiques vía mail. También recibimos propuestas, compuestas, quejas, arvejas, saludos, amores y licores. No se hizo ni se hará el depósito que impone la ley, se incentiva su reproducción total o parcial por cualquier medio como así también su préstamo y/u obsequio sin permiso del editor o de sus señores padres. Besos.

> This book was made entirely using free software. This free software was operated by human beings that live, coexist, bear and commit humanities. Humanities, by definition, are imperfect, so if you find an error in the book we ask that you please let us know via email. We also receive propositions, compositions, complaints, peas, greetings, loves, and liquors. No legal registration was, or will be, completed for this book. Total or partial reproduction by any media is encouraged, as is the borrowing or gifting of this book without the permission of the editors or your parents. Kisses. (Malatesta 2010)

This statement is playful in tone, humorous even, but the process described here—inscribed on the product—is at once humble and bold. There is an acknowledgment of the imperfections that may appear in the book but also an affirmation of the significance of the collective human effort that went into it. Like the workshop, the free software the collective uses is an open process, a set of tools that anyone can use and modify to leave their mark.

Combined with the next six pages that precede the original text, this part of the book acts as a sort of map of some of the relations that make this object. First, the editors and printers of this edition are introduced. Next, the editors of the digital file used to make this book explain the significance of this text and their imagined audience: "el que no entiende de política, el que no es anarquista, . . . y el desocupado y el que está tan ocupado que no tiene tiempo para leer un libro" (the person that doesn't understand politics, the person that is not an anarchist, . . . and the unemployed [unoccupied] person and the person that is so occupied that they don't have time to read a book). The imagined reader is and isn't many things—this is to say, the imagined reader is anyone who wants to read the book. But while this description is intentionally open and vague, it is also firmly rooted in a particular political genealogy made visible by the references to radical Argentine subjects: the anarchist, which could be of a past era or of the present, and the *desocupado*, the *piquetero* of the turn of the twenty-first century. Next, the author is introduced and his connections to Argentina are described. Finally, I learn about the editors who compiled the original pamphlet in Santa Fe in 1935, and I am introduced to those responsible for the digitization in Rosario nearly seventy-five years later. A web of relations appears before me as I read the introductory pages that precede the text itself, and it spans across different centuries and territories. The workshop I visited in Buenos Aires in 2011 suddenly appears as part of something much bigger: a long radical history in which materiality and politics are continually interconnected.

A few weeks after my visit to the workshop, my friend asked me to send him some of the photographs I took in the shop so they can use them on their website. As I scan through the thumbnails, I notice a detail I had missed when I was there. The shot is of one of the walls in the workshop. Between colorful posters of all shapes and sizes, a single sheet of paper hangs. The sterility of its nondescript font and letter-size computer printer paper is interrupted by broad strokes of watercolor paint. As I zoom in on my laptop, I can make out the text of a poem titled "Copyleft":

Qué es de tu gloria; tu fama, tu pan,
si nace de lo muerto, la obra quieta
congelada en el tiempo
Qué es de tu honra, tu vida diaria,
si solo quieres acumular logros
uno tras otro tras otro
hasta que te caigan encima y tomen tu
lugar
todo ese trabajo, el esfuerzo,
perpetuar el YO, inútil, vano.
El *árbol* no se jacta de su flor
ni el pájaro de su canto
la araña de su tela se alimenta

la nube cambia de forma maravillando un
instante
Eso la hace eterna.
Pues en la naturaleza
bajo el reinado del sol
solo nosotros, ajenos a ella
concebimos algo llamado derechos de autor

What becomes of your glory; your fame, your bread,
if it is born from what is dead, the still work
frozen in time.
What becomes of your honor, your daily life,
if all you want to do is accumulate achievements
one after another after another
until they fall on top of you and take
your place
all that work, that effort,
to perpetuate ME, useless, vain.
The tree doesn't brag about its flower
nor the bird about its song
the spider is nourished by its web
the cloud changes shape marveling at an
instant
That is what makes it eternal.
For in nature
under the reign of the sun
only we, foreign to it,
conceive of something we call
copyright[14]

The copyrighted book—isolated and static—is what this poet calls the "still work frozen in time." This is the book produced as a commodity, as private property to be controlled by its owners and sold for monetary gain. It is not made by a "modest inventor," to borrow from Marianne de Laet and Annemarie Mol (2000), but rather a "vain" author whose principal concern is with control of the boundaries of his creation. This approach to managing the things we produce, says the poet, is foreign to "nature" and the organic way that things grow and expand and interact. The "copyleft" book (which we could also call the "generic book," the "workshop book," or the "organic book"), in contrast, represents a rupture with the conventions of production and property.[15] It is made not in the factory, with its standardized process and rules of efficiency. It is made in the workshop through collective processes of learning and experimentation. Like the spaces where it is crafted, this book is filled with the imperfections of life and is infinitely connected through its relations to other objects, to people, to spaces. Its mutability is what makes it so useful, and its utility is the source of its value.

I understand the workshop book to be an example of what de Laet and Mol (2000) call a "fluid technology." Characterized by vague and moving boundaries, this kind of object is "adaptable, flexible, and responsive" (226). The mutability of the workshop book is an effect of the practices through which it is made and used: through experimentation with the technical, economic, and political dimensions of this object, the book changes. But it continues to be a book, perhaps even the "same" book, if the title remains unchanged. The books made in the open cooperative I visited, or at the pop-up street workshop, might have the same pages carrying the same text bound together. But as different configurations of relations and different sets of hands come in contact with those pages—stitching, gluing, trimming, painting—adapting the process to meet their needs and their skills, the book changes. Riffing on Bruno Latour's notion of the immutable mobile, John Law and Vicky Singleton (2005, 339) call this kind of object a "mutable mobile," explaining that "an object or class of objects may be understood as a set of relations that gradually shifts and adapts itself rather than one that holds itself rigid." In the workshop, there is no rigid pattern to follow. The book itself may be "bound," but its boundaries are not fixed—they are provisional and temporary, like the practices of the actors that craft it.

"ROMPER CON EL MOLDE PARA TERMINAR CON ESTE MODELO"

On a small side street in the Flores neighborhood of Buenos Aires, a massive old house has been transformed from an orphanage run by a socialist party to an autonomous social center referred to simply as La Cazona de Flores (The Flores Mansion).[16] The run-down installations of this old, long since abandoned institution are slowly being renovated, with bits of paint and plaster going up, holes being patched and cracked and water-stained walls recovered. The massive sweeping staircase in the foyer is now lined with a spray-painted graffiti-style mural of an urban hillside, with hundreds of small colorful houses clustered together. No longer populated by the children who once lived here, today La Cazona is home to nearly a dozen different projects and collectives organized as an assembly. A few groups provide basic services to the neighborhood, such as the barber shop on the ground floor. Others include a range of media and art collectives, each group occupying its own space within the massive house. A compact room on the second floor is set up as a small artisan textile workshop: a sewing machine and a serger are set atop two crooked wooden tables, scissors and spools of thread are strewn about, and bags of fabric scraps clutter the cozy space. But the collective that runs this workshop doesn't create any of the usual products—clothing, accessories, upholstery—associated with these particular tools. Instead, they make books: "libritos de tela y cartón" (little books made of cloth and cardboard), as they describe them. Their chosen materials for the crafting of their book covers are *retazos* (scraps of fabric), and the name of their press is derived from this symbolic material: Editorial Retazos.

One of the things that first caught my eye as I walked around my new neighborhood on my first morning in Buenos Aires were the massive plastic bags of bright colored fabric scraps that lined the sidewalks. I then noticed dozens of wholesale fabric shops in just the few blocks surrounding my apartment, but I knew from the size, shape, and quantity of these scraps that this was not their immediate source. These scraps had to come from somewhere else: someplace where the heavy, long bolts of fabric are transformed into hundreds of identical items, as the meters of cloth get cut up and reassembled in different shapes. A few days later, I met a new friend for drinks in the neighborhood and asked about the fabric scraps. He explained that the city of Buenos Aires and its peripheries are home to more than twenty-five thousand garment factories (called *talleres textiles*, textile workshops because most are made up of fewer than fifty workers)—some clandestine, some not. These workshops employ close to a million workers (mostly Bolivian immigrants), often in precarious conditions, producing apparel for national and export markets. While the wholesale fabric shops are visible to anyone walking down the street, the textile workshops are not. They make up a marginal, nearly invisible world of work that most residents of the city only see in the bags of fabric scraps they walk past on the street. The products of these workshops, the clothing items themselves, lose their association with the labor that produces them once they hit the shops and market stands where the average consumer buys them. But the scraps of fabric—messy and partial, hastily discarded in bulk—retain traces of the workers who made them.

The book covers made by Editorial Retazos intentionally retain these same traces. Each book cover typically includes at least three different fabrics. A large piece serves as the background, attached to the thin corrugated cardboard base with a contrasting overlock stitch along the edges. A smaller, odd-shaped piece of another print is appliquéd as an accent. Two smaller patches that have been printed by silkscreen are stitched on off-center: one on the front with the book title and one on the back with the logo of the press—itself a collage hodgepodge of fonts on odd-shaped blocks, recreating the effect of *retazos*. Some of the accent pieces have straight lines, while other have rounded edges. A member of the collective explains to me that they always try to keep the original shape of the fabric scrap in an effort to preserve the presence of the worker who cut it, though this may not be apparent to the reader who acquires the book. A scrap from cutting a sleeve pattern may have the rounded edge where the sleeve connects to the bodice. A scrap from a skirt may have the bias-cut of an A-line. A blog post in early 2012 explains the use of the scraps and the symbol of the *retazos*: "para Retazos, identificados con el afuera del molde, las telas que sobran, percibidas como trapos, son ahora transformadas en tapas de libros que problematizan el sistema de los talleres, profanando el esquema vital del cual reniegan. Los mismos trozos de tela despreciados por el diseño preconcebido, son ahora aguijones que desmembran la máquinaria de aquello que los engendra" (for Retazos, who identify with that which lies outside the box, the fabric scraps that are leftover and perceived as rags, are now transformed into the covers of books that problematize the workshop system, profaning the very scheme that they disown. The same scraps of fabric that are spurned by the preconceived design, now dismember the very machinery they are born from; Andrés 2012). Editorial Retazos is part of the now well-known transnational phenomenon of the *cartonera* movement. But while Retazos identifies as a *cartonera* press, as the above quoted text indicates, it emphasizes a second recycled or reclaimed material as its primary symbol— the fabric scrap—and in this way articulates itself to two particularly iconic sectors of marginalized workers in post-2001 Argentina: cardboard collectors and textile workers.

The single book I take home from my first visit to the Retazos workshop, where I paid fifteen pesos for it (less than four dollars), has a cover composed of a gray background, a single black and white leopard print stripe, two white patches, and red and yellow stitching. The photocopied pages inside are bound with two heavy duty staples. The patch on the front is printed with an image of a woman working on a sewing machine next to the title *De chuequistas y overlockas: Una discusión entorno a los talleres textiles* (Of seamstresses and sergers: A discussion about the textile workshops). As the prologue explains, this book is part of a "siempre abierto y político" (always open and political) collaborative research project between two collectives in Buenos Aires that interrogates "el sistema de producción de jerarquías en el mundo del trabajo y de la migración" (the system of production of hierarchies in the world of work and the world of migration; Colectivo Situaciones and Simbiosis Cultural 2011, 5). This is a recurring theme in Retazos publications, and the young people that make up the collective are themselves Bolivian immigrants or children of immigrants, most of whom have worked in and around the world of the textile workshops in Buenos Aires.[17]

Their first publication, *No olvidamos!!* (Estrada Vázquez 2010), recounted the story of the six immigrant workers who were killed in a fire in a textile workshop in 2006. *De chuequistas y overlockas* was published in 2011 and presented on the five-year anniversary of the tragic fire. The prologue, titled "Prólogo-conversación," explains that the book "retoma los efectos del paso de Silvia Rivera Cusicanqui por Buenos Aires para presentar *Ch'ixinakax utxiwa. Una reflexión sobre prácticas y discursos descolonizadores*. Fue entonces que nos convencimos de la necesidad de profundizar el encuentro entre su perspectiva y nuestra tarea" (takes up the effects of the footsteps of Silvia Rivera Cusicanqui through Buenos Aires when she came to present her book *Ch'ixinakax utxiwa. Una reflexión sobre prácticas y discursos descolonizadores*. Following her visit, we felt the need to delve deeper into the encounter between her perspective and our work; Colectivo Situaciones and Simbiosis Cultural 2011, 7–8).[18] The encounter between the Buenos Aires–based Bolivian youth who make up the Colectivo Simbiosis Cultural (some of whom are also part of Retazos) and the La Paz–based sociologist Silvia Rivera Cusicanqui opened a dialogue around not only what happens in the textile workshops in Buenos Aires but also about what happens when those who work in Buenos Aires return to Bolivia—temporarily or permanently—as well as how this influences the divergent perspectives on what really occurs in the worlds of work populated by Bolivian migrants in Buenos Aires. The authors insist that they do not write "as Bolivians" or "as Argentines" because "más que nacionalidades, tenemos 'trayectorias.' Algunas incluyen atravesar una frontera. Son trayectorias que dan que pensar" (more than nationalities, we have trajectories. And some of these include the crossing of a border. They are trajectories that help us to think; Colectivo Situaciones and Simbiosis Cultural 2011, 14).

In a text simply titled "Conversación con Retazos" (Conversation with Retazos), the project is described as emerging from a collective "inquietud de hacer algo," a phrase that requires more explanation than a literal translation can provide (Andrés 2012). The idea of *inquietud* clumsily translates to English as the rarely used cognate "inquietude," meaning restlessness, uneasiness, or agitation—all of which can be imbued with political significance. *Hacer algo* carries two possible meanings, and in this case, the phrase clearly refers to both: to *do* something and to *make* something. Retazos emerges from the desire to *do something* more than just labor in the textile workshops. But it also comes from a desire to *make something*—to make something with the discarded scraps of fabric and to do things in a different way. What is at stake in this project is not a recycling of materials into objects distinct from their original design, in the style of the now ubiquitous *cartonera* phenomenon. Rather, the form of the scraps is intentionally conserved to make their source visible in an effort to "problematize articulations" and make something of "the unworkable," which is how the collective describes the *retazos* themselves. To be sure, they insist that their objective is not to expose or denounce the textile

FIGURE 2.5. Editorial Retazos, Buenos Aires, 2011.

workshops. Rather, they are concerned with problematizing the social relations and dynamics that shape this world of work and the lives of those caught up in it. The question posed continuously by their practice and their products is: what does it mean to organize work, time, and life differently? In this sense, as a small artisan press and a political press, Editorial Retazos problematizes the concept of the *workshop* in its compound sense; the project is an ongoing experiment with both the idea of *work* and the idea of the *shop*. The chosen material and symbol of this press—the *retazo*, the fabric scrap—connects two distinct workshop spaces: the small-scale industrial textile workshop and the artisan book workshop. In this way, the materiality of the books functions as an active expression of the political position of the press. On the last page of each of their books, a text appears describing the function of the *retazo*:

> Se junta la tela, se la corta y se deshechan los sobrantes,
> los que ya no sirven,
> quienes no entraron en esos moldes de quienes diseñan y cortan.
> Están allí en una bolsa en medio de la vereda, uno arriba de otro, con las
> cicatrices abiertas aún, mientras que, quienes se metieron o aceptaron estar
> dentro de esos moldes están en pleno proceso de confección, en una cadena
> que funciona así desde hace mucho en un modelo que excluye, explota e
> impone.

Allí encontramos a estos retazos, excluidos y exiliados, en la vereda.

Pero resulta que no dejan de ser parte de ese todo.

Ahora esos retazos encontraron distintas formas de no sentirse solo eso, sino también se propusieron formar entre todos ellos, los excluidos, los exiliados, un todo.

Un todo que a diferencia de otros todos, incluya, contenga y fortalezca a los demás retazos.

A esos demás retazos de vida, de sueños, ilusiones, frustraciones, anhelos, rebeldías y luchas.

Ahora los retazos estamos dispuestos a crear muchos más completos para vencer a este molde.

Romper con el molde para terminar con este modelo.

The fabric is gathered and cut, and the scraps are thrown away,

pieces that can't be used for anything,

that didn't fit into the patterns of those who design and cut.

There they are in a bag in the middle of the sidewalk, one on top of another, with the scars still open, while those who were included in or agreed to be a part of those patterns are in the process of being assembled, in a chain that has functioned this way for a long time, as part of a system that excludes, exploits and imposes.

That's where we find those scraps, excluded and exiled, on the sidewalk.

But it turns out that they don't stop being part of that whole.

Now those scraps find different ways of feeling like more than that, they also propose that all of them, the excluded, the exiled, should form a whole.

A whole that, unlike other wholes, can include, contain, and strengthen the other scraps.

The scraps of life, of dreams, illusions, frustrations, desires, rebellions, and struggles.

Now the scraps are willing to create many more wholes to defeat this pattern.

Break away from the pattern to bring an end to this model. (Estrada Vázquez 2010)

The patterns used to cut the fabric in the textile workshops ensure that thousands of pieces of apparel have the same shape, the same design, the same form. The offcuts, the *retazos*, that remain on the cutting table or the shop floor are the negative of the pattern but a negative that is not intact—it appears in fragments, like puzzle pieces that could be put together to recreate the outline of the pieces that moved on to the sewing room. But put together in different combinations, mixed with scraps from other patterns, they create something new, a different whole. And for Editorial Retazos, these new, other "wholes" include the books that they craft. They want each book to function as "a whole that, unlike the other wholes, can include, contain, and strengthen the other scraps" (Estrada Vázquez 2010). These scraps and wholes have various manifestations in the texts themselves: testimonies of the migrant workers, analyses of the transnational socioeconomic system of the workshops, stories about migration and the transborder communities that link Bolivia and Argentina, historical studies of the colonial legacies that shape these worlds, and more. In the book-objects, the function of the scraps and wholes is evident in their materiality. The fabrics are put together in different combinations; the color and lines of the stitching vary; the different hands that touch the book leave their marks. In this sense, the books can be thought of as multiple. But they can also be thought of as the products resulting from and making a process that is multiple in form, meaning, and effect.

The launch of the Editorial Retazos book *De chuequistas y overlockas* was paired with the presentation of a magazine and a documentary that also examine forms of production and spaces of consumption on the margins of the formal economy. The event was titled "La potencia del trabajo multiforme" (The power of multiform work),[19] and in a text published with the same title, the concept of the "multiform" is described: "Lo multiforme es una potencia, decimos, porque está creando formas múltiples cuando ya no hay *una* forma de trabajar, ni de conseguir dinero, ni de darle sentido a nuestro labor, ni mucho menos de conquistar dignidad. Lo multiforme es potente porque es experimentación viva" (We say that the multiform is a power/potency because it is the creation of multiple forms when there is no longer *one* way to work, nor to make money or make sense of our work, and certainly not to conquer dignity. The multiform is powerful/potent because it is live experimentation; "La potencia" 2011). The multiform, which we see in the Retazos books themselves as well as in their technical and social practices is evidence of *experimentation*. Significantly, their books connect different worlds of work in their materiality and their content. The Retazos workshop is connected to other workshops—the textile workshops, of course, but also different kinds of "workshops" like the collective spaces of theorization and knowledge practice in the ongoing research project between the collective coauthors of *De chuequistas y overlockas*, Simbiosis Cultural and Colectivo Situaciones. This particular title exemplifies the significance of "the multiform" as an effect of *provisoriedad* in several ways: first, as a text about the necessary transformation of work through experimentation; second, as the product of an ongoing experiment with collective knowledge practices connecting two groups; third, because the edition produced in the Retazos workshop is itself multiple, in that each handcrafted copy looks different and carries in its materials the presence of many other workers; and finally, because this title has also been edited and published by another press in a more conventional format (printed and bound in a commercial print shop), so it circulates in different ways. Experimentation makes both the materiality and the content of this book. But the book is never alone; it is never isolated. And in this case and others, as the next chapter explores in greater depth, the connections are not just effects of the books. The connections make the objects themselves.

THE WORKSHOP IN THE WORLD

In the various statements made by members of the book workshops, a common sentiment is expressed: we do things differently because that is how we've learned to make useful things. This means things that are useful not only to the consumers (the readers) but also to the producers (the book crafters) and the communities and movements from which the books emerge. De Pósfay's manifesto asserts that the more important the book, the more affordable it should be. Hugo explains the quirks of his process and the ways he puts his craft to work for his comrades. The cooperative workshop members in Buenos Aires consider the learning that happens in the shop to be an integral part of why their books are so useful. The rogue street bookbinders identify their practices as part of an effort to create more possibilities than those put forth by the mainstream publishing industry. And for the migrant youth their workshop is a space where something generative and critical emerges from the scraps of a system that has exploited and displaced them. The utility of a book cannot be measured objectively. A book is not only useful because it teaches you something or because it entertains you or even because you can trade it for something else. A book is useful when it is part of a practice of *doing*. And the creation of possibilities for *doing* is what happens in each of these workshops, where the distinction between intellectual and manual labor is collapsed. In this sense, use-value acquires a slightly different meaning than it has in conventional Marxist political-economic terms, as it points to the usefulness of *doing* as much as to the finished product. The possibilities that are imagined and enacted in the organic book workshop connect that space of craft to other spaces and other worlds.

As the books move out of the workshop, they carry the desires of their crafters not only in the words printed on the pages but also in their texture, their weight, their design. As they craft the books, the producers of these workshops are imagining the ways they hope the books will be used. They say they make books that can be shared, that can be reproduced, that can travel, that can be acquired with little money. The practices they put to work to create these objects are evident in their material form. But what happens when the objects that leave the workshop cannot be controlled by the crafters or their predicted uses? All the crafters can do is create the possibilities for these desired and imagined uses. Rather than lay claim to the potential effects or the future forms that their books may have, these "modest inventors" are creating objects that keep the provisionality of their process active in their materiality. They are creating "fluid objects," "multiform" objects that are not "frozen in time," recalling the warning of the "Copyleft" poem. The organic book is just that: a product of experimentation and movement. These books, made through experimentation and a commitment to continual provisionality, are mutable, living, social objects that propose other ways of doing and being together not driven by efficiency or accumulation but by the creation of possibilities. The crafting of durable products allows for the materialization of political and economic desires, but the crafters of these books express no concern with *their* object being the only form these ideas can take. In the following chapters, I explore what happens as these books move beyond the workshop. What happens as they circulate between presses, booksellers, and readers? What else is produced in the process? And how is the process of making things—specifically organic books—*in* the shop related to the process of making other spaces, relations, worlds *out there*?

THREE

THE UNBOUNDED BOOK

Es de todos y no es de nadie.

It belongs to everyone and no one.

—A MEMBER OF THE ORGANIZING
ASSEMBLY OF THE FLIA-CAPITAL, 2011

Any printed book is, as a matter of fact, both the product of one complex
set of social and technological processes and also the starting point for
another.

—ADRIAN JOHNS, *THE NATURE OF THE BOOK*

EVERYONE'S AND no one's. The end result and the starting point. These
apparent paradoxes shape the organic book. As my exploration of workshops
where inefficient practices yield affordable books shows, organic books are not
produced through necessarily consistent or coherent methods. They are the
products and the processes of inconsistent, provisional, and messy practices
that emerge from and contribute to the realm of wild politics (Tapia 2008),
rather than that of institutional politics. While previous chapters focused on
the earlier stages of production of organic books—in the spaces of collaborative knowledge practices or the printing and bookbinding workshops—this
chapter focuses on processes that are somewhat akin to what Christopher
Kelty (2008, 2), in his discussion of free software, has called "distributed collective creation." Rather than focus on the initial point of production through
which a manuscript becomes a book for the first time, a process I showed in
chapter 1 to be a matter of distributed knowledge practices, here I examine
what happens when books travel as they are shared between presses, leading
to the creation of new editions. In this sense, the focus will be on the ways that
organic books are not only opened up for what Chris Atton (1999) has called
"distributive use," but also for what we might call *distributive production*.

Organic books, in various formats both print and digital, often move beyond the context of their first publication through improvised and continuously shifting transnational networks that are characterized by their relative disregard for capitalist principles like ownership and property. These networks take a distinctly multidirectional and multidimensional form. They could be described as *transversal,* which is to say neither vertical nor horizontal, with the articulations cutting across spatial and temporal planes (Viveiros de Castro 2008, 158). This mode of networking and connection in editorial networks is yet another way that we can see the organic quality manifest itself, as the political-economic ethics of the broader social movements are materialized in the book's production and circulation. As Guiomar Rovira (2017, 10) asserts in *Activismo en red y multitudes conectadas:* "La red se ha vuelto el paradigma de las luchas emancipatorias contemporáneas y sus anhelos de horizontalidad. Es a la vez la forma mínima de organización y la infraestructura de comunicación" (The web has become the paradigm of contemporary emancipatory struggles and their desires for horizontality. It is at the same time the minimum form of organization and the infrastructure of communication). While she primarily examines the role of online media, what she describes is clearly visible in the print form of the organic book—an old medium renewed by its relationship with digital technology.

As the books travel, they are unbounded in multiple senses: as they move and are taken up by different actors in different contexts, they are modified materially and politically. They become multiple through the connections that they form and that form them. The possibilities for what they can do are not limited by the conditions of their initial production. There is no central root defining subsequent editions that emerge, no unitary reference point for a book's trajectory. As an extension of the qualities described in chapter 2, the absence of centralized proprietary control over the books can be understood as another aspect of their generic quality, in the sense proposed by Guillermo De Pósfay.

Gary Hall has written about the "unbound book," focusing on the transformations generated by electronic publishing. While it has been asserted, as Hall notes, that there is no such thing as an unbound book—since binding is what makes a text or a set of papers a book—he takes up this idea to work through the implications of open licensing and self-archiving in electronic publishing. His concern therefore is with how the book is unbound from "one of the other senses in which books can be said to be tied": its legal contracts (G. Hall 2013, 7). As I explore what happens to books as they are opened up through alternative copyright practices and moved across territories, I consider many of the themes Hall (2013, 32) raises, especially those related to the management of intellectual property (IP) and the "defamiliarization effect produced by the change in material support." But with my focus on *print* books, I am also interested in how books are unbound more literally—that is, how they get taken apart, modified, and recomposed by decentralized—and often uncoordinated—networks of different actors in different spaces. While Hall analyzes the *unbound* book as one that is set free from its material or legal constraints, I examine the *unbounded* book as one that is limitless and uncontrolled.

Through a series of narratives that move between Buenos Aires, Oaxaca, Mexico City, and La Paz, this chapter analyzes the ways that books get reedited and reprinted repeatedly by different presses to consider what happens when books travel across the continent, through networks that are constantly shifting with no centralized or institutionalized coordination. Materially, how do organic books simultaneously become everyone's and no one's, to borrow from the epigraph above? What are the relations that make the books and that the books in turn make? And what happens if we begin to imagine the books themselves as relations? Organic books move in ways that other books cannot or simply do not. While chapter 4 will follow the print books as they circulate among consumers through informal distribution networks, this chapter looks at the ways books move among different presses who produce new editions. I am interested in the mechanisms that facilitate this sharing, as well as the ways that the books are transformed both materially and politically as they are translated to the local contexts of their reedition. To this end, this chapter focuses on two interconnected themes: the management of IP practices (copyright, anticopyright, Creative Commons, copyleft, etc.) and the sharing of texts between presses contributing to the broader circulation of ideas. In examining what happens as books travel and are reproduced in different spaces, I explore the tension between the apparent disorder of the decentralized networks that facilitate the books' movement and the underlying coordination that drives the common commitment to see the ideas contained in the books circulate widely.

As Adrian Johns (1998, 3) asserts, "Any printed book is, as a matter of fact, both the product of one complex set of social and technological processes and also the starting point for another." With organic books this is especially apparent, as the books and their ideas are always connected to other books and ideas—they are the product of and the tools for collective thought and action. Organic books are never alone, never isolated. In what follows, I first examine the ways that intellectual property practices are reconfigured and reinvented by the producers of organic books as they strive to make the books open and accessible. I then examine the ways that this opening of the book is accompanied by a process of recomposition in which the objects and the ideas are modified and transformed as they get taken up in different contexts and "local cultures of the book" (Johns 1998).

But before presenting my description of *organic IP*—which is how I refer to the expressions of what are commonly called intellectual property practices in organic books—it is important to briefly situate these approaches in a longer history of copyright and IP. In *Authors and Owners*, Mark Rose (1993, 140) asserts that "the institution of copyright stands squarely on the boundary between private and public." He goes on to explain that this understanding of copyright as "mediator between private and public" makes it possible to see the ways that while it sometimes appears as a mode of private property, it also acts as a tool of public policy (140). This tension which underlies the institution of copyright today can be traced back to the seventeenth century and the friction between the "communal order" (Johns 2009, 11) of book crafters and the "emergent ideology of possessive individualism" (M. Rose 1993, 15) of which the monarchy and the state came to act as stewards. Whereas copyright as a practice of crafters was the product of a "regime of regulation" beginning in the late eighteenth century, with the formation of the modern figure of the individual author, copyright started to shift into a "regime of property" (M. Rose 1993, 15). The convergence of what Foucault named the modern "author function" with the advanced marketplace society of the eighteenth century led to copyright becoming embedded within a framework of intellectual property. But just as the concept of copyright was initially unrelated to individual property rights, so too was the notion of the author. As Nicholas Thoburn (2016) notes in his rereading of Foucault, the author function predates its attachment to a regime of property, first appearing in relation to penal law used to punish authors. The institution of copyright as it is understood today, then, is a specific manifestation that depends on its relation to individualism and property. Rose (1993, 142) explains: "Copyright is not a transcendent moral idea, but a specifically modern formation produced by printing technology, marketplace economics, and the classic liberal culture of possessive individualism. . . . And it is an institution whose technological foundation had recently turned, like a vital organ grown cancerous, into an enemy. Copyright developed as a consequence of printing technology's ability to produce large numbers of copies of a text quickly and cheaply. But present-day technology makes it virtually impossible to prevent people from making copies of almost any text . . . rapidly and at a negligible cost." What he outlines here is the way that the modern institution of copyright is a product of the confluence of technology, property, and individualism. The organic book is born from experiments with and across each of these, as its producers challenge the norms and conventional modes of production, circulation, and consumption of print books.

Picking up where Rose's 1993 work ends, with his 2010 monograph, *Piracy*, Adrian Johns expands our understanding of the evolution of copyright and IP. He anchors his analysis of piracy in the twenty-first century—which he defines as an economic order premised on knowledge and creativity, in contrast to the twentieth century's emphasis on energy and the nineteenth century's concern with manufacturing. In doing so, he develops a historical concept of piracy as a practice that predates both IP and copyright but which has come to represent the antithesis to both (Johns 2010, 3). For Johns, piracy is "about objects in space" (2010, 13) and is a question of production *and* reception. The distinction he establishes between the order within which printing occurs (what he identifies as the patriarchal order) and that within which reprinting occurs (an order that exceeds conventional morality) is crucial to my understanding of the unbounded and transversal production and reproduction of organic books. The organic book proliferates through precisely the kinds of unconventional ethical and technical practices that Johns associates with "reprinting" as the practice of pirates.[1]

In this chapter, I follow the ways that books move through networks of editors and presses. In addition to mapping the books' physical appearance and reappearance at different moments in different spaces, I also pay close attention to the marginal elements of the objects: the covers, the copyright pages, the prologues, forewords, and epilogues. By zooming in on the paratexts, evidence of the trajectories and relations of organic books comes into relief. As Gérard Genette's (1997) work has shown, paratext is "what enables a text to become a book" (1). Working with his idea of the paratext as threshold, not boundary, I look at these marginal elements as essential to understanding the unboundedness of the organic book. As I examine the ways that the books get reedited and republished, I ask, what happens when we bring this "zone of transition and translation," this "place of pragmatics and strategy" (Genette 1997, 2), to the center of our analysis and make paratext primary?

DISORDER AND THE APPEARANCE OF ORGANIC IP PRACTICES

Almost two years before I arrived in Argentina, some preliminary research about small presses based in Buenos Aires led me to the website of the FLIA, a roving, alternative book fair that I would later learn has flourished across Argentina (and beyond) since 2006. The FLIA logo—a pop art design of an open, smiling mouth with a tiny book on the tongue, positioned like a hit of LSD or maybe a communion wafer—appears as the banner on the somewhat chaotic Blogspot site that acts as a portal for any and all versions of the FLIA. A page titled "¿Qué es la FLIA?" (What is the FLIA?) offers a basic overview. The first paragraph reads: "La feria del libro independiente y alternativo (F.L.I.A) es un encuentro de intercambio de escritora/es, lectores, editoriales y distintos grupos autogestionados, además de compañeros de todas las expresiones artísticas. No tiene ningún tipo de patrocinio, es gratuita para expositores y asistentes, y su organización es abierta y horizontal para toda la gente que quiera participar, sea con creaciones o sólo con su cooperación y entusiasmo" (The FLIA is an encounter of exchange between writers, readers, presses and various *autogestionado* groups, as well as comrades from all kinds of artistic forms of expression. There is no sponsorship of any kind, it is free for both exhibitors and visitors, and its organization is open and horizontal for all those who want to participate, be it with their creations or simply with their cooperation and enthusiasm; "¿Qué es la FLIA?" 2015). Perhaps anticipating questions about who speaks for the FLIA, a comment at the bottom of the page explains the collective authorship of this text: "Este texto fue armado con textos que diversas FLIAs publicaron por Internet. Flia Rosarina, Flia Bogotá, Flia LaPlata, Flia Chaco, Flia Oeste, Flia Paraná, Flia Corrientes, Flia Mar del Plata, Flia Necochea, Flia Catamarca y más (This text was assembled from various texts that different FLIAs have published online . . .) The following commenter, username Flia Rosarina, remarked: "Muy bonito y emocionante leernos a todxs allí" (How beautiful to read all of our words here). I signed up for the email updates, added the various FLIAs as friends on Facebook, and over the next year and a half distantly followed some of the activity of this book fair that was both puzzling and exciting. From a distance, the FLIA appeared to be many things in many places, and in this sense it stood completely apart from the other book fairs I knew of and encountered over the months that followed.

Shortly after arriving in Buenos Aires for the first time, I attend my first FLIA in Lomas de Zamora, a city in the southern periphery of Buenos Aires. This particular fair is somewhat special as it is the first-ever FLIA-Sur: a newly organized fair for the southern region of the province of Buenos Aires. The fair crowds a large open space with tables and improvised stands crammed in, creating a sort of messy labyrinth of narrow pathways that snake around the room. Along the walls, narrow doorways lead to a few smaller rooms that look like they must have been offices in the building's former life. Since being *recuperado* or reclaimed by the popular assemblies of the neighborhood in November 2002, this former municipal government building has functioned as an autonomous social center used by dozens of organizations and groups for political and cultural projects including a screen-printing workshop, a free library, a women's self-defense school, and a theater troupe, among others. As the organizers describe it on their Facebook page (La Toma Centro Cultural), this "espacio recuperado" (reclaimed space) is run "de manera autogestiva" (through self-management) by people and organizations of "vocación militante" (militant persuasion). On the day of the fair, the space is doubly transformed from its original design as a government building: it is not only "La Toma" ("The Occupation," as the social center is called) but also "La FLIA-Sur."

As I walk toward the end of the room, I see some familiar faces, including several members of El Colectivo—a collectively run press dedicated to

FIGURE 3.1. FLIA newsletter, Buenos Aires, 2011.

publishing books that contribute to "the struggle for social change," as they say—who I met a few weeks earlier when a friend invited me to one of their meetings. They look like they're just standing at the end of a row of tables, but as I get closer, I see that they are in fact working their own stand—composed of a piece of cloth spread out on the ground with dozens of books on display. El Colectivo is one of the most prolific alternative presses in Buenos

Aires, with a large catalog of books featuring works by the "new generation" of radical intellectuals that emerged in the wake of the 2001 rebellion. Of the dozens of radical presses to pop up in the last decade, El Colectivo is one of the most consistent and established in both its production and editorial profile. Yet their presence at the FLIA-Sur is not what I had expected—this hastily improvised stand laid on the ground in the farthest corner of the fair doesn't correspond to my previous impressions of the group, based on their impressive catalog, their highly functional website, and their hefty, beautiful, polished books. I know from my conversations with members of the collective that the FLIA is an important point of sale for them—they don't rely on bookstore sales but rather direct sales in alternative spaces like this. But here at the FLIA, there is no hierarchy or seniority in the layout of the space—those who arrive first choose their spots (and pay nothing for them) and use whatever materials they've brought or find on-site to build their stand. As one member of the organizing assembly of the FLIA-Capital remarked to me, referring to both the books and the fair, "Es de todos y no es de nadie" (It belongs to everyone and no one), a statement that immediately made me recall the Zapatista slogan "Todo para todos, nada para nosotros" (Everything for everyone, nothing for ourselves).

El Colectivo, it seems, arrived late today, so they are left with a small patch of dirty floor in a dark corner, where they display their acclaimed and unique catalog of books. And so here I'm confronted with a puzzling moment, where my ideas of how things should be (that is, based on norms and conventions either real or imagined) don't line up with how they really are. After chatting with them for a moment, I crouch down to scan the selection of books, deciding to buy only one today, and settle on *De Cutral-có a Puente Pueyrredón: Una genealogía de los movimientos de trabajadores desocupados* (From Cutral-có to Puente Pueyrredón: A genealogy of the unemployed workers movements) by Mariano Pacheco. This hefty volume is nearly five hundred pages long, and it will end up being my most expensive purchase by far at the FLIA-Sur, at forty-five pesos (approximately ten dollars).

I leave two hours later energized by the effervescence of the fair and the conversations I've had, though weighed down by the ten new books stuffed in my bag. In total, I spent 144 pesos (approximately $35). I received one free book, a gift from one of the authors after I purchased a book he edited. Another vendor sold me his newest novel with a money-back satisfaction guarantee. Another book I purchased came with an apology from the editor because the price has gone up "significantly" from last year, from 3 to 5 pesos ($0.70 to $1.20). On my long ride home, I begin to skim through some of the books, looking more closely at details I missed in the frenzy and din of the FLIA. I feel their varied textures. One is handmade with a hot pink cardstock cover and a stapled binding, its spine sealed with brown duct tape. Another is more like a polished zine than a book, with a glossy inkjet-printed cover binding the fifty or so pages of text. Several others are small and smooth with matte covers and pages printed on an offset machine. Only one is printed on high quality bond paper, several are printed on a kind of heavy newsprint, and two appear to be xeroxed onto ordinary printer paper. But it's not until I arrive back at my apartment and settle into my seat at my kitchen table to write up some notes that I begin to examine the first few pages of the books.

Of the ten books I have spread out in front of me, only one is marked with the © of copyright—the others all bear some combination of copyleft (with the signature backward ©), Creative Commons, and original statements urging readers to copy and share the text. There is no consistency. One of the copyleft notes appears to have been lifted from a website, the resolution a bit grainy, with the backward © accompanied by the text "Copyleft. La creación se protege compartiéndola" (Copyleft. Creation is protected by sharing it). Others simply bear the backward ©: one is tiny and easy to miss, another is massive and oversized, taking up nearly a third of the page. This one seems to scream: "THIS BOOK IS COPYLEFT!" Another book has the backward © Copyleft above a Creative Commons Attribution-Noncommercial-ShareAlike license. But these two approaches to open IP don't make much sense together. Creative Commons was designed with the specific intention of normalizing and standardizing non-copyright licensing. While copyleft refers to a range of open and free IP approaches, Creative Commons refers to a formally consti-tuted set of licenses, some significantly more restrictive than others. Yet here they appear together. Why not? It seems to serve the purpose of showing that the publishers of this book have no interest in policing the reproduction of this work—they just don't want people to make a profit from it, and they want to insure that others will maintain this same open policy.

A different approach appears in the form of original statements proclaim-ing the openness of the works. One reads: "No sólo está permitido reproducir lo escrito en estos libros: es necesario" (The reproduction of the text in these books is not only permitted, it is necessary). This statement—which seems to be applied to all of the books made by this particular press—interpellates the reader as an accomplice in their effort to spread the ideas contained in each text. It says to me: "You cannot simply be a reader of these works. You are now an agent in the process of their enactment." Other books convey a similar call to the reader—though in somewhat less forceful terms. One de-clares: "La reproducción total o parcial de este libro es alentada sin necesidad de ningún tipo de autorización" (The total or partial reproduction of this book is encouraged; no authorization is necessary). Here the message is more sub-tle—nothing is *required*, but the reader is *encouraged* to do more than just read the book. This particular statement continues to make a pretty radical claim: "No existe la propiedad intelectual" (Intellectual property does not exist). Finally, in contrast to the standard statement in most Argentine books "Queda hecho el depósito que marca la ley 11.723" (The deposit in accordance with law 11.723 has been made), this press asserts that "No queda hecho ningún depósito según marca la ley 11.723" (No deposit has been made in accordance with the law 11.723). This statement is by far the most assertive in its repudiation of copyright. This press's message is layered: (1) unauthorized reproduction of the work is encouraged; (2) the very concept of intellectual property is refuted; and (3) the laws of intellectual property and publishing imposed by the Argentine state are rejected. A bit of research confirms my suspicion that this text—a translation of a well-known work by an Italian theorist—was previously published with a formal IP license. But while I expected to find it marked with a copyright, it is in fact "protected" by a version of Creative Commons that requires that the license appear with all subsequent reproductions. So in the edition I'm holding, with their bold denial of the existence of intellectual property, the press is not only breaking with dominant IP conventions but also with formal alternative IP practices.

A similar gesture appears in another book that I bought at the FLIA-Sur, also a title I'm certain has been published elsewhere and is definitely "protected" by copyright. Interestingly, this also happens to be the only book that is marked by a copyright symbol. The second printed page of the book says in small print: "© No te tomes tan enserio, 2007." The name of the press (which translates literally as "Don't take yourself so seriously") in combination with the profile of the author (and the other well-known authors whose works were on display at the same stand) clues me in to the fact that there is no way that anyone paid for or otherwise acquired the rights to reprint these works. The copyright itself essentially says "this is not a copyright," recalling the famous painting by surrealist painter René Magritte of a pipe accompanied by the text "Ceci n'est pas une pipe." And with this playful twist, I'm led to assume that not only is the copyright fake but likely the press name is too. More than an alternative approach, the moves made by the presses publishing these two books appear to me as acts of defiance—bold gestures of disregard for and denunciation of what they consider to be the restrictive and indefensible category of intellectual property. As Richard Stallman (2002) and others have argued, the very concept of intellectual property elides the differences between information and objects, and for this reason, he lists "IP" as one of his "words to avoid."[2] While I agree with him, I use the term "IP" as a placeholder to refer to the range of practices used to attend to matters of authorship, ownership, or copyrights in publishing.

The spread of books I have in front of me excites me, and I haven't even gotten past the paratexts of most of them. Clearly, the main content of these books is what inspired me to buy them—a broad array of creative and analytical descriptions of the political and cultural underground of Argentina. But what I find as I make my initial survey of these objects is unexpected. I am fixated on the many statements I encounter that challenge and complicate my conception of intellectual property practices—both dominant and alternative. I work through the pile, one by one, opening to the copyright page and photographing the contents. After I have worked through all ten, I compile the images on my computer and crop them, chopping them up into squares and rectangles of different dimensions, creating a collage of whites and beiges and ivories, all marked by black text and symbols in various sizes and fonts. Staring at this montage, my usual position as a reader and collector of books is disrupted. I feel called on by these books and the actors responsible for their production to take on a different role—to become another "publisher" of these works myself by sharing, reproducing, and spreading these texts. As in the workshops I traveled through in the previous chapter, here the roles usually neatly divided in the world of books—author, editor, publisher, printer, reader—are again blurred and crossed.

There is no consistency in the IP practices of the books I collected at the FLIA-Sur. From the range of copyleft logos to the "fake" copyright, these books represent more than simply an alternative approach to copyright. While this inconsistency could be attributed to the differences between the various presses who produce the books, a distinctive characteristic of this particular book fair is the frequent and continuous interaction and exchange that occurs among the presses, authors, and consumers who create and sustain this autonomous project. Often called "La FLIA Infinita" (the infinite FLIA) to recognize its semipermanent status, this event is held more frequently than most book fairs (several times a year in Buenos Aires proper, and at least monthly if you count the fairs held in the urban peripheries, across Argentina, and now as far north as Puerto Rico and Oaxaca). To a certain degree, it could be said that the presses that make up this fair do not function as discrete projects but rather as a network of collaborators. And since this initiative, which dates back to 2006, is one of the most visible expressions of the booming *cultura libre* movement in Argentina, it is not surprising that such an array of alternative IP practices would be found there. But I'm left thinking that, like the books themselves, the kind of adaptation and remixing of existing alternative IP practices I found here, as well as the invention of new ones, could also be described as *organic*—as a product of the unique conditions and relations from which it emerges rather than an importation or reproduction of something external to it, or something institutionalized. Organic IP, as I see it, is distinct from the various discrete alternative IP practices that appear and clash and overlap in the books

I brought home from the FLIA-Sur. It is distinct because, unlike Creative Commons or even copyleft, it is not only open and non-institutionalized—it is messy. There are no clear boundaries between the alternative (copyleft) and the dominant (copyright) and the remixes, crossings, and clashes that organic IP generates disorganize both orders. Rather than understand the IP practices of the FLIA-Sur as an alternative order, I am interested in exploring them as *disorder*, to borrow from Raquel Gutiérrez Aguilar, whose writings circulate at this and other fairs. She uses the idea of disorder to describe the form and effect of the politics and networks not only in Bolivia, where she was writing from, but also across the continent. I am less concerned with the consolidation of alternative practices than I am with the possibilities that the messiness of the disorder enables, and specifically how it relates to the intersecting networks—of presses, of ideas, of politics—that stretch across the continent. To this end, I am also interested in how copyright proper is used and, perhaps, misused.

COPYRIGHT AGAINST COPYRIGHT?

Back home in Oakland, staring at the tall bookcase that is now home to my archive of organic books, I pull a small volume off the shelf to begin a broader survey of the copyright pages of the archive I compiled in two years of field-work. This particular book seems like an obvious place to start, as its title is *Contra el copyright* (Against copyright) (Stallman et al. 2008). When I turn to the fourth page of the book, however, not one but *six* ©s hit my eyes: © Tumbona Ediciones; © 1996 Richard Stallman; © 2002 y 2003 Wu Ming 1; © 2003 César Rendueles; © Kembrew McLeod; © Éramos Tantos. Six individual copyrights, held by the press, the individual authors, and the book's designer. This page also includes the original titles of the essays, the press's contact information, the ISBN, and the printer's information. And at the bottom, two more bits of text appear. One acknowledges funding from the Fondo Nacional para la Cultura y las Artes. The other is a brief statement that reads much like an Attribution-NonCommercial-ShareAlike Creative Commons license. The text states: "Se permite la copia, ya sea de uno o más artículos completos de esta obra—excepto cuando se indique lo contrario—o del conjunto de la edición, en cualquier formato, siempre y cuando no se haga con fines de lucro, no se modifique el contenido de los textos, se respete su autoría y esta nota se mantenga" (Copying of one or more of the articles in this work—except when otherwise noted—or of the complete edition is permitted in any format, as long as it is not for profit, the contents of the texts are not modified, authorship is respected and this note is maintained).

This book is a bit of a hodgepodge of intellectual property practices: on the one hand we have copyrights attributed to any and all parties that could claim ownership of some element of the book, while on the other hand we have a statement opening the book up and making it available to anyone who wants to reproduce it for any purposes that are not for profit. On the opposite page, the authors' names, the name of the series, and the title loom large in a font and style reminiscent of a handbill for a boxing match: "Versus-Round 10: Against Copyright." I'm initially a bit baffled by this mash-up of IP politics: with the title and the permission to copy, the publishers make one statement. Yet with the list of copyright statements, another position seems to appear. Do these elements constitute a paradox? Or are they symptomatic of a different way of approaching the practice of intellectual property, one that doesn't subscribe purely to either conventional or alternative practices but rather mixes and crosses and disperses modes of attribution? And if this is the case, does this constitute a subversion of IP conventions as it both dilutes and confuses the very mechanisms usually used to make clean distinctions between authors, owners, and pirates? As a reader, I'm left a bit puzzled by the mash-up and somewhat jarred by the glut of ©s.

I bought *Contra el copyright* while attending the thirtieth International Book Fair (FILO, Feria Internacional del Libro Oaxaca) in the capital city of Oaxaca, Mexico, in November 2010. I found it at an oversized double stand dubbed the FLIO (Feria del Libro Independiente de Oaxaca, Oaxaca Independent Book Fair). This alternative fair was quite curious. Like "alternative" or "other" book fairs I've attended or followed elsewhere, it occurred parallel to the "official" book fair.[3] And like some of these alternative fairs, it was scattered out across the city with events held at several sites: the stand at the FILO, a bookstore and cultural center, a contemporary art museum, and a graphic arts institute. But unlike these other fairs, it also existed formally *within* the official fair. The FLIO's website states that it was convened by both La Jícara (a bookstore and cultural center) and the FILO (the official book fair), leading me to ask: what does the "independent" in the name FLIO refer to? The fair? Or the books themselves? In both English and Spanish, the event name is ambiguous: the Independent Book Fair/Feria del Libro Independiente. This is a recurring, though probably unintentional ambiguity in the naming of alternative book fairs, and in Oaxaca I found the blurriness all the more interesting given the overlap (both temporal and spatial) with the official fair. Because it didn't actually have a separate fair site for the sale and display of books, the FLIO was primarily enacted through the stand at the FILO and different events (book readings, signings, talks, exhibits) held at the various participating locations, with La Jícara serving as the main space for events. And so the resulting fair was made up more of the events than of the actual physical space of books around which we would imagine a book fair to be arranged. This ambiguity of both the significance and the physical condition of the independent fair generated a productive set of contradictions for me that later helped me think through other paradoxes in the world of organic books.

I arrived at La Jícara for one of the many FLIO events. The speakers that night were the founders of the small press out of Mexico City that published *Contra el copyright*: Tumbona Ediciones. A free-standing projection screen had been set up at one end of the open-air patio in the center of the building—an architectural feature typical of the colonial houses that line the streets in the center of Oaxaca and are now filled with restaurants, galleries, and shops of all sorts catering to the throngs of tourists that swarm the city. The press's logo appeared on the screen: a pin-up style silhouette figure of a women lying down reading a book. *Tumbona* is a Spanish term for a piece of patio furniture—like a chaise longue—used to recline in a leisurely position, perhaps alongside a swimming pool. Tumbona (as the name might suggest) is not a particularly militant or radical press—it's a bit of a fluke that the only book of theirs that I pick up is *Contra el copyright*, as most of their titles (even others within the Versus series) are far less overtly political: mostly short fiction in various formats. As the event began, one of the speakers explained that Tumbona's slogan is "el derecho universal a la pereza" (the universal right to laziness), which clarifies the logo for me. To be clear, this is not about some anarchist position against work—it really is a celebration of laziness and leisure.

In explaining the origins of their press, the speakers described the deep influence of their experiences in Buenos Aires in the context of the political and cultural crescendo following the economic crisis and popular uprisings of 2001—the very context that led to the founding of the FLIA. The society they encountered there, they explained, was saturated with independent literary and artistic projects of all kinds, including small presses like the one they would later found back at home in Mexico City. But unlike their Argentine counterparts, the context surrounding their experiment with alternative publishing was flat—for them, Mexico in the early 2000s lacked the cultural and political effervescence they had felt in Buenos Aires. Nevertheless, their press was part of a larger landscape that linked them to autonomous projects and spaces beyond Mexico, bringing them into contact with certain tendencies in alternative culture—copyleft among them. They spoke at length about the history and evolution of copyright, morphing from a mechanism intended to protect authors and readers to a tool that favors publishers' commercial interests. They described the challenges they faced trying to "convince" authors to adopt copyleft for their works, insisting that, contrary to what one might think, they've found the free circulation of their publications to be commercially beneficial: "por cada descarga, se genera una venta" (for every download, you make a sale).

As I sat listening to the couple at the front of the patio talking about the importance of the "circulación libre del conocimiento" (the free circulation of knowledge) and "precios justos" (fair prices), I flipped to the front of the tiny book I bought earlier at the fair to refresh my memory about just how many pesos I doled out for this slim pocket-sized volume. On the first page I saw the price written in my own handwriting: ninety pesos (roughly $7.50). This doesn't quite line up with the formula they present about how to price books: a book shouldn't cost more than a beer, they say. Ninety pesos for a book this size is far from accessible, and a quick scan of the cover reminds me that this book could hardly be considered an independent publication: the logos of two different government agencies appear alongside that of the press, indicating official sponsorship of the project. As I look down at the book while listening to the editors speak, it's hard to reconcile the words I'm hearing with the object I'm holding in my hands. An hour later, I leave the event drawing two conclusions—or perhaps better stated, sketching two ideas—about this mishmash of statements, including the copyright/pseudo–Creative Commons combination that appears in the book: (1) perhaps the Mexican context is less conducive to autonomous cultural production than the Argentine context for a variety of both political and economic reasons; and (2) *cultura libre* sometimes manifests more as a fashionable discourse than a material reality. But while the question of context is significant, it is also important to pay attention to the ways these different spaces—like Mexico City, Oaxaca, and Buenos Aires—are connected and the multidirectional and multidimensional flows of ideas and practices between them.

In the stories I've presented of organic IP in practice, sharing, cooperation, and modification and adaptation are key threads that connect them and that make visible the practice of autonomy driving and being driven by the organic book. Whether the presses are modifying the books' content or form or adapting the alternative IP licenses that help them to travel, the lack of concern for any centralization of control over the sharing of these books is significant. The presses exercise something like the "productive freedom" that Gabriella Coleman (2012) describes in her ethnography of hackers and that other scholars of IP politics and information technology highlight in their work. In *Two Bits: The Cultural Significance of Free Software*, Christopher Kelty (2008, 2) analyzes what he describes as a "reorientation of power with respect to the creation, dissemination, and authorization of knowledge in the era of the Internet." This reorientation of power dynamics in knowledge production is directly tied to efforts to expand availability and encourage modification or adaptation—the two elements that Kelty identifies as characteristic of anticopyright practices. Similarly, Severine Dusollier (2002, 287) asserts that such practices "offer a dissenting logic based in sharing and proffer an economic model premised upon giving." And Yochai Benkler (2006, 9) connects this "networked information economy" to a phenomenon of "enhanced autonomy" in which "the newly expanded practical freedom to act and cooperate with others. . . . improve[s] the practiced experience of democracy, justice and development, a critical culture, and community."

Like these broader innovations in decentralized network cultures, the experimental IP practices in organic books present exciting challenges to the assumptions of possessive individualism that underlie dominant IP practices. But perhaps what is most interesting about organic IP is precisely the way it manifests so messily, so full of tensions. The stories of organic IP that opened this chapter leave me with questions. What does copyright mean when it is paired with a statement that resembles a Creative Commons license? What does the copyright symbol do when it appears next to a fictitious name? What happens to its legitimacy when the lineage of a work's origins is inaccurately depicted? And what does it mean when the same work appears across different territories with multiple copyrights? The practices that prompt me to pose these questions are related to another way that the book becomes unbounded as editorial autonomy is exerted: the variations in the materiality and content of distinct editions. The editions are not only distinct in the ways they are packaged and licensed (or not) but also in the range of elements that the presses choose to modify as they translate the object for their own contexts and realities. Organic books do not follow set paths. Their maps are made as they move. The following sections follow that movement, examining the ways organic books travel through networks of presses, getting unbound and remade through practices of adaptation and translation.

NOT PIRATED BUT FREE

The map of *Contra el copyright* expanded for me in a surprising manner six years after I acquired the original Tumbona edition. While browsing my favorite bookstore during a brief trip to Buenos Aires, I came across the book again. This time, it was completely different. Tumbona Ediciones has some distribution to Argentina, and I had seen the press's books in stores (including this one) and at fairs in Buenos Aires before. The book I found in 2016, however, represented a different kind of movement of the book. Whereas the Tumbona edition is pocket sized, with the cover art matching the rest of the titles in the Versus series, the edition I came across in Buenos Aires, published by a press called Cospel, is bound as a more standard B-format paperback, with a solid red cover bearing the title, the authors' names, and a modified version of the series logo.[4] But the most striking shift from the design of the original edition is the large, oversized copyleft icon that appears in the style of a rough stamp in the center of the cover. The reverse © is accompanied by the word "copyleft" in a font of equal size to that of the book's title. In this way, this cover art appears and acts almost like a second title, creating uncertainty about which is the main title of the book. The cover itself is made of an inexpensive glossy paper, and upon opening the first page, the artisanal and low-cost quality of the edition becomes more obvious. The first page is marred by stray black marks, of the sort left by a dirty xerox job. And the glue holding the spine together clings to the cover and the first page, evidence of a hand-glued binding, like those I witnessed in many of the print shops described in chapter 2. The second page bears some centered, italicized, and bolded text that is not sourced from the Tumbona edition. It reads:

> Nota de la presente impresión/Edición: Cospel ediciones es un proyecto que se desarrolla en el nordeste argentino, precisamente en una región donde la inquietud por los temas relacionados con la Cultura Libre va de la mano con un escaso acceso a bibliografía especializada. Nuestro emprendimiento no tiene fin de lucro alguno, simplemente buscamos difundir y hacer circular conocimiento, compartiéndolo con quienes ven en este paradigma una posibilidad de franquear la barrera impuesta por los usos privativos de los bienes culturales.

> Note of the present printing/Edition: Cospel editions is a project that is developed in the northeast of Argentina, precisely in a region where the concern with issues related to *cultura libre* goes hand in hand with limited access to a specialized bibliography. Our project is not for profit, we simply seek to disseminate and circulate knowledge, sharing it with those who see in this paradigm a possibility of crossing the barrier imposed by the private uses of cultural goods. (Stallman et al. n.d.)

Several elements stand out. First is the use of two different terms to describe the object at hand: a "printing" but also an "edition." With these terms, the Cospel editors highlight a nebulous area in the decentralized and disordered editorial networks of the organic book. The book made by Cospel is something between a reprint and a new edition. It is quite literally a reprint in the sense that aside from the cover and two pages of text at the beginning of the book (one of which is repeated as the last page), the Cospel edition is simply a bound photocopy of the complete Tumbona edition, including the original copyright page which I described above. But it is also a new edition, produced in a different time and place than the original. And while the interior of the book is completely untouched, there are significant transformations in this object: the cover, the size, the texture, the price, and the overall aesthetic. But perhaps most significantly, the added pages, with the original statements penned by Cospel, imbue this object with new meaning and a distinct use-value.

The second element of the Cospel statement that stands out is the editors' direct identification of the political economy of knowledge and print culture as they relate to the praxis of *cultura libre*.[5] For Cospel, *cultura libre* presents a challenge to the barriers and dynamics of isolation that are a legacy of the colonial lettered city. A tool of the contemporary lettered city's underground, *cultura libre* is often limited to the urban centers, like Buenos Aires and Mexico City, that have historically been the privileged spaces of European writing and reading cultures in the Americas (Mignolo 1994, 227). Cospel Ediciones is a project based in the capital of the northeastern Argentine province of Chaco, a city remarkably named Resistencia. Like its neighbors Formosa and Santiago del Estero, Chaco is one of Argentina's most marginalized provinces, and in many ways it has more in common with Paraguay (which it borders) than with its own national capital, Buenos Aires. Through analysis of the networks connecting Bolivia and Argentina, the previous chapter addressed the ways the organic book in a sense provincializes the lettered city by challenging the center-periphery dynamics endemic to commercial and academic publishing. Here, with the case of Cospel, we see a project within Argentina that highlights and seeks to disrupt these dynamics of exclusion by mobilizing *cultura libre*.

The diverse practices of *cultura libre* are conceived as a mechanism capable of "crossing the barriers" imposed by proprietary approaches to IP, but they are also imagined as a means of constructing and extending social relations not based on capitalist or colonial principles. Following the statement about the new printing/edition quoted above, there is an invitation to contact the editors for more information. Below that, the following appears:

> Cada libro nos acerca un poco más.
> Muchas gracias a todos los que hacen y crean
> pensando en los demás, porque si alguna vez
> se revisa la historia serán los que de esta
> época han tenido el gesto libertario, la
> conciencia plena, los comunes, los artífices
> de una humanidad más justa y plena.
> Impreso en Argentina, para uso educativo.

> Every book brings us a bit closer together.
> Many thanks to those who do and make
> thinking of others, because if history is ever revised,
> it will be those of this era who have the libertarian spirit,
> full conscience, the majority, the creators of a more just and full humanity.
> Printed in Argentina, for educational use. (Stallman et al. n.d.)

The book here is figured not only as an educational tool, a conduit of knowledge and information (the *bibliografía especializada* referenced earlier), but also *as a relation*. Books connect us, they say. And books (and other things) made with a communal and collective ethic are even more effective in the efforts to create a more just and humane world. The other Cospel books I've acquired don't include this page, though they do include a different *noticia* (notice) that similarly expresses this spirit. The *noticia* gives a specific name to the practice of *cultura libre* employed by Cospel: "Freez(by)." The note explains that the project is "basado en la premisa del intercambio y el trabajo colaborativo" (based on the premise of exchange and collaborative work), and the name refers to: "Free: Free Culture, Cultura libre / Z: indicación, abertura, letra incómoda, etc / (By): Compartir del mismo modo, refiere al acto de pasar mano en mano, boca a boca, considerando lo que sus autores haya dispuesto" (Free: Free Culture, *Cultura libre* / Z: direction, opening, uncomfortable letter, etc. / (By): Sharing in the same way, referring to the act of being passed from hand to hand, mouth to mouth, considering what the authors have provided; Stallman et al. n.d.). Rather than adopt an existing approach to IP (copyleft, Creative Commons, etc.), as others do, Cospel instead chooses to invent its own, a sort of remix of elements of Creative Commons and other elements of the shared vocabulary of *cultura libre*. Significantly, with its reference to "mano en mano" (hand to hand), the explanation of "(by)" asserts the particularity of the materiality of the print book, as a specific kind of cultural good that takes up space and relies on face-to-face relations. Here, the ethics and practices of *cultura libre*—both born from and centered in digital culture—are attached to a specific kind of object, one that travels differently than its digital counterparts. The short description that follows extends this idea as it elaborates on the intervention Cospel aims to make with their publications, which is "promoviendo y difundiendo un modo de relación con los bienes culturales" (to promote and disseminate a mode of relation with cultural goods; Stallman et al. n.d.). Finally, the note clarifies (perhaps anticipating assumptions based on the aesthetic of the edition) that this "no es un libro 'pirata' o ilegal, es uno que entiende a la libertad como constitutiva del mismo" (is not a "pirated" or illegal book, it is one that understands freedom as constitutive of itself; Stallman et al. n.d.). Cospel's edition of *Contra el copyright* transforms a book that could otherwise have remained within the conventions and circuits of (independent) commercial publishing into one with a new life, filled with new meaning. As it is reread, reedited, remade, and reprinted by Cospel in the northeast of Argentina, it creates new relations and new maps, all connected to those of the original Tumbona edition. This is a clear expression of the productive disordering that characterizes the organic book's networking function. In the next section, another book's story makes visible other ways that organic IP comes to life, making, shifting, and extending maps and relations.

Unusually wide and hefty in weight, the first edition of *Los ritmos del Pacha-kuti* (2008b; *The Rhythms of Pachakuti*, 2014) by Raquel Gutiérrez Aguilar was published in Bolivia—the site of the popular rebellions it analyzes.[6] On the back of the bright purple cover are the logos of two presses. But on the copy-right page, a single © appears, floating next to not the presses' but the author's name. The next edition was published just a few months later in Buenos Aires and is similarly marked by multiple logos: Tinta Limón Ediciones and UNIA, the Universidad Internacional de Andalucía. While the former's role as the publisher of this book is obvious for various reasons, the latter's is unclear, as nowhere else in the book is there any mention of this European university. I'm left to assume that UNIA provided some funding for this publication. On the copyright page, the words "Rights reserved" appear followed by "© 2008 Tinta Limón." The final edition was released about six months later in Mexico City. The number of logos has increased, though none are repeated from either of the preceding editions. As I flip through the first pages, I notice that the copy-right page more closely resembles the Argentine edition than the Bolivian edi-tion, though in place of one copyright symbol, there are three.

As *Los ritmos del Pachakuti* moves swiftly across the continent being picked up, reedited, and modified by different presses, the IP licensing seems to get progressively more restrictive, with the most recent edition from Mexico bear-ing not only multiple copyrights but also a formal statement threatening le-gal sanctions against anyone violating the law. Of the three presses that have published this book, the group in Mexico, Bajo Tierra (which literally means "under ground"), is the one I'm closest to and know best. Bajo Tierra is also the press that most explicitly self-identifies as anticapitalist and autonomist of all those I encountered in my research. So what happened here? How did an anti-authoritarian, anticapitalist youth collective end up in the position of reinforcing the very structures of capitalism and state power that it so compel-lingly denounces and critiques in its writings and organizing efforts?

I look back over the list of copyrights. The first is to the author and the sec-ond is to the press. The third copyright holder is where I suspect the restrictive language and licensing originated: the university of Puebla, the Benemérita Universidad Autónoma de Puebla (BUAP), where Gutiérrez Aguilar complet-ed the doctoral thesis that would later become this book. But I know from conversations with Bajo Tierra that this relationship is far from symmetrical. While the labor of editing, designing, and getting the book printed fell wholly in the hands of Bajo Tierra, the BUAP's participation was exclusively financial. Yet as the more powerful (economically, politically, bureaucratically) agent in this transaction, BUAP's will to not only copyright the work but mark it with such restrictive and imposing legalistic terms trumps the political desire of the small youth collective who, together with the author they identify as a "comrade," are the true architects of this book. But to paint the collective as a passive actor in this transaction would be too simple—and this is confirmed through my conversations with collective members. They explained that they agreed to the terms of the copyright because the collaboration with the BUAP is useful in other ways. And rather than see the copyrighting of one of their books as a political contradiction, they acknowledge it as a bureaucratic detail with little if any actual legal or material impact on the circulation of this work. They insist, after all, that they are not "istas"—that is, they are not dogmatic in their politics. They adapt their practices to meet their current needs and possibilities (interview, Mexico City, 2010).

My impression of the print editions of this book is quickly complicated by a simple Google search for the title. Among the first results is the Tinta Limón website, where I notice a bit of text accompanying the description of *Pachakuti*: "Algunos derechos de esta obra están liberados por sus autores y/o editores para su disfrute público y gratuito sin fines de lucro. Haz click aquí para ver los detalles de la licencia" (Some of the rights of this work have been liberated by the authors and/or editors for free and public, noncommercial, use. Click here for the details of this license; Tinta Limón Ediciones). The link leads to a description of the Attribution-NonCommercial-NoDerivs Creative Commons license. So this book, while copyrighted in its print edition, has been "liberated" in its digital form: a PDF file is available for free download. Why the press has chosen not to use the same license in the print edition is unknown to me, but this partial liberation of the digital file has the effect of complicating their otherwise typical IP approach.

The Bajo Tierra website, in contrast, does not offer any downloadable files or even any view of the contents of its books. Yet within the results of my web search I notice a PDF of the Bajo Tierra edition of *Los ritmos del Pachakuti*. The link takes me to a website I know well: Scribd, "the world's largest digital library," which purports to only host "legitimately" sourced texts—that is, in no violation of copyright. However, I, like any Scribd user, know the reality to be quite different, as there is little enforcement of this policy. The only way users can download files for free is by uploading a file in exchange. This is how the archive grows. So anyone can upload just about any file—and many scanned books and, I assume, leaked PDFs of copyrighted books have been added to the Scribd archive.

The link I click on from my Google search takes me directly to the Scribd page where a full PDF of all 288 pages of the Bajo Tierra edition has been uploaded by a user in Mexico City who I know is not a member of this press. I expect it to be a scan of the print book, but the sharpness of the title page tells me otherwise—this is an original PDF file. And what I see as I scroll down to the second page looks quite different from page two of the print book I'm holding next to my computer screen. There is no mention of the BUAP, and the ISBN number is incomplete. But the most significant difference is the conspicuous absence of the copyright icon. In its place is a Creative Commons license, Attribution-NonCommercial-NoDerivs 2.5 Mexico.

How did this PDF end up on Scribd? I suspect that this file is an early proof of the book, compiled before the legal and technical details—including the copyright licensing and ISBN—had been negotiated and finalized. But this file is not just incomplete. The differences between this page and its analog in print are more than mere technical details. They suggest that Bajo Tierra's (as well as perhaps the author's) desire may have been to publish the book without copyright, using a less restrictive IP license. But with the involvement of the BUAP—a major academic institution with proprietary claims to both the published book and the research contained in it—this became impossible. Both the Tinta Limón and Bajo Tierra digital files appear to me as something like the freer, more open and mobile sisters of the print editions. Or, better yet, something like the digital alter-egos of the print book—like an alternate persona with its own set of ethical engagements.

What this bibliography conveys is a sense of how the book is unbounded as different presses share the text and reprint their own editions across Latin America.[7] In describing the book as unbounded, my intention is not to suggest that the book is necessarily becoming more and more free or public or to ascribe some telos of progressive radicalization to its trajectory. Rather, I want to explore it as a way to see power being dispersed, to borrow Zibechi's idea. He explains that, "Durante los momentos insurreccionales la movilización disuelve las instituciones, tanto las estatales como las de los movimientos sociales" (Zibechi 2006, 39; During moments of insurrection, mobilizations dissolve both state and social movement institutions. Societies in movement, articulated from within quotidian patterns, open fissures in the mechanisms of domination, shred the fabric of social control, and disperse institutions [Zibechi 2010, 11]). In this translation, the main idea comes through: these moments of what he calls "societal movement" produce a disordering of *everything*, not just the dominant but also the alternative. And here, quite starkly, the "dispersion of power" cannot be romanticized and ascribed some telos of progressive radicalization. When power is dispersed, what is at stake is a lessening of centralized control or authority over a thing, a space, a community, an idea, a process. Although Zibechi does state that, ideally, the dispersion of power is accompanied by a degree of social cooperation, not fragmentation, that cooperation may not be clearly legible as following a unified and collectively determined path. Rather, the social cooperation at play in the dispersion of power may simply be an expression of what Gutiérrez Aguilar (2009) calls a "collective horizon of desire." But desire for what? She is careful not to name anything in particular—and in doing so she suggests that what is important is the collective effort of disordering, with a new order only emerging through practice, not design. In the words of her comrades in the Colectivo Situaciones (2007, 88), "commonality emerges in (and from) difference."

In the case of organic books, what emerges from this dispersion of power is an expression of editorial autonomy. There is no center, no authority in the life of this book—except for the author. And even the author sometimes slips out of the equation, becoming yet another decentered actor in the process. What these stories suggest is that the practices not only disrupt conventions of IP and commercial or academic publishing but also disorganize the power dynamics that guide them. And the presses do just this: they disorganize the logic of intellectual property by both disregarding or subverting their mechanisms (copyright, for example) and also—and perhaps more interestingly—using them messily and inconsistently. What the underground worlds of organic books reveal is not the existence or consolidation of alternative IP models or institutions but rather organic IP, which disperses modes of attribution and disorganizes the foundations of capitalism—property and individualism. This produces distributed and decentralized practices of both production and consumption.

DISTRIBUTED PRODUCTION IN THE MESS OF NETWORKS

The stories that brought organic IP practices to my attention and led me to name them as such are stories of books that are unbounded. In chapter 2 I described how print books are physically bound by thread or staples or glue. But here I explore how they also become unbounded, and to what effect, as they are opened up and reassembled by other actors who pick up the pieces that move across territories. In this movement, they are not bounded as single editions controlled by single owners or authors. They are not bounded as objects that transmit ideas and practices consistently in their content or their form. They are not bounded by the places from which they emerge. These books are unbounded in their meaning and in their movement. The varied editions of *Los ritmos del Pachakuti* (*Rhythms of the Pachakuti*) or *Dispersar el poder* (*Dispersing Power*) described in the previous section show this. What could be interpreted as a technical or logistical detail in the production of a book—the copyright—becomes a space where we can begin to follow the tensions between the coordination and collaboration that connects presses and the editorial autonomy they each exert. These are books that—in part because of the organic IP practices enacted by their publishers—travel widely, moving through networks that they also help to create. But just how do they travel?

How do the different editions come to exist in different places? How do different actors contribute to expanding the circulation of the books? And what happens—politically and materially—when the book is set into movement, traveling beyond its initial site of production? As the previous sections have shown, organic books are produced through practices aimed at opening these objects, which is to say, aimed at making them more accessible through lower prices and (more) open IP so that the ideas held in their pages might circulate more widely. In what follows, I describe some of the ways that the ideals printed on the opening pages of the books—through statements like those that insist that the reproduction of the books is permitted or encouraged or even necessary—are enacted as books get reedited by presses in different spaces. In doing so, I consider not only the ways that editorial autonomy is exerted by the presses as they produce new editions but also the ways that their practices contribute to the formation of networks like those that the books and their politics aim to expand.

In 2008 the Mexico City youth collective Jóvenes en Resistencia Alternativa got wind of news that the Italian autonomist theorist Franco "Bifo" Berardi was planning a trip to Mexico. While some of the members of the group knew of his work, many others didn't. Through discussions in the general assembly about the nature of his work and his relevance to their projects, it was agreed upon that his visit was an opportunity to continue building the kinds of networks they had been developing in recent years. The collective, which had formed some six or seven years earlier as an offshoot of a student organization at the Autonomous University of Mexico, had been deeply immersed in a series of projects aimed at building relationships with other organizations and movements across Mexico. They clearly identify themselves as members of a generation of urban youth politicized by the influence of Zapatismo and the related alterglobalization movements around the world. And in 2008 they were coming off a wave of organizing linked to the Zapatistas' Other Campaign, launched in mid-2005 to articulate all those "from below and the left" in Mexico who identified with the need for a "national plan of anticapitalist struggle." One of the collective's most ambitious projects was its Other Seminar, which included a series of workshops in different parts of the country where members of different organizations and movements would convene around a certain topic, which could be skill-oriented, like popular education or alternative media production, or more thematic, like the workings of capitalism or antisystemic movements. With this experience behind them, they felt, as one member commented, "la preocupación de continuar tratando de establecer los contactos o las redes o plataformas de trabajo" (the concern about continuing to establish the contacts or the networks or platforms for work; interview, Mexico City, 2010). This meant finding ways to extend the kind of spaces of collective knowledge practices and encounter that the Other Campaign and later the Other Seminar had provided, through which the collective developed deep ties with others similarly engaged in anticapitalist organizing.

Bifo's visit to Mexico presented itself to the collective as an opportunity to do just that: to continue to build and share with their growing networks. And suddenly, in addition to their plans to organize events with Bifo in different political spaces, the possibility emerged for publishing one of his books, *Generación Post-alfa: Patologías e imaginarios en el semiocapitalismo* (Berardi 2008; Post-Alfa Generation: Pathologies and Imaginaries in Semiocapitalism), which had been translated and published by the Colectivo Situaciones and its press Tinta Limón in Buenos Aires. A friend of the collective put JRA in contact with the Argentine group, which offered to share the PDF for publication in Mexico. Colectivo Situaciones sent the file via email for free, asking only that they be credited in the Mexican edition. In a footnote to her prologue, Raquel Gutiérrez Aguilar (2008c, xi) describes and valorizes the significance of this relationship between the Mexican and Argentine collectives: "Hoy se edita en México a partir del esfuerzo hecho por jóvenes mexicanos quienes se acercaron a otros jóvenes argentinos, el Colectivo Situaciones, para entablar relaciones de cooperación y reciprocidad. Agradezco a *Jóvenes en Resistencia Alternativa* la invitación para escribir este prólogo, que me vincula con este esfuerzo común de difundir herramientas para el pensamiento crítico, haciéndolo todo, además, de manera autogestionaria y autónoma" (Through the effort of Mexican youth working with another group of youth from Argentina, the Colectivo Situaciones, this book is edited today in Mexico to build relationships of cooperation and reciprocity. I thank JRA for the invitation to write this prologue, which connects me to this common effort to disseminate tools for critical thought, all produced through autogestion and autonomous practices). What is significant here is not only the dynamic of interaction, collaboration, and sharing that Gutiérrez Aguilar describes occurring between Colectivo Situaciones and JRA but also the ways that she understands herself as becoming a part of that connectedness. She sees herself as contributing to this "common effort" of production and, more importantly, dissemination of "tools for critical thinking" through autonomy and *autogestión*. While Situaciones and JRA alike tend to prioritize the publication of works that come directly from social movements, Bifo's book, while more abstract, is nonetheless important politically in their estimation, as precisely this kind of tool. In an interview, a member of the Tinta Limón/Colectivo Situaciones project explained this distinction, explaining their decision to publish works by Bifo, Paolo Virno, Félix Guattari, and other European theorists: "Que si bien no surgían de luchas directas, ni próximas, podían estimular la imaginación al-

ternativa y resistir lo que nos parecían los momentos más oscuros de la hege-
monía" (Even if they didn't come directly from struggles, or even from close
to them, these books could stimulate the alternative imagination and help us
resist what seemed like the darkest moments of hegemony; interview, Buenos Aires, 2011). And when an author like Bifo travels to Latin America to
dialogue with these collectives and movements, that work acquires another
dimension. In the original Spanish edition, Colectivo Situaciones included an
interview they did with Bifo, in which they connect his ideas with their political context—post-2001 Argentina. When Bifo arrived in Mexico City, he
joined local militant thinkers like Raquel Gutiérrez Aguilar and members of
JRA to discuss the conceptual and political challenges facing popular movements there. The very names of these two presses convey the idea of the complexity of the tools they seek to produce and disseminate: Bajo Tierra refers to
all that is just below the surface, underground, and not immediately visible or
apparent; Tinta Limón is a reference to the clandestine practice of writing in
lemon juice to keep a message invisible except to those who know it is there
and know to heat it to reveal it. Both suggest that reading is more than just
seeing what appears on the page—it is a process of looking deeper, reading
between the lines, reading through and past the paper.

The process of publishing Bifo in Mexico—through exchanges and dialogues that spanned continents—is what set the press that would later be
named Bajo Tierra Ediciones into motion, adding a new dimension to the
work of the larger collective, JRA. Significantly, it was not the result of some
long-standing plan to make books, nor was it the manifestation of a desire
to publish their own writings or those of their comrades. The press came
about through a combination of relationships that make visible the activity
of networks that extend beyond Mexico, while in turn also contributing to
the expansion and strengthening of these multidimensional relationships.
Bajo Tierra's story, as recounted to me by members of the collective, is one of
relationships, collaborations, encounters, and exchanges that create organic
networks. Borrowing from Annelise Riles (2001, 3), I use the term "network"
to refer to connections that extend beyond just human actors to include the
knowledge practices and objects that "internally generate the effects of their
own reality by reflecting on themselves." She writes: "Networks . . . are systems
that create themselves" (173); they are not fixed models or structures. Rather,
in her approach, the network is both the object and the subject of analysis
and inquiry; it is "both a means to an end and an end in itself" (51)—which
is why she says that it can be turned inside out, as in the title of her book.
The network is not instrumental but generative and self-generating, and this
view is echoed in the ways the members of Bajo Tierra describe their relationships with other presses, writers, movements, and organizations. While

certain formations that they work with are formally named "networks"—such as the Red Autónoma Anticapitalista formed in 2010—all of their work, both within and beyond the collective, is network driven and transversal in its orientation. As I have mentioned in other chapters, transversal networks, neither vertical nor horizontal, cut across layers and dimensions and intersect and take flight. Colectivo Situaciones (2007, 92) discusses the work of articulation as "de-centering the networks," "open[ing] oneself towards stretches of the network that have not been *made explicit*" (emphasis in the original). What is key here is the idea that the network is not already made; it is continually expanding—not necessarily in size but rather in what it reaches. The tensions that emerge when commonality seems to have reached its limit are precisely the moments that allow new nodes to form. In discussing the difficulties social scientists have faced in trying to account for such dynamism, Knox, Savage. and Harvey (2006, 131) assert that "the network's power and importance is tied to its mutability and shifting form."

One member of Bajo Tierra/JRA remarked: "creo que nuestra capacidad de redes nos ayuda" (I think our network ability helps us; interview, Mexico City, 2010). What she named their "network ability" or skill is their fundamental political practice—gathering, encountering, sharing, connecting, exchanging through networks—be it in the books they publish, the workshops they put on, the benefit concerts they organize, the statements they release, the street actions they lead, or simply their own internal assemblies. Bajo Tierra's catalog of books can be read like a map of the networks they are engaged in. But it is not just a representation of those networks: *the book is the network*. Like the Bifo book that articulates a generation of Italian autonomists, Argentine militant intellectuals, and Mexican anticapitalist youth, other titles in their collection act similarly, simultaneously creating and describing the relations of their informal networks. Just two of their eight titles are original publications—all the others are titles they have reprinted or, better stated, reedited. While "reprinted" would be the more common term to describe a press publishing a book that has previously been published elsewhere, what is occurring here is more than simply a reprinting. There is, in fact, an original editorial process at play, with not only formal changes but also content modifications.

In a lecture at the Universidad de Buenos Aires, Matías Reck, an editor for the press Milena Caserola, remarked to a class in the publishing degree program: "El editor tiene un rol fundamental en la construcción del libro: mientras el texto sigue siendo el mismo en cada edición distinta, el objeto va cambiando" (The editor has a fundamental role in the construction of a book: whereas the text stays the same in each new edition, the object itself changes; Buenos Aires, 2011). What Reck is referring to is much broader than what might usually be recognized in the work of the editor—the editor here is the person, or group of people, who compose the book as a compound, social object defined not only by the main text but also by the decisions made about any added text (back cover, prologue, notes), design, materials (paper, ink, binding), IP licensing, and print run quantity, to name just a few. In this way, as he says, "the object changes." It is not just a reprint, as each time it is reedited a different object is produced, carrying in it the influence and traces of its editors, past and present. It becomes a network. To be sure, while each edition is unique, we are not talking about discrete objects. Each edition is connected to past editions in ways that may or may not be immediately evident. While what occurs is a reedition, those actors engaged in this work often don't see themselves as "editors," in the sense that they find little affinity with the career editors of the commercial presses, or even the students in the class where Reck gave his talk. A member of a different alternative press in Buenos Aires remarked that "hacemos libros, pero no somos una editorial. . . . Que tengas ediciones no quiere decir que edites, que seas editorial. . . . Yo no me considero editor" (We make books, but we are not a publishing house. . . . The fact that you have editions doesn't mean that you edit and that you have a press. . . . I don't consider myself an editor; interview, Buenos Aires, 2011). This tacks back to the theme of how roles get blurred in the production of organic books. The clear divisions of labor in commercial publishing that the category and prestige of the editor is built on don't hold up here. Further, some, like the "editor" quoted above, firmly reject that title.

Bajo Tierra's first publication, *Generación Post-alfa*, demonstrates this double character of the reedition clearly: it is at once derivative and original. Originally written in Italian, the Spanish edition of Bifo's book was produced in Argentina by eight translators, one copy editor, and the members of Colectivo Situaciones and their press Tinta Limón. The Argentine edition is not copyrighted but bears a Creative Commons Attribution-NonCommercial-NoDerivs license. The Mexican edition, however, bears two copyrights: one to Tinta Limón Ediciones, 2007, and a second to Bajo Tierra Ediciones in coedition with Sísifo Ediciones, 2008.[8] Below these notes, a small text appears that reads, "El espíritu de trabajo de bajo tierra ediciones es la publicación con licencia copyleft en acuerdo a las partes involucradas. Sin embargo, para la publicación de este libro, Tinta Limón Ediciones cedió los derechos a bajo tierra ediciones en coedición con Sísifo Ediciones para su primera edición en México" (The spirit of Bajo Tierra Ediciones's work is to publish with copyleft licenses with the agreement of the different parties involved. However, for the publication of this book, Tinta Limón Ediciones ceded the rights to Bajo Tierra in coedition with Sísifo Editions for its first edition in Mexico;

Berardi 2008). As in previously discussed cases, despite the Argentine edition's inclusion of an alternative IP license designed to make possible precisely this kind of reproduction, the Mexican edition carries a completely distinct political statement on its copyright page. Bajo Tierra is committed to copyleft, but in order to publish this particular title they had to get the rights from Tinta Limón and maintain the copyright license, which did not actually appear in the first edition. While this inconsistency is not unique, as the books discussed in the first part of this chapter demonstrated, it is worth noting the distinct political character that the Bajo Tierra edition acquires in just this one page: two copyrights make visible a relationship between the two presses, and the accompanying statement sets JRA apart from Tinta Limón, as JRA insists that its commitment is to copyleft, despite the fact that this is the group's first publication and it has no prior experience with licensing a publication.

As Bifo's book traveled from Argentina to Mexico, other material and political aspects were transformed in the reedition. While the design of the guts was mostly preserved, a different cover was created by a designer within JRA. The Tinta Limón edition, as do others in their collection Nociones Comunes (Common Notions), bears a cover with a monochromatic tinted reproduction of an old drawing—presumably something so old that no credits are required, since none appear in the book. The design of this cover and the others in the collection, composed of works of political philosophy by a host of mostly European authors, suggests a sort of classic quality. The ink drawings look antique, and while I recognize none of them, it seems like they could be recognizable as classics. While the bold color tints—lime green, magenta, violet, bright orange, and yellow—give the covers a modern touch, the overall effect in my eyes is one of seriousness and even stodginess, as if to warn or alert the potential reader of the density of their prose. This collection has a distinct aesthetic in comparison to the books that make up the more popular Mano en Mano (Hand in Hand) or Pensar en Movimiento (Thinking in Movement) collections. Those books, with titles such as *Mal de altura: viaje a la Bolivia insurgente* (Altitude sickness: A trip to insurgent Bolivia) and *¿Quién habla? Lucha contra la esclavitud del alma en los call centers* (Who's calling? Struggle against the slavery of the soul in call centers), have vibrant covers featuring stylized photographs and a street art aesthetic. In contrast, the cover of Bajo Tierra's edition of Bifo's book is composed of an extreme close-up of the upper half of a young, indistinctly gendered face. At first glance, I wasn't sure what I was looking at. My eyes met textures, lines, a high contrast between the two halves of the cover. Closer inspection revealed two dark eyes, almost completely covered by a thick fringe of straight black hair, and the curve of a prominent nose, the edges of the photograph slightly pixelated. The title is stamped in white over the dark hair; all caps in a rough industrial font. Even though so little of this face is visible, something about it in combination with the font and the title screams "YOUTH!"

While the Tinta Limón edition might be on the surface less attractive to a nonacademic reader, particularly if juxtaposed with a title from Tinta Limón's other collections, in the Mexican edition, Bajo Tierra creates an aesthetic and cultural translation of the object for their own context and audience: the realm of politicized urban youth in one of the world's greatest megalopolises. In the note mentioned above, Raquel Gutiérrez Aguilar names both Situaciones and JRA as "youth," and while both emerged from student organizing and maintain a political perspective as youth in the sense of belonging to a new generation of activism, they have very distinct contexts, trajectories, and audiences. Colectivo Situaciones, as a "militant research collective," has gained currency among intellectuals and academics not only in Argentina but across Latin America, Europe, and the United States through its original writings, which are quite theoretically dense. For the first ten years, their work was centered around collective research and writing projects. JRA, in contrast, initially built its networks in Mexico through the organization of massive benefit concerts featuring hip-hop, reggae, and rock artists organized annually to raise funds for the Zapatista communities and later for an autonomous social center that they hoped to build in Mexico City. Consequently, JRA's principal audience is an extension of its work from the university: high school and university students and the fan bases of the politically savvy musicians JRA works with, including Bocafloja, Panteón Rococo, la Maldita Vecindad, and others. In this way, while JRA's primary audience is students, they are not necessarily academics or intellectuals. And the group's proximity to its audience is evident in the aesthetic of the books and other media it produces.

The sort of aesthetic translation that I identify in the various cover designs is significant inasmuch as it makes visible the effects of a book's publication in a different time and place. But they are also significant in the ways they remind us that a book is composed of much more than the textual content of its pages. While the cover undoubtedly contributes to readers' experience with a book, it certainly should not be interpreted as signifying anything about the book's content. Rather, the book cover's transformations across editions is perhaps the most obvious way we can see the materiality of the organic book in flux as it is unbounded and rebound. Together with the other, less obvious material elements of the print book—the paper, the binding, the typeset, the layout— the cover communicates the ways in which the publishing experiments that make the organic book unsettle and mobilize what Nicholas Thoburn (2016, 1) calls the "full materiality" of the book. As he argues, "Materiality is not a fixed property of books but a mutable product of their physical, signifying, temporal, and affective materials and relations, including relations brought to them in acts of reading and other forms of productive consumption" (110). In a different context, Marcy Schwartz (2014, 418) has argued that the circulation and consumption of used books highlights the ways books are remade as they circulate, gaining new meaning through "every change of hands." The movement of organic books between editors and presses represents a particular space of reading in which not only the text but the full materiality of the book-object acquires new meaning. With my discussion of the material and aesthetic translation, I demonstrate how the practices through which the organic book is unbounded and remade are a kind of productive consumption, not unrelated to the idea of distributive production referenced in the opening of this chapter.

While the formal elements—like the copyright page and the cover design—are material evidence of a political and cultural translation of the book to its new context, other aspects of the Mexican edition of Bifo's book demonstrate this translation more directly.[9] All of Bajo Tierra's publications include a short, collectively authored text that introduces the book and its significance for the press. Given that most of Bajo Tierra's publications are reeditions of books published elsewhere, this is an important way the press situates the ideas within the collective's work, which it identifies as committed to "autonomía, autogestión, y horizontalidad." In the Bifo book, the "Nota de bajo tierra ediciones" outlines the "tres impulsos [que] nos empujan a reproducir en México *Generación Post-alfa*" (three impulses that push us to reproduce *Generación Post-alfa* in Mexico): (1) the effort to "difundir, socializar, debatir, exponer, reproducir ideas, provocaciones, insinuaciones, hipótesis y textos que aporten al pensamiento autónomo" (disseminate, socialize, debate, expose, reproduce ideas, provocations, insinuations, hypotheses, and texts that contribute to autonomous thought); (2) their interest in exploring and understanding the complex transformation of capitalism since the 1970s; (3) the commitment to discussing subjectivities and aspects of life typically relegated to the realm of "the personal" by "izquierdas y antagonismos acostumbrados sólo a privilegiar frías racionalidades materiales e instrumentales" (lefts and antagonisms accustomed to only privileging cold, material and instrumental rationalities; Berardi 2008). With these statements about the collective's engagement with Bifo's ideas, Bajo Tierra/JRA locates itself both politically and historically. The collective distances itself from the "traditional" left while situating itself as part of the generation raised in the era of neoliberalism, influenced by feminisms and indigenous movements, and committed to autonomist, anticapitalist praxis. In this way, it indirectly signals its place in the generation politicized in the aftermath of the Zapatista uprising. While thinkers such as Bifo and to an extent the Colectivo Situaciones no doubt share this inspiration, they emerge from very different contexts than JRA. With this introductory note and the transformation of the book, the Mexican editors make their particular position known.

The exertion of editorial autonomy in the inclusion of different paratexts is of course not unique to Bajo Tierra. And the ways they appear and disappear has significant effects on the overall form of each edition. Some texts are carried over from edition to edition, while others are unique to a single edition or disappear in others. These texts, which transform each edition of the book into both a local and translocal book, connect political conversations and practices across disperse sites. A book that has traveled widely with nearly a dozen editions in circulation is Zibechi's *Dispersar el poder*. The prologue to the first edition (which has been included in the majority of reprints since) suggests this dynamic of plurality in its title: "Los múltiples significados del libro de Zibechi." As the book moves and is remade, rethought, reprinted, reread, it becomes multiple while simultaneously producing spaces of encounter where relations are extended or at least made visible. The Mexican edition, published by Guadalajara's Casa del Mago press, features a small text on the back cover addressing the local audience, suggesting the usefulness of the text for understanding and strengthening the popular rebellion in progress at the time in Oaxaca. In 2007 the Editorial Quimantú in Santiago de Chile released the first Chilean edition, which was followed by a second run in 2011, for which Zibechi penned a new introduction reflecting on the complexity of antistate relations in Bolivia after the election of Evo Morales. In between, several presses in other parts of Latin America reprinted the book, and translations began to surface in Europe and the United States. Strikingly, the forewords featured in translations published in the north call out the more privileged reader, stating, "This is a book about you" (Holloway 2010b). A relationship is created between the presses and the readers through these texts that situates the book and its ideas in their local realities.

This political translation also occurs through invitations that the presses extend to friends and comrades of the collective to write prologues or epilogues for the books, as in the case of Raquel Gutiérrez Aguilar's contribution to the Bifo book published by Bajo Tierra/JRA. In this way, the political translation of the books becomes a process that extends beyond JRA to engage broader networks. Later, these friends and comrades are the guests invited to participate in the presentations of the books, dialoguing with the authors, JRA, and their audience and communities. This process of material and political translation repeats itself in all of Bajo Tierra's publications. The books acquire a unique identity and tenor as they are reedited and recomposed for the local context and the realities of the producers and imagined consumers of these objects.

TERRITORIES OF (EDITORIAL) RESISTANCE

In the spring of 2010, I traveled to Lima for a gathering of intellectuals and social movements organized by a group whose publishing project I had been following. In a conversation with one of the organizers, also one of the editors of their book series, we began to talk about the circulation of Raúl Zibechi's work. I brought up the Mexican edition of a title they had also edited, and explained a bit about my ties to Bajo Tierra. The Peruvian press, Programa Democracia y Transformación Global, had published the first edition of *Autonomías y emancipaciones* (Autonomies and emancipations) in September of 2007. In the foreword, the press describes its relationship with Zibechi: "una colaboración muy fluida y agradable que ha resultado en un libro importante y original" (a fluid and pleasant collaboration that has resulted in an important and original book; 2007a, 13). This "original" book quickly began to travel, but in this case it was not the presses that were circulating the files but rather the author himself. He shared the PDF of the Peruvian edition with comrades at presses in other places, including Bajo Tierra in Mexico City. The Peruvian editors didn't even know that the book had been reedited until much later. The copyrights on the Peruvian edition are held by the author, the press, and university with which the press collaborates. The author clearly had the right to do as he wished with his work, but the reaction of the Peruvian editor was one of a bit of surprise at not being informed of the trajectory of what he considered to be their publication. Before the file arrived via email in the inbox of the collective in Mexico City, it first passed through several other (virtual) hands. Zibechi wanted the book to be published in Mexico, so he activated his networks to find a way to do it. Zibechi contacted an old friend from Montevideo, who now lived and worked in Mexico City, to see if she could explore the possibility of publishing it with the press of a well-known intellectual who is close to the Zapatistas. When this did not pan out, she began to think of other possibilities. She had been loosely working with JRA as an informal collaborator (the general category for those who participate in public events and workshops with JRA but are not members of the assembly). Unaware of the new publishing project, Bajo Tierra, she asked one of her friends in JRA if he had any ideas of presses that might be interested in Zibechi's book, to which he replied, "Well, yeah, us! We have a press now!" The Bifo book hadn't even been published yet, and the press was still nameless, but Zibechi promptly sent her the file, and they went to work on it, taking on the labor of reediting it: collectively reading and discussing it, thoroughly copyediting it, reconceptualizing the design, and so on. And the result was a book that looked very different from the Peruvian edition, inside and out. Again, as with the Bifo book, the cover design developed by Bajo Tierra had a distinctly urban and youthful aesthetic: the background was an image of a worn stucco wall, the shape of Latin America appearing where the paint was chipped revealing the terracotta foundation. A red star to one side, a single exposed light bulb hanging overhead, and leaning against the wall, on a grassy ground, a collection of objects suggesting the varied tools of the range of movements discussed in the book: a machete, a miner's helmet, a staff with feathers on one end, two corn cobs, a hammer, a slingshot, a bicycle gear, and a can of spray-paint. And as with the Bifo cover, the same stylized rugged stencil font was used for the title and author.

This particular book has run wild across the continent as it has been shared by the author and the many presses with whom he collaborates. But unlike other books that have also had such rich, plural lives with reedition upon reedition, this particular book has really become unbounded, perhaps more so than any other book I've found. With each edition, in addition to the changes in basic elements like the cover and interior design, the content of the book has been transformed significantly. Not only have new introductions or prologues been added, but in several cases entire chapters or sections have been added or omitted. The book—in its range of versions—has appeared with several titles: *Autonomía y emancipaciones: América Latina en Movimiento* (Autonomies and emancipations: Latin America in movement); *Territorios en resistencia: Cartografía política de las periferias urbanas latinoamericanas* (Territories in resistance: Political cartography of the Latin American urban peripheries); and *América Latina: Periferias urbanas, territorios en resistencia* (Latin America: Urban peripheries, territories in resistance). In fact, as I started to collect different editions, it took some investigation to confirm that they are all in fact "the same book," though of course they also aren't.

Every edition is produced in conversation with the author, though ultimately the presses are the ones composing each new version. The copyright licensing also shifts with each edition, reflecting each press's distinct approach to IP. Whereas the first edition from Peru is copyrighted, few (if any) of the subsequent editions that I have identified are. Some simply have no licensing at all, others bear more formal Creative Commons licenses or informal statements encouraging reproduction. On the last page of the Colombian edition, below the printing date and a list of the fonts used, the following text appears: "El conocimiento es un bien de la humanidad. Todos los seres humanos deben acceder al saber. Cultivarlo es responsabilidad de todos" (Knowledge belongs to humanity. All human beings should access knowledge. Cultivating it is the responsibility of everyone; Zibechi 2008a). The publishers of these varied editions are doing just that—they are not only reproducing the work to increase its circulation, they are in fact creating new meaning in the editorial choices they execute with relative autonomy. For these reasons, this particular book exemplifies the unboundedness of the organic book: its pages are literally taken apart as each edition is formed for the local context of its publication, and the possibilities for its remaking appear limitless. While the way books circulate often figures them as discrete, singular objects whose dissemination brings them unchanged to different contexts, the networks through which organic books travel operate as a mechanism of distributive production: they are produced anew in these networks and as such become multiple.

Through a kind of material semiotic analysis of the organic book, I have examined how the very same books become multiple as they become assemblages of different elements in different contexts. Organic IP practices mark not simply an alternative intellectual property practice but a disordering or disorganizing of the institution of intellectual property as a product of the unique conditions and relations from which it emerges. In some cases, this transforms the conventional notion of intellectual property by enrolling what would be considered the reader in the production, reproduction, and dissemination of the book. To repeat, sharing and modification or adaptation are key threads that connect different organic IP practices, as well as a lack of concern for any centralization of control over the sharing of these books. In this sense, the presses exercise a productive freedom in the distributive production of organic books. The unbounded book is an expression of the decentralized network as both material form and political ethic.

With my discussion of the material and aesthetic translation, I have shown how the practices through which the organic book is unbounded and remade are a kind of productive consumption. Rather than simply following the reprinting of various versions of the same book, each time it is reedited, a different object is produced, carrying significant traces of its editors, past and present. But more importantly, as it is recomposed, "partial connections" (Strathern 2004) are made visible in the object. Rather than some consistent, clearly defined relation between the various actors (presses, writers, etc.) involved in its production, there are connections and divergences at play, coordination and disorder. In this sense, I wonder how relations are made in objects: what happens when the thing becomes the relation? In chapter 4, the networking agency of the organic book is further revealed through the distribution and marketing practices that connect the writers and presses to readers.

FOUR

THE NETWORKING BOOK

Otros somos, otras, lo otro.

Si el mundo no tiene lugar para nosotr@s, entonces otro mundo hay que hacer.

Sin más herramienta que la rabia, sin más material que nuestra dignidad.

Falta más encontrarnos, conocernos falta.

Falta lo que falta. . . .

We are others, the other.

If this world does not have a place for us, then another world must be made.

With no tool other than our rage, no material other than our dignity.

We still must encounter each other more, know each other better.

What is missing is yet to come. . . .

—EZLN, "Comunicado del CCRI-CG del EZLN"

THE MARKETPLACE of the organic book is not the bookstore but rather just about anywhere else. Certainly, organic books sometimes appear in shops, but more frequently they circulate through alternative networks of distribution that take up space in the street, the plaza, the campus, the festival, the *encuentro*, the okupa, the café. Organic books also make their own markets—itinerant markets that appear and disappear with varying degrees of regularity. In the twenty-first century, book fairs, like just about everything else, have become monstruous corporate events. The annual international book fairs held in Guadalajara and Buenos Aires receive close to a million visitors each, charge admission, are held in massive convention centers, and are sponsored by major transnational publishing corporations.[1] And just as more and more alternative presses have emerged in response to the expansion and concentration of corporate publishing (Bell 2017), in the second decade of the twenty-first century, alternative book fairs have begun to appear with greater frequency across Latin America. My fieldwork coincided with several "first" alternative book fairs in Bolivia and in Mexico, including the one I discussed in the previous chapter: the "independent" book fair (FLIO) nested in the official Oaxaca book fair (FILO). This is not to say that alternative book fairs hadn't ever happened in these sites before—certainly there is a long history of alternative book culture in both countries. But it is striking that 2010 and 2011 would see a new surge of alternative book fairs in the region, particularly because of what this might indicate about the economics of publishing and book distribution in the context of widespread contestation of capitalism and neoliberalism. The book market, as this chapter shows, becomes mobilized as a site of *encuentro* in the broader struggle to reclaim dignity and hope through practices of autonomy in the continent in movement.

MAKING BOOKS AND MAKING SPACE

This chapter is about the exchange and encounter generated by organic books as they move from producer networks to consumer networks. These roles (and others related to organic books) are often blurred and merged, with organic bookmaking occurring through complex and fluid arrangements of actors. This chapter focuses on what could be considered the final stage in a book's movement—the moment when it reaches the hands of its readers. But just as previous chapters have shown that organic books are made by collective knowledge practices, "worlds of work" (Johns 1998) not limited to the authors and printers, and distributive production networks, this chapter argues that the books are also made—and remade—through the encounters and exchanges their circulation generates. Vendors (often but not always the writers and presses themselves) and readers also make the organic book through the practices of encounter they engage in. Therefore, rather than maintain the dichotomy of producer and consumer that guides commercial markets, as I zoom in on the markets organic books form I am interested in thinking about the range of crafters who affect the lives of organic books. But while the focus of this chapter is indeed the moment when the book is made available to potential readers, my analysis here is limited to the distribution practices that aim to increase the movement of and access to organic books. In this sense, my discussion does not extend to examine the reception of organic books by readers.[2]

As I follow the organic book into the spaces it travels through as a printed and bound object, I explore its marketing and distribution as a space-making practice. When these durable objects move, they literally create spaces: the book fair, market stand, book display, or book shop are all physical sites where people, ideas, objects, and places connect. And significantly, the spaces produced by the marketing and distribution of organic books are at once (temporarily) bounded and (infinitely) connected. The crafters of organic books conceive of their objects as articulated to other projects—other movements, other writers and thinkers, other presses, other print editions, other media— which all have the potential to move across territories and create other spaces. As the previous chapters have discussed, the organic book is never alone, never isolated. The organic book market, as the site where the crafters of books come together most visibly, is an instance of what Michal Osterweil (2005) has called "place-based globalism." She writes: "'Place-based globalists,' . . . work to completely reinvent what counts as political as well as what has global reach. They seek to constitute a global movement by creating dense networks of specific struggles and actualized alternatives that in their proliferation and their redefinition of potent political sites, fragment, multiply and thereby reconstitute the time and space of Western Capitalist Modernity. In so doing, they work in the present to make its domination impossible" (26). In signaling the experimental and shifting practices of place-based politics, Osterweil makes evident the significance of their networked form—they operate through a combination of connectedness and dispersion (both spatially and conceptually). The organic book is an object in movement: it is not produced through fixed practices, nor does it circulate through linear trajectories. Examining its distribution and marketing requires an alternative conception of space to account for the rhizomatic character of its networks. Henri Lefebvre's (1991) theorization of space as a process of continual production offers a starting point for understanding space as relational—neither bounded nor fixed. J. K. Gibson-Graham (1996, xxxviii) push this non-Euclidian approach further with their notion of "feminist spatiality," which "embraces not only a politics of ubiquity (its global manifestation) but a politics of place (its localization in places created, strengthened, defended, or transformed). This powerful imaginary gives us the perhaps unwarranted confidence that a place-based economic politics has the potential to be globally transformative." Organic books, as political-economic practices of a kind of "place-based globalism," make networks: not static, fixed networks but always-becoming networks that are continually created through *encuentro*. Organic books are *networking books*. They carry ideas and practices and make relations as they move in and out of places. Organic books are in this sense "multi-scale and network-oriented" (Escobar 2001). In contrast to the increasingly fragmented and globalized character of commercial publishing (with Latin American presses working with printers in China and distributors in Spain, for example), the organic book is a product not of global but rather "trans/local practice" (Casas-Cortés 2009).

The distribution circuits of organic books are organized differently from the capitalist markets of commercial publishing. The broad dissemination of ideas and the formation of collective practices (thinking, working, creating, etc.) are privileged over any metric of commercial success, reflecting "a politics of collective action . . . our conscious and combined efforts to build a new kind of economic reality" (Gibson-Graham 1996, xvii). In my exploration of the markets of organic books, I work with this recuperation of the economy from a strictly capitalocentric vocabulary. The project of Gibson-Graham of "rethinking the economy" is grounded in three political dimensions—language, subjectivity, and collective action—which they argue are necessary for understanding and developing the economy as "a site of ethical praxis," a space rather than a model.[3] In this way the economy becomes a space of possibilities, and the market can be understood as both a place and a practice. Following Arturo Escobar's (2010) reading of Gibson-Graham for the Latin American context, I understand solidarity and autonomy to be the overarching ethics that orient such economic practices.

The markets made by and for organic books are informal, open, and public, and they form a relation between producer and consumer, where different forms of making have effects in the same book. Just as an important process of making occurs in the workshop where it first takes shape, as the book reaches the hands of its many readers, they use it to think and act, making other processes come into being. In this sense, the organic book market is an instance of *encuentro* politics: processes and spaces of noncapitalist exchange through which relations are formed, transformed, opened, or extended. The twenty-first century ushered in new forms of transnational grassroots political engagement, premised less on programmatic forms of organization and more on facilitating dialogue, exchange, and collaboration: *encuentro*. In the context of Zapatismo, *encuentro* has been described as "an ethic of opening oneself to others" (El Kilombo Intergaláctico 2007, 12) and often takes the form of gatherings of people and ideas. When accompanied by a material practice of exchange—as in the distribution of organic books directly from producer to consumer—the relations and networks formed through *encuentro* have the possibility of enduring beyond the temporary moment of the face-to-face interaction. I follow the organic book as the thing that allows for the proliferation and endurance of *encuentro* beyond the transitory interactions between people.

In this chapter, as I travel between organic book markets in Mexico City, El Alto, Santiago de Chile, Buenos Aires, and beyond, I examine the spaces and relations the organic books make as they move, considering their role as political and material agents in the "wild networks" that sustain the continent in movement.[4] Combining insights from J. K. Gibson-Graham's theorization of economic diversity with the Zapatista concept-practice of *encuentro* politics, I explore how the pairing of the noun-verb concepts of *encuentro* and market might open new possibilities for thinking about the materiality of political exchanges and networks. Just as the *encuentro* or the market can be a place (noun), they are also active concepts as verbs: as in, to encounter and to market, or to make a market. Marketing, in the sense of offering a good and of creating a marketplace, makes space. *Encuentro*, as both the act of encountering and the site of encounter, also makes space. Marketing, here, is the *encuentro* of people, ideas, objects, and practices. This chapter examines the particularities of the organic book market as an *encuentro* that materially forms and extends networks that span and cross territories. The way books are made affects how they move. Organic books are made *differently*, in the sense that they are not made in the usual way and that they are made in many different ways. Consequently, as this chapter shows, organic books move differently too.

"SON LIBROS DIGNOS"

"La feria de libros confirmó 'que la gente lee si los libros son baratos'" (The book fair confirmed that "people do read if books are inexpensive"; Paul 2010).[5] This headline in the newspaper *La Jornada* accompanied a review of the first Alternative Book Fair in Mexico City held in October 2010. The quote is attributed to Paloma Sáiz, an organizer of the fair. Just weeks into the first phase of my fieldwork, I spent a few afternoons at the fair which was held over five days in the Alameda Central in the heart of Mexico City. The alternative fair coincided with the massive Feria Internacional de Libros in the Zócalo just a short walk away. The timing was strategic—alternative book fairs are often held parallel to official or commercial book fairs in an effort to seize some of the energy generated by the larger events. And this particular book fair had an explicitly articulated objective: to advance the struggle "contra los libros caros y la literatura chatarra" (against expensive books and junk literature; Rodríguez 2010).

I was struck by the very official aesthetic of this alternative fair: color printed programs, large tents, fancy banners, an army of volunteers. And the back of the program provided a key to understanding what made this infrastructure possible. There were two logos: one for the Brigada para Leer en Libertad (Brigade to Read Freely) and the other bearing the yellow sun of the Partido Revolucionario Democrático (PRD, Democratic Revolutionary Party) of Mexico City.[6] Despite this institutional affiliation, there was something of an antagonistic relationship to the official book fair being held concurrently in the Zócalo, put on by the secretary of culture and the PRD-controlled city government. And as a newspaper article stated, the organizers' intention was to create a fair "fuera de la estructura burocrática oficial" (outside of the official structure of bureaucracy; Rodríguez 2010).

A few weeks later, I went to the home of two of the *feria* organizers, Paloma Sáiz and Paco Ignacio Taibo II, to learn more about the project. Not unrelated to the reach and scale of the *feria* is the fact that Taibo—who is considered the founder of the *neopolicial* genre in Latin American literature—is one of the most commercially successful writers in Mexico today and an influential figure on the left. Sáiz worked for many years in the secretary of culture and was the brain behind a variety of public reading initiatives including Para Leer de Boleto en el Metro, which put free books for loan in the metro stations around Mexico City. But her frustrations with the obstacles posed by the seemingly endless and self-defeating bureaucracy—not uncommon in these kinds of public initiatives given the lack of stability in muncipal government—led her to leave her prestigious government position and launch the independent project of the Brigada para Leer en Libertad, which includes the Feria Alternativa, as well as much more frequent smaller fairs across the city called *tianguis de libros*.[7] Sáiz and her team conceive of the project as one of militancy, a political intervention through book culture. The Brigada carried over some of the foundations of her work in the government, most centrally, the push to produce accessible books with the goal of changing the culture of reading. Accessibility, for Sáiz and the Brigada, carries multiple meanings. She reiterates how crucial it is to bring books and reading to high traffic, popular, public spaces: the metro, the Alameda Central, or the Reforma corridor. Accessibility also refers, of course, to the cost of books—hence the Feria Alternativa's stated struggle "against expensive books." The prices at bookstores in Mexico City, Sáiz explains, are generally prohibitively high, and the Zócalo book fair doesn't offer discounted books "the way a book fair should." This is in part due to the fact that the fee for stands is so high—the Feria Alternativa's rate for stands is roughly one-sixth of the Zócalo rate. But the question of accessibility also has to do with the *kind* of books the Brigada thinks should be circulating.

Their intervention in local book culture extends beyond just facilitating a space for affordable, quality books to circulate—they have a publishing project built into their mission. The Brigada has published and distributed hundreds of thousands of small books for free, with dozens of titles, including anthologies of short fiction, popular Mexican history, anthropological texts, and analyses of current popular movements.[8] The books they publish and distribute at their events are the materialization of their holistic vision of accessibility: these books are free, publicly distributed, accessible, and of popular interest. At her home, Sáiz pulled book after book from her shelf, showing me the complete collection of free books that the Brigada has produced and circulated. And as the Brigada insists time and again, while they are low-cost books and distributed for free, these are "libros muy dignos."

The Brigada para Leer en Libertad has many elements of the government literacy programs that Sáiz herself directed for many years. Anchored in Mexico City, largely in the most central parts of the capital, the project does little to challenge or disrupt the center-periphery dynamics that have shaped literary and book culture in Mexico for centuries. These are the same dynamics that have maintained the marginalization of non-urban cultural practices since the colonial period and that have been promoted through government campaigns and nation-building efforts aimed at linguistic and cultural homogenization. But there are also ways in which the project reflects new—or perhaps merely heightened—concerns about public space in the twenty-first century. With its emphasis not just on the promotion of reading but on the production and circulation of print books, the project highlights the importance of making a public space for political and cultural debate. It's not just about publishing or circulating free reading material but about creating a space for people to come together to talk, think, dialogue. And with their hope that the books might also help to build small home libraries, the physical space for *encuentro* the books make in the streets has the potential to be reproduced on a smaller scale in a more personal space. The *tianguis*, like the Feria Alternativa, take up public space with the stands and tents they install temporarily. In doing so, they transform that stretch of sidewalk or that park into a different kind of space that creates the possibility for a kind of *encuentro* that might not otherwise happen.[9] Those who make a trip to the *feria* or the *tianguis*, or perhaps were just passing by, leave with a free book in their hands. Through these small books, the dynamics of that temporary public space have the possibility of extending to other spaces and lasting a bit longer. The hope is that they share the books with the friends and families, telling the story of where and how they got the book.

The Brigada's proposal—making inexpensive, quality books accessible to a public that might not otherwise buy books—is compelling. But the kinds of voices that the publications bring together and disseminate are, for the most part, the same voices being published and distributed by the major, commercial publishing houses that dominate in Mexico and Latin America. So while the Brigada is promoting a more public approach to reading and book culture, with a degree of autonomy vis-à-vis the *federal* government, the vision of this party-funded project has its limitations—it does little to problematize the broader cultural politics of commercial publishing in Mexico or the troubling government campaigns that have historically used literacy and reading as biopolitical tools of assimilation. Nevertheless, the project emerges at an important juncture in the politics of the city: street vendors in the center of the city have been evicted from their historic sites of informal commerce in consecutive waves over the last ten years, and multitudinous protests have retaken the streets and public plazas with semipermanent encampments. Certainly, the Brigada has a much greater degree of privilege than the itinerant vendors or the camping protesters—it has the seal of approval (and pesos) of a major political party and has no problems acquiring permits for events. With its mainstream authors, government permits, and party dollars, the Brigada is not an expression of the kind of autonomous politics that characterize organic books and their producers. But there is a contestatory, oppositional element to the project that comes from the founders' decades of intimate involvement in the political economy of book culture in Mexico. Their histories with state cultural projects in particular have motivated them to create something different than the "establishment" initiatives, like the Zócalo book fair, which they see as crippled by institutional bureaucracy and allegiances to publishing powerhouses. Nevertheless, in the context of the increasing privatization and disciplining of urban space (not only in Mexico) and the progressive monopolization of publishing, the Brigada finds resonance in other initiatives elsewhere in the city and across the continent, where books are on the frontlines of efforts to reclaim the streets as a site of popular dialogue, debate, and *encuentro*. As the sections that follow will explore, the tension between institutional and autonomous politics is a recurring theme related to the marketing of organic books.

"Place can be a political project," write Gibson-Graham (2002). The place of the Brigada is the city street. The specific site shifts, as the *tianguis* or the *feria* moves with each installment, but the place remains constant, and it is politicized. The Brigada project merges the kinds of liberal cultural politics that Sáiz developed in her former position in the government with a politics of what David Harvey, following Lefebvre, calls the "right to the city." In an interview, Harvey explains this idea: "The city is increasingly a gated community for the very rich. So out of the streets comes this notion that this is not our city anymore and we want to take back our city. . . . So there is a sense that something is going wrong with urbanization right now. 'The right to the city' idea comes out of that, but 'the right to the city' as an idea is what I call an 'empty signifier'—it can mean anything to anybody" (Composto and Rabasa 2011). The space that the Brigada wants to make in the streets of Mexico City is public, diverse, and accessible, and it aspires to create possibilities for dialogue and debate by filling that space with books, which it considers crucial tools for those processes. The Brigada's project is alternative, as the name of the *feria* conveys, but this concept is also entirely relational—its meaning is dependent upon its locus of enunciation. Responding to critiques of their use of the term "alternative," Gibson-Graham write (1996, xxii–xxiii): "The word is not wimpy but threatening. It signals that there's something wrong with the status quo and that the advocate hopes to change things. . . . What's problematic . . . is not the word itself, but the idea that it will always work for us, that it can, in other words, be context-free." The form and scale of threat associated with an alternative project varies. In the case of the Brigada, the very elements that make it less alternative—its institutional connections, its relationship to intellectual and political elites, and so on—might in fact make it a more tangible threat to the status quo. It directly and explicitly challenges its official counterparts (the Zócalo book fair and the secretary of culture's initiatives) but does so through relatively conventional institutional channels. Another "first" book fair in Bolivia tells a different story of the challenge posed by an alternative.

"NO QUEREMOS IMPORTAR LA FERIA. . . . QUEREMOS HACER UNA FERIA ALTERNATIVA, DE AQUÍ"

The geography of the twin cities of La Paz and El Alto is something of a spatial inversion of the neocolonial power relations, with the Aymara city of El Alto towering almost two thousand feet above the colonial city of La Paz, with its wealthiest and most elite neighborhoods situated nearly another thousand feet below the city center in the exclusive Zona Sur.[10] That the Feria Internacional de Libros de La Paz (FIL La Paz) is held in the Zona Sur—at a significant remove from the center of La Paz and even further from the more than one million, mostly Aymara, residents of El Alto—is not surprising. But it only exacerbates an already pronounced intellectual and cultural hierarchy that can be traced back to the colonial period. The FIL La Paz, like other major international bookfairs, charges admission, has high fees for exhibitors, and serves primarily as a platform for transnational publishing corporations. As many people I spoke with stated, within Latin America, Bolivia is often erroneously—and problematically—thought of as lacking a culture of reading or publishing.[11] And within Bolivia, and certainly from the perspective of La Paz, El Alto is similarly characterized as peripheral. But a bus ride away from the FIL and the Zona Sur, in El Alto a vibrant, if marginal, world of books can be found everyday—at street fairs, market stalls, cultural centers, neighborhood organizations, cafés, and the Universidad Pública de El Alto. While book fairs have certainly been held before in El Alto, in 2011 the first Feria del Libro de El Alto was organized.

I learned about the book fair while attending an event at the Museo Nacional de Etnografía y Folklore in La Paz, which frequently hosts lectures and book presentations for small independent presses. A few days later, I went to La Ceja (the central district of El Alto) to meet with the fair's organizers at the office of the Asociación de Representantes de Editoriales de El Alto (AREA). The presses represented by AREA are mostly publishers of textbooks, children's books, and popular press books. At first glance, there was nothing inherently alternative about the fair. It was being supported by the municipal government, had several corporate sponsors, and was billed as an event "de promoción de la lectura" (for the promotion of reading). The poster for the fair had several slogans: "Movemos tu mente y el mundo a través de los libros" (We move your mind and the world through books) and "Apague la televisión y encienda un libro" (Turn off the television and turn on a book). But the very site of the book fair, El Alto, imbued it with an alternative or contestatory quality. In our conversation, one of the organizers expressed why she felt the fair was so significant: "No queremos importar la feria de La Paz, queremos hacer una feria alternativa, de aquí, de El Alto, de nosotros que vivimos y tragamos cada día el polvo de las calles de El Alto" (We don't want to import the fair from La Paz, we want to make an alternative fair, for El Alto, for and by those of us who live here and who breathe the dust of the streets of El Alto every day; interview, El Alto, 2011). Her tone was more melancholy than militant, but there was a sense of defiance underlying her comments. Her use of alternative suggested that what was being built with this fair was a space for that which is marginalized and invisibilized in La Paz (and elsewhere) and that the fair was an opportunity to create "algo de nosotros" (something of our own). She emphasized the significance of the participation of many Alteño writers as something that would set this fair apart. So while the fair itself was far from independent or autonomous with its corporate and state sponsorship and the participation of major transnational publishing corporations, it did in fact pose a threat (to return to Gibson-Graham's characterization of alternative)—not to capitalism explicitly but to other (certainly related) dynamics of power and exclusion that characterize the relationship between La Paz and El Alto.

The fair was not without tensions, however. The stated desire to not "import" the La Paz fair did not mean that other importations would not occur. The opening ceremony for the fair closed with a champagne toast, and as the emcee announced the *brindis* (toast), a group of older men at the back of the crowd proclaimed "¡Hay que ch'allar! ¡Nada de brindis!" (We have to *ch'allar!* Not make a toast!). Here the European *brindis* was challenged with a call for a *ch'alla*, a term originally from Quechua that refers to an act of honoring, recognizing, or blessing, often accompanied by some sort of offering to the Pachamama. But the elders in the crowd demanding a *ch'alla* weren't signaling the clash of different worlds per se. What they were calling out was the replacement (or displacement) of the shared world of the Alteños—the world in which ceremony means *ch'allar* with strong alcohol—with the world that La Paz represents relationally—the world of Euromodernity where a champagne *brindis* is the standard.

Once inside the fair, the alternative or contestatory quality again appeared in tension with elements of that other world typically represented in the La Paz book fair: most notably the massive Grupo Santillana stand or the elaborate installation by the office of the vice presidency of the Plurinational State of Bolivia.[12] But between these and all around them, a different kind of *encuentro* was taking place. There were stands representing well-known independent

FIGURE 4.1. Feria del Libro de El Alto, El Alto, 2011.

presses like Gente Común, as well as stands shared by several projects, like the one set up by Textos Rebeldes in collaboration with the Colectivo 2 and a local artist. Various local NGOs participated in the fair, such as the Centro Gregoria Apaza, as did cultural and political projects like Wayna Tambo and Mujeres Creando.

Ten days later, the fair concluded with a closing ceremony that included the presentation of the first Yuriwi ("birth" in Aymara) prize given in recognition of an Alteño writer. As the award was being introduced, I assumed—erroneously—that it would be given to one of the many literary authors present at the fair. Given the organizers' repeated gestures toward a sort of depoliticization of El Alto's militant indigenous legacy (and present), I was stunned when they announced that they were awarding the prize to sociologist Pablo Mamani Ramirez, in recognition of his works *Microgobiernos barriales* and *El rugir de las multitudes*, studies of the social infrastructure of El Alto and the 2003 rebellion, respectively. Mamani Ramirez's work has been published by the small presses that print at the La Paz printing workshop I described in chapter 2, including Textos Rebeldes. And his works are an important source informing Zibechi's analysis of El Alto in *Dispersar el poder*. The moment of surprise at the book fair award ceremony was a reminder to me of the multiplicity and complexity of El Alto that the fair had made especially visible. Despite efforts to make the fair *just* the El Alto book fair, it was indeed an *alternative* book fair in various senses. As one editor of a small press later told me, "Esta feria de El Alto, me gustó mucho. Yo estuve en la feria de libros [de La Paz] el año pasado y es fría. Es una cuestión fría, es puro negocio. Sino en cambio aquí ha sido más un encuentro, ha sido un encuentro de todo. Ha sido bien interesante, bien distinto" (I really liked this fair in El Alto. I was at the book fair [in La Paz] last year and it's cold. It's a cold affair, it's pure business. In contrast, the fair here was more of an *encuentro*, an encounter of everything. It's been interesting, very different; interview, La Paz, 2011).

Each of the contexts I move through in this chapter has unique spatial and material conditions within which the alternative worlds of books emerge. What I aim to demonstrate across the different sites are the diverse expressions of alternative economies of ideas, practices, and objects that the organic book makes possible. The point of reference for the articulation of the alternative shifts from site to site, project to project, but the emphasis on reimagining spatiality, materiality, and social relations remains constant.

NUESTRA DIGNA RABIA

In the last days of 2008, thousands of people convened in Mexico City to participate in the Primer Festival Global de la Digna Rabia (First Global Festival of the Dignified Rage).[13] While the Zapatistas have a long tradition of bringing their politics to the capital city in the form of marches, caravans, rallies, and dialogues, this event was unique since it was the first formal *encuentro* held in Mexico City.[14] The Digna Rabia came on the heels of the Zapatistas' Otra Campaña (Other Campaign), and the Mexico City *encuentro* was set to be followed by related events in the Caracol de Oventik and the Universidad de la Tierra–Chiapas the following week, both common sites of major public Zapatista activities.[15] On the morning of December 26, I arrived at the Lienzo Charro de Iztapalapa, in the far eastern section of the sprawling city. As the name indicated, this was in fact, the home of Los Reyes Charros, an organization of men, women, and children who participate in the national sport of Mexico, *charrería* (equestrian sports that include rodeo). Initially, it appeared to be an unlikely locale for the Zapatista festival, but in the opening ceremony, the president of the association quickly assured us that they are indeed "adherents" to the Zapatista "Sexta Declaración" and that the organization was proud and honored to share its space with the many who traveled from near and far to attend the festival. Over the next four days, we came to know the dusty equestrian center well, as it was temporarily occupied by activists, artists, journalists, and scholars from dozens of countries.

The Lienzo Charro is run by an organization that at the time was known as Los Panchos, the Frente Popular Francisco Villa Independiente–UNOPII, then the largest organization of adherents to the Other Campaign in Mexico

City. Now known as the Organización Popular Francisco Villa de la Izquierda Independiente, the organization has been constructing urban autonomy since the 1980s. In the past twenty-five years, it has grown to include more than a thousand families across eight autonomous neighborhoods in Mexico City (Navarro Trujillo 2016 123). The neighborhoods, or *predios*, emerged in response to an escalating housing crisis in Mexico City and have evolved into an ongoing experiment in urban autonomy that is unparalleled in scale elsewhere. The spaces created and maintained by this organization are sometimes referred to as Zapatista territory in Mexico City. The Digna Rabia was held at the recreation space run by Los Panchos—a dusty pocket of rural life tucked into the dense and bustling reality of one of the world's largest cities.

When I arrived at the festival, I was still unsure about whether *compañerxs* from the autonomous Zapatista communities would be present or if any members of the EZLN leadership would attend. The announcements had invited collectives and individuals from all over the world to attend, and unlike at previous *encuentros*, the Mexico City event was set to include a space for anyone interested to set up a stand with information, items for sale, exhibits, and so on. It was only upon arriving at the festival that I had a real sense of what this entailed. The space of the Lienzo Charro was divided into various areas, including a tent for roundtables, two stages for theater and music, a tent for film screenings, and a small market-like space organized into little lanes complete with street names that, in the style of Latin American cities, referred to significant dates in revolutionary history—for example, 17 de noviembre, the date of the founding of the EZLN in 1983. This temporary marketplace was the space dedicated to the hundreds of collectives that had answered the call and reserved a space to share their work and their materials with the festival participants. I had assumed the roundtable sessions of activists and intellectuals would be the most fruitful part of the event, yet as I walked through the fair where dozens of collectives had set up stands, I quickly realized that an important *encuentro* was also happening here, one that would outlast the festival. With its steel-framed and tarp-topped stands, the fair looked like the countless *tianguis*, informal markets, that pop up across Mexico every day.

Walking through the long narrow lanes, I was immediately confronted with fragments of the vast experiences of the diverse participants who had come to share a bit of their struggles. This included San José Brown Berets, Basque autonomists, Italian slow foodies, Mexican anarcho-punks, Nahua campesino activists, Triqui liberation activists, sex workers, and various feminist collectives. It was in this *tianguis* that I collected a number of books written by grassroots intellectuals and collectives from across the Americas and published by small presses. The *tianguis* became a site where experiences and perspectives were exchanged—reflecting the far-reaching and long-standing influence of Zapatismo. And crucially, walking through the numerous lanes, the festival participants acquired a multitude of printed materials (books, pamphlets, posters) compiled by activist writers and collectives: some for sale, some for barter, some for free. These printed materials are what enabled the *encuentro* to extend beyond the site of the festival, as the thousands in attendance filled their pockets with these pieces of the *encuentro* and carried them home to share and discuss in their own communities.

The Digna Rabia was an *encuentro* of people but also of struggles and of the rages that propel them. Rage is the word used here to name a common "no," a common *grito* (scream or cry), as John Holloway stated in his talk at the festival. This rage is the expression of a protest, a refusal, but it becomes dignified as it is articulated in a process of making and doing something else, something more. This common rage against the system that destroys, consumes, homogenizes, and fragments (some of the verbs the Zapatistas use in the "Sexta Declaración" to describe what capitalism does) is expressed in the print materials the fairgoers took home from the Digna Rabia. But, as previous chapters have shown, the books are more than mere conduits of a message—they are objects that make life differently, and they do so through the spaces, practices and relations they make. While various other kinds of print media were circulated in the *tianguis*, the books stand out for their durability; pamphlets and flyers are likely to end up lost or discarded, but books last. Their durability instills them with a certain value, regardless of their price.

The *tianguis* is a space where we can see relations forming through the exchanges and encounters that it enables. A *tianguis* is a commercial marketplace, but like the precolumbian *tianquiztli*, it is a space of exchange of all sorts, not just commercial buying and selling. In this sense, the concept of the *tianguis* is useful for understanding the market as a space of *encuentro*, where noncapitalist relations can emerge. On the relationship of markets to capitalism, Glyn Daly writes: "There is nothing . . . which is essentially capitalist about the market. Market mechanisms pre-exist capitalism and are clearly in operation in the socialist formations of today. It is clear, moreover, that a whole range of radical enterprises exist within the sphere of the market" (cited in Gibson-Graham 1996, 141). While the term *tianguis* is particular to Mesoamerica, I find the concept useful for thinking about markets differently, which is to say beyond a logic of capitalocentrism. A *tianguis* is a market, but it is temporary, contingent, and most of all, popular. It is a space, but it is not fixed or stable. And what is exchanged and produced in this space are not just goods and services but also experiences, ideas, and practices. In the pages that follow, I travel through various other *tianguis* of organic books to explore how they act as sites of *encuentro*.

"HABÍA QUE CAMINAR DE MANERA DISTINTA"

"Nosotros nacimos en 2002, en medio del seno del neoliberalismo. En prome-dio en ese momento un libro costaba 8 lucas, 10, 15. No existía el libro barato" (We were born in 2002, in the thick of neoliberalism. At that time, the average book cost eight, ten, fifteen lucas. There was no such thing as an inexpensive book; interview, Santiago de Chile, 2011).[16] So began the story of the Editorial Quimantú, as recounted to me during a visit to the home of two of the found-ers in Santiago de Chile in 2011. As we sat there talking, a massive crack in the living room wall kept catching my eye, a reminder of the massive earthquake that had violently shaken the region just a year earlier. Over coffee, the five collective members took turns filling in bits of their story: a story of a multi-generational group of people who came together to make affordable, political books—something they saw as desperately missing in Chile at the start of the twenty-first century. On my way from Bolivia to Argentina, I had arranged to spend a week in Santiago to meet the Quimantú collective and learn more about their project. I had been introduced to them over email by Raúl Zibechi just a few months earlier, as he had urged me to contact them to see how their work fit into the networks of presses I was researching. Zibechi had published a few of his books with them and insisted that their approach to alternative publishing was one of the most interesting in Latin America. And as I started to scour the internet for information about them, I quickly saw why.

The Editorial Quimantú founded in 2002 borrowed its name from a leg-endary publishing project that had been violently shut down by the military dictatorship in 1973. The Editorial Nacional Quimantú was a project of the Unidad Popular, occupying an industrial press seized by its workers in the first days of Salvador Allende's government. In the three years of its short life, this press published and distributed millions of books and magazines, with dozens of collections aimed at all generations and sectors of Chilean society.[17] One collective member explained: "entonces el libro de la Quimantú valía luca 200, luca 300 que era el precio de la cajetilla de cigarros. Eso hacía de que tú estu-vieras en el micro en esa época, y había cualquier obrero, cualquiera dueña de casa, o estudiante con el libro en su bolsillo o leyendo, todos los chilenos leían. Lo que pasó, lo que se hizo en el fondo, fue una revolución cultural" (at that time, the Quimantú books cost two hundred or three hundred lucas, which was the price of a pack of cigarettes. That made it so that if you were on the bus, you would see workers, housewives, students with books in their pockets, reading—all the Chileans were reading. What happened, deep down, was a cultural revolution; interview, Santiago de Chile, 2011).

With millions of affordable, accessible, quality books produced and dis-tributed on a massive scale, the place of books in public life was momentarily transformed by the Editorial Nacional Quimantú. But following the coup on September 11, 1973, Quimantú was one of the first sites targeted and raided by the military. Recounting this violent period, they described the response of the people to this attack on the press: "la gente se asusta mucho. Esconde el libro y lo quema. La mayor cantidad de libros no es que los hayan quemado los milicos, sino las mismas personas que los compraron. Es muy fuerte el tema, de como desaparecen los libros Quimantú" (people got really scared. They hid their books and they burned them. The greatest number of books burned were not those destroyed by the army but by the people that had bought them. It's a really heavy issue, how the Quimantú books disappeared; interview, Santiago de Chile, 2011). The language of the books "disappearing" is chilling—just as thousands of people were disappeared during the dictatorship, so were the archives of the revolution.[18]

Some of the collective members were politically active during Allende's time and were forced into exile following the coup. Identifying his own "juventud acumulada" (accumulated youth) one member recalled his experiences with the books produced by the original Quimantú, explaining that his mother burned his collection, while a friend hid books in a brick wall, where they remained for years. Given the literal flames with which the orginal Quimantú was destroyed, it's hardly metaphorical when they say that "la Quimantú de hoy es como el ave fénix, porque nacimos de las cenizas" (the Quimantú of today is like the phoenix, because we we were born from the ashes; interview, Santiago de Chile, 2011). Nearly thirty years later, the name Quimantú was brought back to life by an autonomous collective with no formal ties to the original project. The group came together around a shared interest in producing "political books for the left" and a common desire for more "herramientas para construir esta sociedada que queremos" (tools to construct the society that we want; interview, Santiago de Chile, 2011). They discovered that there was no active registry for the name Quimantú and decided to bring back the spirit of Allende's project, though with a new perspective and strategy for the current national context in which they were living and working. It was not an effort to revive the earlier project but rather to make something new while activating the popular memory tied to the Quimantú legacy. But there was one concrete element that they wanted to maintain: "el libro al precio del paquete de cigarrillos. El libro barato, popular, para la gente, no el libro mercancía" (the book that costs the same as a pack of cigarettes. The inexpensive book, the popular book, for the people, not the commodity book; interview, Santiago de Chile, 2011).

The name Quimantú was inspiring, full of the energy and dynamism of the Allende years, but it was also a "weight on their shoulders." Their relationship to the past is heavy—both because of the traumatic recent history of Chile

MAGALÍ RABASA

and because of the trajectory of the Chilean left, institutionalized as the Concertación, with its strategic deployment of an official discourse of collective memory and revolution (Lazzara 2006; Stern 2010).[19] They faced resistance and criticism for their use of the name, and some even accused them of having a lack of respect for Allende's legacy. But this weight was something they willingly carried with them as they forged a new path. In both their approach to politics and their approach to publishing, the new Quimantú shares with other projects of their time a tendency toward prioritizing experimentation over any programmatic or dogmatic mode of doing and thinking. They say that the Quimantú, as well as the Chile that struggles *desde abajo* (from below), "se construye a pulso. . . . se va experimentando en el hacer" (it is constructed in practice. . . . it is experienced through doing; Interview, Santiago de Chile, 2011). In our conversations, in fact, the "caminando preguntando" (walk while asking questions) slogan of the Zapatistas was referenced directly, as they described their collective process:

> Cuando miramos al horizonte, había que caminar de manera distinta, hacia otro futuro. Igual que los zapatistas, lentito, como hormiguitas, y en lo cotidiano. No podíamos avanzar más, porque si avanzábamos más nos metíamos en el sistema capitalista, nos metíamos en el banco, armábamos nuestras máquinas, nuestra empresa. Y nos metíamos en la dinámica de Chile, que lo podríamos haber hecho. Y no lo hicimos. Ni banco, ni préstamo, ni Estado, ni institución, ni Fondo del Libro, ni Municipalidad. Ni políticos, ni nadie. Nosotros solitos.

> When we looked toward the horizon, we knew we needed to walk differently, toward a different future. Like the Zapatistas, slowly, like ants, and in the day-to-day. We could not advance more than that because if we moved faster we would get caught up in the capitalist system, we'd be caught up in the banks, we'd be setting up machines, making a company. And we'd be getting caught up in the dynamic of Chile—and we could have done that. But we didn't. No banks, no loans, no state, no institutions, no book fund, no municipality. No politicians, no one. Just us on our own. (Interview, Santiago de Chile, 2011)

The new Quimantú is figured, above all, as autonomous. And in the context of their emergence—"en el seno del neoliberalismo" (in the heart of neoliberalism)—this autonomous positioning is conceived of as foundational to any popular struggle from the left.

What they call "la dinámica de Chile" (the dynamic of Chile)—the culture of banks, loans, and credit that the neoliberal experiment generated—is contrasted with the other ways of doing together that were emerging, most visibly among the youth, at the start of the twenty-first century.[20] And this *other* Chile is where "los Quimantús" (as I heard them called) felt resonance with their project: "Con la forma de los pingüinos, con transversalidad, con horizontalidad, con discusiones en asamblea, con participación" (With the form of the Pingüinos, with transversality, horizontality, assembly discussions, with participation; interview, Santiago de Chile, 2011). The 2006 movement of high school students, known as La Revolución de los Pingüinos (the Penguin Revolution—a reference to the black and white school uniforms), for many signaled a new period of political struggle in Chile. A new generation, born at the tail end of the Pinochet dictatorship and coming of age in the so-called transition to democracy, took to the streets by the hundreds of thousands and occupied their schools, demanding lower costs and greater access to higher education. The Pingüinos, who would grow up to be the university students marching and striking across the country in 2011, ushered in a new wave of politics not contained by the dichotomy of right and left nor limited to the usual practices of electoral and party politics. The students, in their struggle to defend and reclaim public education, represent a direct threat to the stability of the political-economic order that has shaped Chile since the 1970s. The way that the economy has been figured in Chile (and elsewhere) has perpetuated a sense of capitalism as an underlying determining system. But as many have argued, the economy is "not a transcendental, but a project, or set of projects" (Gibson-Graham 2008, 621), and by calling into question this concept of the economic as an "autonomous domain" (Mitchell 1998), diverse possibilities emerge for recognizing activities that might otherwise be called non-economic. In distancing itself from "la dinámica de Chile," the Quimantú project is asserting itself as enacting a different kind of economic reality—one in which diverse principles interact, including ethics of solidarity and collective well-being.

Much could be said about the kinds of books the new Quimantú publishes, which its members describe as works of "pensamiento político de izquierda" (leftist political thought). Their catalog is vast, with over a dozen collections that focus on topics like popular education, feminisms, land and housing, and radical Chilean history. In addition to the dozens of original titles, they also have reedited many books published elsewhere in the Americas. These include the sorts of texts that put their project on my radar: works by writers like Raquel Gutiérrez Aguilar, Gloria Muñoz Ramírez, Raúl Zibechi, and the like. But similar books are published by other alternative presses in Chile, most notably Lom Ediciones, though at much higher prices than those of Quimantú. What is unique about Quimantú's catalog is not only their unparalleled low prices but also the books that emerge from their networks of relations: collections of writings about the recent movements around education in Chile or the struggles around housing rights in the peripheries of Santiago. These relations are the energy that drives the Quimantú project, which its members playfully call "esta locura" (this craziness). But these relations generate much more than just the books that Quimantú edits, designs, and prints, by functioning as the basis of Quimantú's distinctive distribution strategy.

When I arrived in Santiago for the first time, I was surprised to learn that Quimantú books are not sold in bookstores. In my earlier fieldwork in Mexico and Bolivia I had seen the ways that alternative presses deploy a range of unconventional distribution strategies—but all the presses I encountered *also* sold their books in local bookstores. They just don't rely on bookstores as their only, or even primary, point of sale. These presses recognize that, between the huge price mark-ups and the way small presses' books tend to get lost in large stores, bookstores are one of the least effective modes of distribution for these projects. But Quimantú's position vis-à-vis the bookstores in Santiago is unique: the press dismisses them completely, refusing to participate in the "dinámica de Chile" as they called it—which is to say, the complete commodification of everything and an economy in which books are just another good to be sold for profit. The high taxes on books and the bookstore mark-up combined with the inaccessibility of bookstores to the average Chilean all make it impossible for Quimantú to sustain the central commitment of its project: producing "popular, inexpensive books." When I asked if their books were available in *any* bookstores in Santiago, they replied that two stores carried their books. But my visits to these two shops made me understand that the answer, in fact, is no. The two shops that sell Quimantú books are very unconventional, and the reason they carry their books is because they are small businesses run by close friends of the collective. The first, Sarri-Sarri, is a small, ten-by-ten-foot enclosed stand in a galleria: really just a tiny punk kiosk that sells zines, music, patches, and t-shirts. The second, Librería Proyección, despite the name, is not *really* a bookstore, as the founders explained to me during a visit.

"LA IDENTIDAD SE VA CONSTRUYENDO COLECTIVAMENTE"

My second night in Santiago, before I even met the Quimantús, I was invited by friends of friends to attend an event at a space they had collectively founded the year before: Librería Proyección.[21] I walked across the center of Santiago to the address I found on the website: just a few blocks from the Casa Central of the Universidad de Chile, tucked behind an old church off the Alameda, the main thoroughfare that runs across central Santiago. It was mid-July 2011, just a month into the massive student protests that had paralyzed official operations at the universities and schools across the country. The walls in the area around the Universidad de Chile were covered with graffiti and wheatpasted posters, with slogans like "¡Con rebeldía y subversión se libera la educación!"

(With rebellion and subversion education is liberated!) or "¡No endeudes tu cabeza ni privatices tus ideas!" (Don't get your head into debt or privatize your ideas!) or "¡La educación no se vende, se defiende!" (Don't sell education, defend it!). When I arrived, I looked up to see a freshly painted orange façade with a simple black silhouette of a tree next to the words "Librería Proyección." I climbed the stairs, unsure what to expect, and walked into a bright bookstore filled with young people. I saw an open door leading into a packed room where an event was underway. As I approached the door, someone asked if I was there for the film event or the *autogestión* event. There were not one but two packed events—neither of which were directly related to books—happening here on a Friday night, and the space was huge. This was clearly not just a bookstore.

A few days later, I sat down to talk with one of the founders of Librería Proyección, and he explained a bit about how the project had come together over the last few years: "La idea de abrir la librería fue a propósito de la necesidad que sentíamos un grupo de amigos compañeros de crear un espacio donde poder reunirnos. Un espacio donde también otros se pudieran reunir, encontrarse, discutir, articular trabajos políticos que ya estaban andando. . . . Pensábamos que una buena idea era arrendar una casa y volverla sustentable a partir de un negocio" (The idea to start a bookstore came from the need our group of friends and comrades had for a space to have meetings. A space where others could also meet, encounter each other, discuss, and articulate political projects that were already happening. . . . We thought it would be a good idea to rent a house and sustain it with some kind of business; interview, Santiago de Chile, 2011). When I asked why the choice of business was a bookstore, the response raised a similar issue to what the Quimantús named as the reason for their project: the lack of a popular and accessible book culture in Chile.

Librería Proyección resembles many of the kinds of cultural centers or social centers (some *okupas,* or occupied spaces, others not) that I've passed through in other parts of the continent: a collectively run space for political projects and events, often with a café or bookstore to bring in a bit of income to offset expenses. The collective that founded Proyección chose to call their social center a bookstore very intentionally, as a way of avoiding the aggressive quality and the preconceptions that are sometimes associated with social centers or activist spaces: "nos parecía que lo principal no era tener una identidad, sino aportar. Eso es lo más importante. La identidad se va construyendo colectivamente" (what seemed most important to us was not to define an identity but to contribute. That's what's most important. Identity is constructed collectively; interview, Santiago de Chile, 2011). The space that is called Librería Proyección, which would be impossible without the income generated by the bookstore, is a space of *encuentro* where diverse experiences and ideas come together and other engagements emerge. Books are central to what takes place here, but they are also just an excuse for something more.

NOS LANZAMOS EN LA CALLE

Beyond the two unconventional shops I visited, Quimantú's books circulate through the same kinds of wild networks that produce them: the workers, students, neighbors, and families whose stories of organization and struggle are recounted in the pages of many of their books.[22] Within the city of Santiago, the day-to-day sales occur at political, cultural, and academic events where members of the collective set up their mobile stand. Direct sales, "de mano en mano" (from hand to hand), are the principle mode of distribution for Quimantú—and Quimantús value this not only because it allows them to keep prices as low as possible but also because it brings them into contact with their consumers, the readers. Some of their books are also sold at *quioscos*—street newsstands where books are also sold—but without the same overhead costs of the bookstores. Beyond Santiago, the books move through friends and contacts of the collective who carry the books to other parts of Chile when they travel: twenty books here, another ten there. They tell me that they receive requests from time to time to ship books to other countries, but the cost of shipping is usually at least double (and often up to quadruple) the cost of the book itself, making it hugely impractical.

At the heart of Quimantú's project is a desire to intervene not only in the national publishing industry through the production of affordable, accessible books, but also to intervene in the broader cultural politics by contesting the privatization of all aspects of social life that the neoliberal experiment produced in Chile (Harvey 2005). In this sense, the legacy of the original Quimantú project of the early 1970s is reactivated multiply: by taking up this name, the new collective positions itself in firm opposition to all that the Pinochet dictatorship forced on Chile economically, socially, culturally, and politically. Like the Pingüinos in 2006 and the university students in 2011, with their multitudinous marches and occupations of the public schools, Quimantú conceives of the reclamation of public space as central to its contestatory praxis. Playing with the idea of taking the streets and launching books, Quimantú came up with the slogan "Nos lanzamos en la calle," a play on words with a double meaning: "we launch ourselves in the street" (as in book launches) and "we take to the streets." Several years into "la locura" (the madness) of the Quimantú project, they decided to shift their strategy for presenting new publications. Rather than release the books one by one with events for each individual publication, they developed the idea of the "lanzamiento múltiple" (multiple book launch) which allowed them to organize larger events while bringing together a broader range of participants. Since 2006 Quimantú has been organizing an annual event, where they present all the books published that year, called Yo Me Libro.

Always held in an outdoor public space, Yo Me Libro is part book fair, part reading, part party, part street festival, part gathering of social movements. Each year carries a new slogan using the Yo Me Libro name, another play on words, combining books (*libros*) with struggle, release, and liberation (*librar*): "Si tú te libras, yo me libro" (If you free yourself, I'll free myself); "Yo me libro . . . en mi barrio" (I free myself . . . in my neighborhood); "Yo me libro . . . del bicentenario" (I free myself . . . from the bicentennial); "Yo me libro . . . con todas sus letras" (I free myself . . . with all its letters); "Yo me libro . . . no tengo elección" (I free myself . . . I don't have a choice [election]). In some instances, the slogans relate to current national issues, like the bicentennial or the elections, while in other cases it's more broadly expressed in terms of one's personal liberation as connected to others. The suggestion is that the process of liberating oneself from the trauma, repression, and isolation generated by the dictatorship and the neoliberal experiment must be rooted in collective experience. While the Yo Me Libro fairs serve as Quimantú's official book launch events, they are organized and produced by a broader network of people, collectives, organizations, and projects. And this collaborative process of organizing and facilitating the fair is an important part of Quimantú's objective: "para nosotros el proceso de gestación de la feria es tan importante como el evento mismo" (for us the process of organizing the fair is as important as the event itself; El Surco 2012).

Nearly a decade into their project and after six years of Yo Me Libro events, the Quimantú collective decided it was time for something bigger, something that would extend beyond their press and beyond Chile to mobilize the relations they had been building across the continent. During my first visit to Santiago in July 2011, they explained to me that they were in the process of organizing the first Feria del Libro Popular Latinoamericano, which they were naming América LeAtina Desde Abajo.[23] Their desire with this fair was not only to create a broader book fair by co-organizing with other presses and organizations but also, and perhaps most importantly, to connect more deeply with the experiences of other Latin Americans, and to build relations of solidarity, exchange, and collaboration. One collective member described the importance of these connections in terms of combating, and healing from, the isolation that has afflicted Chile for more than three decades: "entre los chilenos, entre la gente hay una necesidad hacia Latinoamérica de conocer otras experiencias, porque nos tienen encerrados. . . . Es muy fuerte el encierro. Si se presenta esa feria de esa manera, cultural, multifacética, de los pueblos latinoamericanos va a ser muy lindo, sano . . . de mucha sanidad para el pueblo chileno" (among the Chileans, among the people there's a need to learn about other Latin American experiences, because we are very closed off here. . . . The isolation is very intense. If the fair can happen like this, a multifaceted encounter of Latin American peoples, it will be really beautiful, really strong . . . and really healing for the Chilean people; interview, Santiago de Chile, 2011). To explain the apparent lack of movement and exchange between Chile and Argentina, people often playfully gesture to the mountain range that marks its eastern border, the Cordillera de los Andes, describing it like a wall. But the way the Quimantús explain this isolation points to something much deeper than just geography. Even the language they use, *encierro*, can mean isolation or seclusion (which can be voluntary) but also confinement or imprisonment, and it is in these terms that they describe the effects of the dictatorship on Chilean society. In this sense, an important part of the process of *sanación*, of healing, is breaking that isolation.

Calle República 517: this was the address given for the first Feria del Libro Popular Latinoamericano in December 2011. This and two neighboring street numbers, República 550 and 580, are hugely symbolic in the collective memory of the Chilean people. All three were torture and detention centers. While they've all undergone resignification—one has become a university, another an occupied social center—Pinochet's legacy continues to infect them more than two decades later. The university is tainted by the neoliberal educational reforms, and the occupied social center was the target of ongoing state repression leading to its eviction in 2009. But on the occasion of the fair, the residents of the República neighborhood came out to express their joy at seeing their streets filled with families, young people, music, art, and books. One neighbor explained that this was the first public event on that street since the May Day celebration held there in 1973. In this sense, the fair brought to life the slogan printed on the posters: "A la calle no hay quien la calle" (No one can silence the street; *calle* is both "street" and the verb meaning "to silence"). Just as the coup transformed Chile from one moment to the next, Calle República had a silence suddenly imposed on it that lasted for decades. The *feria* was embraced by the neighbors and even individuals and family members of those who had passed through 517, 550, or 580 during the dictatorship. Over the next three days, the street came alive with not only dozens of stands selling books and all kinds of print culture, as well as musical performances, parades, live radio broadcasts, and a collective mural project. A standard feature of any book fair, the program included a full schedule of book presentations, readings, and roundtables. Though at the risk of impracticality, these were held in the street, alongside the stands, the music, the food, and the crowds. This single block of central Santiago clearly demonstrates the relational nature of urban space, and the identities and subjects that are forged within it (Massey 2004).

Quimantú's political-economic ethic was a fundamental axis of the *feria*, conceived as a "respuesta a la mercantilización del libro que está incorporado en la cultura chilena" (response to the commodification of the book that is embedded in Chilean culture; "América LeAtina" 2012). All the vendors present at the fair made a pledge to not sell any book for more than five lucas (equivalent to ten US dollars). Given the high prices of books in Chile (and in Latin America in general), this rule immediately excluded a whole sector of independent or alternative presses that might publish political books or even similar titles to those offered at the fair but do not share the commitment to producing low-cost books.

I participated in the fair as part of a contingent from Buenos Aires, where I had been living for the past six months doing fieldwork. Los Quimantús made a trip to Argentina a few months before the fair to personally invite presses and writers to participate in the fair in Chile and to establish more personal contacts with projects they hoped to collaborate with more generally. Since I had been working with the FLIA in Buenos Aires, I helped coordinate their visit, which coincided with the eighteenth FLIA, dubbed the FilosoFLIA, since it was held at the Facultad de Filosofía y Letras of the Universidad de Buenos Aires. Among the FLIA participants and their networks, there was great enthusiasm about the fair in Chile, particularly because of the possibilities for connecting with *proyectos compañeros* (comrade projects) across the continent. While many had hoped to participate, the travel expenses limited the numbers that actually made the trip from Buenos Aires to Santiago. Because I had the means to travel and no books of my own to sell there, I traveled as a kind of mobile miniature FLIA, with books from a half dozen presses I knew from the FLIA. I sold all but five of the eighty books I carried to Chile—the fairgoers eagerly bought up the FLIA books, excited by the variety and the affordability of works they knew they wouldn't find locally outside of the fair.

Just as the FLIA books came into contact with a different audience, they also came into contact with other books that filled Calle República during the three days of the *feria*. As these objects traveled to the *feria* from across Santiago and also from Argentina, Bolivia, Ecuador, and Mexico, different cultures of the book traveled with them and in them. And in the process, the objects themselves shifted as they came into contact with each other. The *encuentro* of this *feria* had material effects—books were exchanged, circuits expanded—as well as political effects. Marres and Lezaun (2011, 495) write of the role of objects in shaping politics as they explore "how things partake in the constitution of political subjects . . . spaces . . . or tools." The objects of the *feria*—as a market of books—enabled diverse encounters and exchanges that directly and indirectly contest the privatization and fragmentation that the participants identify as destructive effects of neoliberalism and globalized capitalism. Just as books were deployed as a material tool capable of intervening in public space along Calle República and "la dinámica de Chile" more broadly, on the other side of the Cordillera de los Andes, the people that make the FLIA were similarly using books to take up and transform urban space.

LA FERIA INFINITA

Since its inception in 2006, the FLIA has used books as a means of intervening in and reclaiming public space.[24] The books that make up the fair transmit experiences and strategies of radical politics, while the space itself constitutes a solidarity network of radical bibliophiles of all sorts in an increasingly privatized and repressive urban context.[25] After the first two phases of my fieldwork in Mexico and Bolivia and a brief visit to Chile, I arrived in Buenos Aires in mid-2011 eager to immerse myself in the practices of the FLIA. Barely settled into my new apartment in the Once neighborhood of Buenos Aires, I started to send off emails to the few contacts shared by friends in Mexico and Bolivia. A few days later, my Facebook newsfeed alerted me that a meeting of the FLIA-Capital was happening in two days.[26] The meeting announcement read: "Este martes a las 20:00hs reunión de la FLIA-Capital. Tenemos que decidir dónde la hacemos, empezar a definir las comisiones. Siempre es bienvenida gente nueva a trabajar en el colectivo, energías renovadas siempre vienen bien" (This Tuesday at 8:00 p.m. meeting for the FLIA-Capital. We have to decide where we're having the next one and start to define committees. As always, new people are welcome to come work as part of the collective—renewed energy is always good). The same announcement appeared on the FLIA blog, though with an added description: "reuniones super archi recontra abiertas" (super, ultra, extremely open meetings; "FLIA Buenos Aires"). The repeated assertions of the openness and the call for new participants left me no excuse not to go.

It was only as I walked up to the address listed that I realized the meeting was being held at a bookstore that I'd been wanting to visit, having seen it on the points of distribution lists of several presses I was following. I walked in to La Libre and asked the twenty-something guy sitting at the counter about the FLIA meeting.[27] He told me there was just one other person there and that the meeting would be starting a bit later. So I awkwardly browsed the shop, excited to see a very different stock of books than what I had found in the dozens of bookstores I wandered through along Avenida Corrientes near my apartment. When the meeting finally began in what appeared to function as a kitchen, meeting space, and stock room, I introduced myself to the small group, and someone immediately offered me a beer and an explanation: "creo que eso te va a parecer más una reunión de amigos" (I think it's going to seem more like a meeting of friends). Someone else asked me how I got there, and I started to say that I took the number 24 bus, only to be interrupted with a clarification:

"No, how did you get *here*, to the FLIA?" I explained my situation, told them I'd been following the FLIA online, saw the call for the new round of meetings on Facebook, and that I was hoping to participate however possible during the six months that I'd be in Buenos Aires. Everyone seemed totally open to my participation, but it seemed that—despite the open calls visible to the fifteen thousand followers of the Facebook page—it had been a very long time since someone new (and someone completely unknown, at that) had come to a meeting.

The meeting began to take a bit more shape as we started in on the topic of the day: where to have the FLIA 18, projected to take place about six weeks later. A few suggestions came up, some I'd never heard of (Parque Brasil, Estación de los Deseos), while others were names familiar to me (IMPA, Ciudad Universitaria). In the hour or so that followed, I learned a great deal about the way the FLIA works, and especially about its use of space. When events are held in public spaces (like a park, a plaza, or a street block), no authorization is requested, no permits are acquired. Rather, the space is just taken, and, they explained, with up to 800 or 1,000 people in attendance, and 100 or 200 stands set up (most, but not all, selling books), any police efforts to evict the fair are essentially futile. In their experience, the FLIA has the critical mass to occupy a public space. The events are advertised for weeks in advance, with times and dates and locations listed. But the police and city officials' response, if any, is just symbolic, and the FLIA is tolerated (though with some, now increasing, resistance). The other kind of location where FLIAs are held, they explained, are spaces held by an organization or a movement. In these cases, the FLIA assembly presents a proposal to have a book fair there. Generally, the response is positive, as the FLIA is a respected initiative and serves as a way of bringing greater visibility and support to the host group or project. I was left thinking that the movement of the FLIA through different locations is as much about constructing a decentralized, open, and horizontal effort to bring alternative book culture to different spaces as it is about articulating the FLIA with different political, cultural, and economic projects across the city.

Despite my silence, the conversation vacillated between discussion of the location and comments directed at me, explaining how things work, sharing anecdotes from the history of the FLIA, and the recent political history of Buenos Aires. As was explained to me, there are very few rules of the FLIA. Organization is open and horizontal, drawing on the assembly model that has become nearly common sense in Buenos Aires since 2001 (Sitrin 2005). The FLIA is always free for both vendors and the public. And you don't organize a FLIA on the same day that a different FLIA is happening somewhere else, since many vendors travel to participate in FLIAs all over the country and even beyond, in Uruguay or Brazil, for example. In addition to the FLIA 18, there was talk of another FLIA before the end of the year. With the ten-year anniversary of the popular rebellion of December 19 and 20, 2001, approaching, members of the FLIA assembly expressed a sense of desire and responsibility to participate in the anniversary. Before we left, one participant remarked to me, "aunque empieza en el 2006, la FLIA es un producto del 2001" (even though it started in 2006, the FLIA is a product of 2001).[28]

"LA FLIA SE PARECE A LO QUE SOÑÉ, A LO QUE MUCHOS SOÑARON"

In 2011, right around when I arrived in Buenos Aires, a documentary about the FLIA was released.[29] When I watched it, it filled in more details of the history that had been sketchily recounted to me at my first FLIA assembly. Titled *Los subterráneos: Voces e historias historias sobre la F.L.I.(A)* (The subterraneans: Voices and histories of the FLIA), this short film was made by Buenos Aires documentary filmmaker and writer Tomás Larrinaga of the Anarkocinema collective. By alluding to Jack Kerouac's 1958 novella, *The Subterraneans*, set in 1950s San Francisco, the director suggests a parallel between the bohemian quality of the FLIA and the Beat scene.[30] This chosen reference links the FLIA to another era, though as the participants featured in the film assert, the FLIA is very much a twenty-first-century phenomenon—it has wild roots that materially and discursively articulate it to earlier moments of alternative cultural politics in Argentina and beyond, but there is nothing nostalgic about the FLIA. It is described as "a product of 2001," but the shape it takes as it grows is uncertain—the wild roots create wild growth.

Composed exclusively of interviews and footage from a number of FLIAs and related spaces in Buenos Aires, *Los subterráneos* offers perhaps the most comprehensive history of the FLIA. It could be interpreted as ironic that the story of a book fair would be best documented on film rather than in print, since that is, after all, the privileged medium of the event. But what the efficacy of the video form points to is the primacy of face-to-face practices and physical spaces, rather than just words and ideas, in the FLIA. The FLIA is made of much more than just books, and the documentary shows this through the direct accounts of those who make this movement, speaking from the very spaces that in some way contribute to making the FLIA. These include the Sexto Kultural, site of the very first FLIA; the Federación Libertaria Argentina, where one participant comments on the undeniable influence of the vibrant Argentine anarchist tradition on the FLIA; the Centro Cultural Pachamama, which hosts Buenos Aires's poetry slam and is a sort of permanent hub for the otherwise itinerant FLIA scene; and even the various FLIA blogs. This last space, a "virtual space," is key to the FLIA's defining quality: it is not a single FLIA, but rather *la FLIA infinita*: the infinite FLIA. As one participant interviewed in the film remarks: "la FLIA sin Internet me parece un fenómeno más difícil de crear. . . . Los mails, los blogs, las páginas, el Face también forman parte de la FLIA" (the FLIA without the internet seems to me like it would be a much more difficult phenomenon to create. . . . The emails, the blogs, the pages, the Facebook: these are all part of the FLIA; Larrinaga 2010). And it is this mess of decentralized communication—massive listservs, blogs with many admins, social media accounts with widely known passwords, and collectively maintained calendars—that make the FLIA multiply. The infiniteness of the FLIA is also found in its name: Feria del Libro Independiente y (A) . . . , as it is often written. The A, written as (A), evoking the anarchist circle-A as it sometimes appears in online communication, stands for any of the many possible words that could be used to describe the FLIA. The most commonly named are: *alternativa, autónoma, autogestiva, amiga, amorosa* (alternative, autonomous, autogestive, friendly, loving). Javito, a FLIA poet and musician, explains: "en la primera feria no se llamaba FLIA, se llamaba Feria del Libro Independiente a secas, y después se la agregó la A, y hasta el día de hoy se sigue discutiendo e interpretando y cada uno pone lo que quiere" (at the first fair, it wasn't called FLIA, it was just the Independent Book Fair, and then the A got added, and to this day there is an ongoing discussion and open interpretation of the A and everyone makes it what they want it to be; Larrinaga 2010). In this way, the very name of the FLIA conveys some of what its practice demonstrates: it is open and continuously shifting. Another participant describes the FLIA with language that also suggests its multiplicity: "La FLIA se parece a lo que soñé, a lo que muchos soñaron" (The FLIA looks like something I dreamed, something many of us dreamed of; Larrinaga 2010). This idea is as much about a shared dream as it is about a plurality of visions.[31]

The documentary offers various narratives of how the FLIA started, most of which point back to the Contraferia organized just outside of the official FIL held each year in Buenos Aires at La Rural, the expo center located near Plaza Italia in the posh Palermo district. The FIL, the largest book fair in Latin America, charges admission (like most large book fairs) and the vendor fees are prohibitively high for small presses and independent authors. Beginning in 1998, a group of writers and editors got together to set up the first Contraferia as an alternative to the official fair, protesting its inaccessibility. The prologue to the book produced collectively on-site at the first FLIA in 2006 narrates the transition from Contraferia to FLIA:

> El comienzo fue continuidad, en este caso de la contraferia del libro que organizaban unos locos lindos allá por el año '98 y que megáfono en mano, libros en piso, corazón en su lugar, se presentaban frente al predio municipal de exposiciones. . . . De ahí en más comenzamos a charlar y decidimos que NO íbamos a hacer una contraferia, que estábamos para la propia feria, para la

feria del libro independiente. Una feria del libro independiente es un espacio donde un montón de nosotros que escribimos o difundimos ideas podemos hacerlo al margen de las limitaciones que el sistema/mercado nos imponen.

The beginning was continuity, in this case of the counter-book fair that some lovely crazies started organizing around 1998, and with the megaphone in hand, their books on the ground, and their hearts in place, presented themselves in front of the expo center. . . . But from there we started to talk and decided that we were NOT going to make a counter-fair, that it was time for our own fair, for the independent book fair. An independent book fair is a place where a ton of us that write and disseminate ideas can do it on the margins of the limitations that the system/market imposes on us. (FLIA 2006, 6)

The first FLIA was organized in May 2006 with the slogan "por el libre y gratuito acceso a la cultura" (for the open and free access to culture), precisely what the FIL did not provide. With the shift from Contraferia to FLIA, the political impetus also shifted: the priority was no longer to intervene in or reform the existing system (the FIL) but to invent something completely new and different, an alternative space of *encuentro* operating with a different logic for marketing books.

The book from the first FLIA, the source of the text cited above, was actually written *at the fair*. One of the stands had a laptop available for anyone to stop and write something—a poem, a narrative, a song. The prologue describes the process, calling it a "live press": "otros locos lindos improvisaron una imprenta en vivo. La compu estaba prendida, se acercaban, escribían un texto, un poema, algo, . . . y se fueron sumando los escritos. Así fue que quedó esta antología poética increíble, que acá les presentamos" (other lovely crazies improvised with a live press. The computer was on, people would approach and write a text, a poem, something, . . . and that's how the texts grew. And that resulted in an incredible anthology of poetry, which we present here to you; FLIA 2006, 8). "El libro de la FLIA," the FLIA book, that was invented at that first fair, was repeated at subsequent fairs. The FLIA book is an extension of another important project that precedes the FLIA: El Asunto.

"NO PUEDE DESTRUIRSE PORQUE NO EXISTE"

In 2001 one of the writers who would later help organize the first FLIAs began compiling a catalog and library of independent books produced in Argentina and called it El Asunto ("the issue").[32] A print booklet accompanied by a website, the *Catalog of Independent Books* includes a wide range of books—poetry, stories, art, novels, politics—and is described as contributing to the debate about "the independent book." The website presents the most up-to-date version of the catalog, but it also includes a page on the "catálogo en papel" (paper catalog), which is subtitled "página de otra época" (page from another era), though the print catalog was last made in 2010, hardly "another era." A summary appears for each edition of the print catalog, including a scan of the cover, the date of its publication (and the respective FLIA that it appeared at), and an overview of the contents—how many books and a breakdown of the numbers by genre. The significance of the print form is suggested repeatedly both in the language of the website and the descriptions of the catalog. Beginning with the fifth edition, the entry includes a description of the physical object: "empieza a salir con número, se agrega una doble hoja, ahora son 12 páginas de 9 × 11 cm" (starts to be published with a number, a double page is added, now there are twelve pages, nine by eleven centimeters). The seventh edition is described in these terms: "Se realiza íntegramente en una impresora casera. 48 paginas encuadernadas artesanalmente, sí, sí, pegadas con un pequeño lomo y tapa de 150 gr" (Wholly produced on a home printer. Forty-eight pages bound artisanally, yes, glued together with a small spine and a 150-gram cover; El Asunto 2012). The last page of the section dedicated to the print catalog narrates the origins and evolution of the catalog in both political and material terms. That the project begins in 2001 is significant, and the project is described as collectively building something from nothing through exchange: "La idea es que no sólo seamos vidriera sino que también vendamos y que entre todos hagamos una construcción desde la nada, a través del canje" (The idea is to not only be a display case, but that we also sell things and that all together we build something from nothing, by trading; El Asunto 2012). The objective is not just to make visible that which already exists but rather to make something new, collectively. As a catalog, El Asunto is both a systematic listing and a marketing tool. But the products listed in the catalog are not static objects that are simply arranged alongside one another. As a project, El Asunto is also an *encuentro* of "independent books," as they describe the broad range of publications gathered in the catalog. And this *encuentro* occupies an array of physical sites, including its print catalog and website, as well as the shifting spaces of the FLIA.

Weeks before leaving Buenos Aires, I spend an afternoon at the El Asunto workshop and archive, located in a small single room just a few blocks from Plaza Almagro, with one of the founding organizers, Pablo Strucchi. As I scan the room trying to take in all the colors and textures that filled the cluttered space, my eyes stop suddenly. A hand-painted wooden sign is leaning against a table. The whimsical design features multicolored figures and swirls with the El Asunto web address in oversized font and two other bits of text. The first says "El Asunto es incorruptible porque no tiene integrantes" (El Asunto is incorruptible because it has no members). The second says "El Asunto no puede

FIGURE 4.2. Archive, Buenos Aires, 2011.

destruirse porque no existe" (El Asunto cannot be destroyed because it doesn't exist). Similar paradoxical assertions appear on other materials for El Asunto, like the poster I notice tacked to the wall. They remind me of the contradictory slogans of the Zapatistas, with their weapons that wish to be silenced and the notion of leading by obeying. I sift through folders and stacks of propaganda from El Asunto and the FLIA, stored in the dozens of boxes and crates that make up their archive. The space is both chaotic and ordered, and Pablo seems to know more or less where everything is. Built-in shelves have been fashioned out of particleboard, with each section labeled by genre and ordered alphabetically: poetry, novels, essays, art, and so on. The countertops are covered with all the tools and provisions that keep this project running: scraps of paper, pens, piles of books and booklets, glue sticks, scissors, thread and needle, old water and beer bottles, bags of yerba mate, tobacco.

I notice a handcrafted box with different shapes and sizes of booklets and bookmarks and flyers stuffed into the various compartments built into it. This box is made of plain, unpainted plywood and held together by glue. I've seen similar boxes in bookstores, cafes, and cultural centers across the city, though these are brightly painted and have an additional panel providing a support on the back end. The box here in the workshop is an unfinished model for DistriBULLA La Cajita: "un proyecto que nace en el 2008 con la idea de unir a artistas, escritores y lugares a través de una cajita, intervenida por un artista, que contiene libros de escritores independientes" (a project that was born in 2008 with the idea of bringing together artists, writers, and places through a little box, designed by an artist, that contains books by independent writers; "Agenda El Asunto" 2012). A play on words connecting "distributes" and "ruckus," DistriBULLA La Cajita is "la pata distribuidora de la editorial cooperativa el asunto" (the distribution branch of the cooperative press el asunto; Gómez 2011). El Asunto, here described as a "cooperative press," is also many other things: a catalog, an archive, a workshop, and a distribution project. Among the materials I've found in Cajitas around the city are coedited publications that bring together multiple collectively run presses in a single book. Some are works of fiction or poetry; others are translations or new editions of works of political theory or analysis. And many, but not all, bear the logo of El Asunto, always written as ")el asunto(" with the inverted parentheses suggesting its boundlessness, alongside sometimes one, sometimes up to a dozen other logos of local independent presses. And these publications, like the Cajita itself, are another physical site for the *encuentro* facilitated by El Asunto. They disrupt the usual logic of publishing with a single, or no more than two, publishers involved in any given publication, as well as the commercial approach to distribution. Rather than move through commercial distribution networks (distributors, bookstores, etc.) they move through La Cajita, face-to-face sales, or events like the FLIA. In this way, even when they do appear in bookstores (generally housed in La Cajita), they avoid the formalities (ISBN registration, copyright) and expenses (mark-up, distribution fees) that often act as barriers preventing independent authors' and publishers' works from entering these more formal spaces. DistriBULLA La Cajita is just what the name suggests: like the many and varied FLIAs, the Mexico City *tianguis*, or the Chilean Yo Me Libro, it is an informal minimarket of books that temporarily occupies a space—in this case, less than two square feet on a table or a counter in a permanent venue.

"VOS SOMOS LA FLIA"

UNESCO named the city of Buenos Aires—long a hub of mainstream and independent publishing in Latin America—the 2011 World Book Capital, making it the site of sixteen months of special activities meant to highlight its significance for the culture and industry of books.[33] The city's famous bookstores, which seem to appear by the dozen in every neighborhood of the capital, all bore the UNESCO insignia in the form of stickers on their doors, and the conservative mayor (later president), Mauricio Macri, made a public declaration at the start of 2011 vowing to support all activities related to book culture through April 2012. In recent years the government of the city of Buenos Aires has emerged as an overt enemy of the poor and the left, as Macri's repressive policies have led to the eviction of many of the popular spaces recuperated in the wake of the 2001 rebellion and the criminalization of the informal sector in all of its forms. In a move similar to recent policies in Mexico City, Macri declared a "war on itinerant merchants" toward the close of 2011, putting hundreds of thousands of vendors—of everything from junk food to handmade crafts—on alert. Just as the new policy came into effect, the FLIA was organizing its nineteenth fair with absolutely no contact with the program of the World Book Capital events.

For this event, the FLIA assembly worked with the Movimiento Popular La Dignidad to occupy the Calle Bonpland over the weekend before the tenth anniversary of the events of December 19 and 20, 2001. Bonpland, interestingly, is a tree-lined street in upscale Palermo. Just as in nearly every neighborhood in Buenos Aires, in the wake of the 2001 rebellion, Palermo too was home to a neighborhood assembly housed on Bonpland, and in the next decade the space held by that assembly changed hands and form multiple times. Today the main building at Bonpland 1660 holds a market space for "economía solidaria" (solidarity economy; now under the auspices of a government agency dedicated to this concept), and the back area holds a community kitchen and three independent cultural projects: Yo No Fui (It wasn't me; a women's prison literature project), Centro Cultural Bonpland, and En Movimiento TV (the video project of the Movimiento Popular La Dignidad).

That the FLIA would take over the street outside these spaces just days before the tenth anniversary of December 19 and 20, 2001, reflects a great deal about the tensions and contradictions of the relationship between autonomous politics and the state in the city of Buenos Aires. On the first day of the FLIA 19, dozens of bookmakers and booksellers arrived at Bonpland in the morning with their boxes and suitcases of books, lining up along the sidewalk to make a loosely coordinated move to take the street and block traffic. Once we collectively decided that we had the critical mass needed to successfully occupy the block, we moved in with our arms filled with books, lugging makeshift tabletops and sawhorses. We had distributed and posted notices the week before advising neighbors not to park their cars along the block over the weekend, but a few cars remained. They become a part of the architecture of the improvised street fair—the neighborhood literally became part of the FLIA. In a matter of hours most of the street was filled with stands, with a third row slowly emerging in the middle. Dumpsters were used to block one end of the street, and eventually a local celebrity art car—the Arma de Instrucción Masiva (an old pickup truck refashioned to look like an army tank made of books)—arrived, serving as the barrier along the other end. As expected, a police car arrived soon after, in a gesture more of routine harassment than actual disruption. The only violation cited was blocking the street; nothing related to unpermitted vending. And when the police demanded to know "who was in charge" to list a name on the citation, the collective response was simultaneously "no one" and "all of us." Here, the participants once again confirmed that the FLIA is *not* an organization but an open assembly with no designated leaders.

Some of the books at the FLIA directly chronicle the stories of the societies in movement in Buenos Aires and the continent—like those covering the wobbly table of La Periférica Distribuidora, a sister project of Tinta Limón and Colectivo Situaciones. Others, like the poetry and fiction being sold by the authors themselves, narrate mundane occurrences, a reflection of the imaginaries of the everyday people who make up these societies. What connects this spectrum of books—some hand-stitched with screen-printed covers, some hastily pasted together with recycled paper, others, like the Tinta Limón titles, printed in commercial print shops—are the dynamic and ever-shifting relations through which these ideas become texts and the texts become objects. In her analysis of the FLIA, editor and sociologist Marilina Winik (2010, 145) discusses the ways that this fair reflects "la fusión entre la metodología de las redes con la necesidad territorial del encuentro" (the fusion between the methodology of networks with the territorial necessity of *encuentro*). The networks at play in the FLIA, and more broadly around the organic book, are at once territorially grounded and globally connected, recalling Osterweil's definition of "place-based globalisms." The networks of readers, activists, writers, presses, artists, and movements that make up the fair rely on the spatiality produced by the books. Without this space, the relations that compose these networks remain ephemeral and invisible. In these spaces, the "materialization of these social collectives" (Hull 2003) acquires a greater dimension. Not only are these relations materialized in the individual books, but they are also made visible and tangible in the spaces where the books encounter and make each other, as they sit side by side on a pop-up table or a bit of cloth on the sidewalk. There is a particular spatiality produced by the books, and it extends beyond the ephemeral moment of the fair or the *encuentro* through the movement of these objects.

Many of the spaces the books make, in this sense, become another "vehicle for navigating politics," which is the language used by one of the founders of Herramienta Press in Argentina to describe a key function of books (interview, Buenos Aires, 2011). As objects, books become the things that make relations and through which we can see and map networks (D. Miller 1995; Strathern 2004). The books that make these spaces are remade in them as well because, despite their apparent fixity as objects, books change as we read them, touch them, move them, rearrange them (Elia 2008). The multidimensional webs of

FIGURE 4.3. Arma de Instrucción Masiva, Buenos Aires, 2011.

crafters of the books connect in the spaces the books themselves make, like the markets where they circulate. The books' mutability has everything to do with their heterogeneity: as the previous chapter revealed, the same book is never made twice. Each book is multiple, as the relations that it creates are continually shifting, which Bolivian writer Oscar Vega Camacho (2011) describes as the book's continuous becoming. This is not to say that every book has this quality, but organic books are made through processes intentionally articulated to what their texts, in some way, describe.

The FLIA creates temporary autonomous zones (Bey 1991) that recuperate previously occupied spaces or overlap with existing autonomous projects. When the FLIA took the street on Bonpland, it contributed to the palimpsestic quality of a space first recuperated by the Asamblea de Palermo and later by the Movimiento Popular La Dignidad. The walls of the alleyway are covered with layers of peeling posters and graffiti, traces of different moments in the space's history. In her discussion of the unemployed workers movements (MTD, Movimiento de Trabajadores Desocupados) in Buenos Aires since 2001, Liz Mason-Deese (2012) highlights the transformations in the territorial forms of organization: "'The neighborhood is the new factory' was one of the principal slogans of the MTDs and other organizations of the unemployed. This slogan carries a double significance: production is no longer centered in the factory but dispersed throughout the territory and, in parallel, labor organizing must be dispersed throughout the neighborhood as well." What connects the struggles centered on the workplace with the neighborhood-based movements "seeking to collectively manage as many of the elements of daily life as possible" (Mason-Deese 2012) is the common emphasis on producing different types of space in which different kinds of social relations can emerge. The FLIA, as Marilina Winik so poignantly states, connects these territorial forms of organization and *encuentro* with efforts to build and extend networks that cross territories.

A poster I came across in the El Asunto archives bears the words "Vos somos la FLIA" (You/we are the FLIA). I immediately recalled the Zapatista slogan "Detrás de nosotros, estamos ustedes" (Behind us, we/you are). The collective and shifting identity of the FLIA is conveyed by the play on words that collapses "us" and "you"—everyone makes the FLIA, we are all the FLIA. The FLIA and the other organic book markets I moved through in this chapter are sites where the spatiality of *encuentro* is merged with the material exchanges that the *tianguis* market mode facilitates. Just as the book makes space in grounded places—as the stands transform a street, for example—the book is also the thing that makes the relations of that space travel and move to other places. The networking character of the organic book is both external and internal—the book creates relations as it is made, but it also opens itself as it encounters other books, other actors, other spaces. Organic books make permanent *encuentro* that is always in movement—relations and exchanges are produced on its pages, within its covers, and in the spaces that exist between one book and the next.

EPILOGUE

Las ideas recorren, como ríos, de sur a norte.

Ideas run, like rivers, from the south to the north.

—Silvia Rivera Cusicanqui, *Ch'ixinakax utxiwa*

WHAT HAPPENS when organic books travel further than the actors who craft and distribute them can or do? What happens when they move beyond the webs of "societies in movement" that zigzag across the continent? And more specifically, what happens when these ideas travel to the North, crossing national, linguistic, cultural, economic, and even epistemological borders?

THE ORGANIC BOOK TRAVELS NORTH

In early 2012, shortly after wrapping up the last phase of my fieldwork, I attended the New York Anarchist Bookfair in an old church on Washington Square Park. Anarchist book fairs are the closest expression I've found in the United States to the underground book cultures of Latin America that I followed in this project. I was eager to refamiliarize myself with this world of books, in part out of something like nostalgia for my recent experiences, but also because I wanted to return to this milieu—a familiar part of my political-intellectual life in the United States—to consider in what ways the practices I had been following in Latin America were and weren't happening, or perhaps weren't even possible, here in the North. As I made my way around the concentric semicircles of tables lined with books, zines, and other print media, I was reminded of the relative dearth of grassroots political publishing in the United States and the distinctly more individualistic tone of anarchism on this side of the Rio Grande. About halfway through, I paused to scan the spread offered by AK Press, whose warehouse happened to be located near my (then) home in Oakland. There I spotted a book that almost jumped out at me, for it was the most direct link between the fair and the book worlds I had left when I came home from my fieldwork: *Dispersing Power* by Raúl Zibechi. This is the book that accompanied me in spirit and in print as I moved from place to place during my fieldwork. Its ideas traveled with me, helping me think through the practices I was witnessing. But it also seemed to appear nearly everywhere I went, with one (or sometimes more) of its many distinct editions appearing in bookstores, fairs, libraries, homes, and workshops in each of the cities I visited. And here it was yet again. But this was not the same book. So much about it had changed. To begin with, it was in front of me as a translation to English, the product of a collaboration between a Chiapas-based Irish exile and a major anarchist press from the United States. Printed on thick, heavy paper, it was marked with a slew of copyright notices and a rather hefty price tag. It seemed worlds away from the first edition I described in chapter 2, with its newsprint pages and handwritten corrections.

The English edition of *Dispersing Power* has two forewords, including one carried over from the German edition. Both address an audience that seems distant from the worlds Zibechi describes. The first, by Benjamin Dangl (2010, xii), closes with the words "With the publication of *Dispersing Power* in English, this new world has expanded." The second, written by John Holloway (2010b, xv), opens with this statement: "If you think Bolivia is a far off country, forget it. Don't bother to read this book. Better give it to a friend. This is a book about you. About your hopes and fears, about the possibilities of living, even of surviving." Here, Holloway conveys the articulatory quality of the book—it is about and made by you, us, them.

The organic book, with its reorientation of theory and politics, opens the possibility of subverting the kinds of North/South knowledge relations that have been so compellingly critiqued in postcolonial and subaltern studies. These books and the networks of movements, people, and ideas that they emerge from and in turn produce create a different geopolitical map of knowledge as they travel—they directly challenge the "asymmetric ignorance" that governs the production and flow of knowledge between North and South (Chakrabarty 2000). Organic books, especially as they are translated to travel from South to North, subvert this "asymmetry": the ideas, concepts, and practices produced in the South enter into symmetric conversations in different parts of the world.

In his foreword, Holloway (2010b, xv) tells us that Zibechi, a Uruguayan journalist, "goes to Bolivia to learn." He is not an indigenous Bolivian, he is not a protagonist of the history he relates through his analysis—his book is the product of relations and dialogues that cross territories. In this way, books like his offer a double lens for seeing a reorientation of knowledge relations that potentially subvert or at the very least make visible both the neocolonial asymmetries that persist within Latin America and between North and South. What is at stake is not a simple inversion but rather a *disordering* of hierarchies.

The next time I encountered the English edition of *Dispersar el poder* was on a syllabus for an undergraduate course being taught in anthropology at my university. Despite its appearance at the New York book fair and its distribution by a relatively alternative press, this book and others like it—works of theory from the South that make their way through translation to the North—primarily get consumed by academics and their students when they travel from América to America. But this is no surprise to those making these books. There is no romantic expectation that Zibechi's book is being bought and read by the Bolivian immigrants who populate parts of Virginia, or that the indigenous economic refugees from southern Mexico living in San Diego County or the Bronx are the audience for the Zapatista Subcomandante Marcos's books that were also sold at the New York book fair.

With the 2014 publication of the first English edition of Raquel Gutiérrez Aguilar's *Los ritmos del Pachakuti*, the dynamics of the South-North travels of organic books are made even more apparent. The publisher of *The Rhythms of Pachakuti* was not AK Press nor any of the other presses selling their wares at the New York book fair but Duke University Press. Duke is arguably one of the most prestigious scholarly presses for all things Latin American and is housed at a top ten private university in the United States. It's difficult to imagine a more elite venue for Gutiérrez Aguilar's first English monograph. But the relations that made this book in the North are composed of actors that appear on multiple maps of knowledge practices. The circuits they participate in and give shape to are not limited to their institutional locations in the US academy.[1] *The Rhythms of Pachakuti* is not just a book made by and for US academics, it is also a set of relations that connects people, ideas, movements, histories, and experiences. And as an object it allows the relations to travel in different ways.

THE ORGANIC BOOK'S BORDER CROSSING

In late July 2011, I had just arrived in what would be my last fieldwork site: Buenos Aires. I was farther south than I had ever been before, and the chill of the austral winter was a steady reminder of how far I was from my home in California and the *compañerxs* in Mexico with whom I had begun my fieldwork. As I opened my email, there were several messages from Mexico City, beginning to coordinate a response in solidarity with Raquel Gutiérrez Aguilar, who had just suffered what she called "agravios y amenazas del gobierno gringo" (offenses and threats by the gringo government) in the title of the open letter she promptly released. In it, she describes her experience: "Anoche tomé un avión para ir a Italia. Tenía que llegar a la Toscana a encontrarme con amigos y compañeros para compartir con ellos experiencias de luchas en América Latina. No pude llegar a mi destino porque al gobierno gringo se le ocurrió que yo no tenía derecho a pasar ya no digamos por su territorio, sino tampoco por su 'espacio aéreo'" (Last night I took an airplane to go to Italy. I had to arrive in Tuscany to meet with friends and *compañeros* to share experiences of Latin American struggles with them. I wasn't able to make it to my destination because it occurred to the gringo government that not only did I have no right to pass through its territory, but through its "air space" as well; Gutiérrez Aguilar 2011). The letter, which goes on to detail the events that occurred, circulated widely, with coverage in major news outlets including *Democracy Now!* and *The Guardian*. Gutiérrez Aguilar was imprisoned in Bolivia in the early 1990s but since 2007 has been cleared of all charges, leading some to conclude that her place on the secret blacklist that barred her from US airspace is "on the basis of [her] ideas rather than [her] actions" (Identity Project 2011).

Gutiérrez Aguilar cannot travel thirty thousand feet above the United States, let alone onto actual US-controlled soil, but her ideas most certainly can, and with the 2014 translation of *Pachakuti* we see their movement through very formal and institutional material circuits. In the foreword, Sinclair Thomson (2014, xii) writes: "for English-language readers, it is not only the Bolivian case that deserves to be studied and understood but also Gutiérrez Aguilar's own political thought." He goes on to affirm that her book "deserves to stand as a key text in the international literature of radicalism and emancipatory politics in the new century" (xvii). The contribution of this book, then, is not only the view it offers of the Bolivian rebellions of the twenty-first century but the originality of Gutiérrez Aguilar's theorization of her own experiences of militancy. Thomson uses subaltern studies founder Ranajit Guha's category of a secondary source to describe Gutiérrez Aguilar's perspective in her writing about the Bolivian rebellions. In his now classic 1988 essay "The Prose of Counter-Insurgency," Guha (1988, 51) explains: "the secondary follows the primary at a distance and opens up a perspective to turn an event into history in the perception not only of those outside it but of the participants as well." For Guha, academic and scholarly writing would constitute a tertiary source, and the secondary category is reserved for those who have some direct experience in the events they describe, though they write about them from a certain distance (not only temporal). It is precisely this position—which bears some resemblance to that of Gramsci's organic intellectual—that makes Gutiérrez

Aguilar's conceptual and analytical work so potent and relevant and, perhaps to some, even threatening, as evidenced by her blacklisting. But while state institutions ban her presence in US airspace, academic institutions facilitate the movement of her ideas to the North.

One interpretation of the effort made to circulate Gutiérrez Aguilar's work in translation through such visible and official circuits as those of Duke University Press is that it represents a subversion of the often acknowledged but rarely challenged geopolitics of knowledge. Another interpretation, however, could be to read it within a different framework for thinking about knowledge flows, like that which Silvia Rivera Cusicanqui proposes in her provocative essay about discourses of decolonization (2010a, 2012). She writes: "Las ideas recorren, como ríos, de sur a norte, y se convierten en afluentes de grandes corrientes de pensamiento. Pero como en el mercado mundial de bienes materiales, las ideas también salen del país convertidas en materia prima, que vuelve regurgitada y en gran mescolanza bajo la forma de producto terminado. Se forma así el canon de una nueva área del discurso científico social: el 'pensamiento postcolonial.' Ese canon visibiliza ciertos temas y fuentes, pero deja en la sombra a otros" (Rivera Cusicanqui 2010a, 68; Ideas run, like rivers, from the south to the north and are transformed into tributaries in major waves of thought. But just as in the global market for material goods, ideas leave the country converted into raw material, which become regurgitated and jumbled in the final product. Thus, a canon is formed for a new field of social scientific discourse, postcolonial thinking. This canon makes visible certain themes and sources but leaves others in the shadows [Rivera Cusicanqui 2012, 102–3]). Earlier in the essay, she presents an argument for shifting from a language of "geopolitics of knowledge" to that of the "political economy of knowledge" in order to "salir de la esfera de las superestructuras y desmenuzar las estrategias económicas y los mecanismos materiales que operan detrás de los discursos" (Rivera Cusicanqui 2010a, 65; leave the sphere of the superstructures in order to analyze the economic strategies and material mechanisms that operate behind discourses [Rivera Cusicanqui 2012, 102]).[2] Her emphasis on the materiality of knowledge production and circulation is compelling, and while her concern here is with academic circuits, her argument resonates with my exploration of the economic ethics of book culture. But this text, like Zibechi's and Gutiérrez Aguilar's books, is a translation made in the North based on a text produced in a radically different context in the South. Rivera Cusicanqui's essay, based on a lecture from the early 2000s, was originally published in Spanish in Argentina as the final chapter in a 2010 dual edition by Tinta Limón and Editorial Retazos. But the English translation I cited above appeared in 2012 in *South Atlantic Quarterly*, a journal of Duke University Press, through a process not unlike that which brought *Pachakuti* to the North. A significant difference, however, between these two texts that both have their origins in Bolivia is the fact that the subject of Rivera Cusicanqui's essay is precisely the movement of knowledge production from the South to the North and its absorption by elite academic networks. More specifically, in her essay, Rivera Cusicanqui names Duke University and specific members of the *South Atlantic Quarterly* editorial board as representative of the extractivist political economy of knowledge that she so sharply critiques. Clearly, both the author and the editors are aware of this apparent contradiction. But rather than read this or other cases of conflictive or complicated border crossings as conceptual or political dissonance, I want to suggest that it points directly to the relationality, instability, and variability inherent to any notion of organicity.

The examples of Zibechi, Gutiérrez Aguilar, and Rivera Cusicanqui's translation and export and import demonstrate just how diverse the many editions of an organic book can be. The organic book is alive, and, as I have endeavored to show, it is never alone—it is always connected to and often in tension with other books, other objects, other spaces, and other actors. The distances—territorial, institutional, linguistic, epistemic—that these books' relations now span are greater than they were in their earlier editions in the South, and with this stretching of meaning and materiality, they acquire new life.

A BOOK ABOUT ORGANIC BOOKS

In closing this book, it would be remiss of me not to recognize the medium through which I present these narratives and analysis of the *organic book*. In each of the chapters, I have highlighted the ways that the organic book is distinct from the *book*, be it the modern book, the academic book, the state book, the commercial book, or any other name we might give to the books that overwhelmingly occupy the shelves of bookstores and libraries. *The Book in Movement* is, of course, an academic book produced in the North. But while this edition might have all the characteristics against which I have sought to define the organic book, the story of this book, like any book, doesn't begin or end in this apparently "final" product, to paraphrase Adrian Johns. Like the many books whose stories have appeared in and across the various chapters, my book is an object that connects a "wide range of worlds of work," to again borrow from Johns. Certainly, this includes the worlds of academic labor that connect the university classroom to the professional association meetings to the offices of the university presses and academic journals, but also the extra-institutional spaces where work and doing are sites of collective experimentation: the organizing meetings that happen near campus, the long-term intellectual conversations that overflow from the rigid confines of professional hierarchies or even geography, the moments where research is blurred with political practice.

As a research project that has now extended over nearly a decade, *The Book in Movement* has had other lives beyond the academy, most clearly in two related projects. The first is my participation as a founding member of a small, alternative publishing collective, a project that was born just a few months after I returned from doing fieldwork. Since 2015 the press has been publishing original editions of small books that bridge anarchist theory and experimental academic writing, as well as translations from Spanish of works written by *compañerxs* with whom I worked during this project. The second and perhaps more punctual project is an actual book. In 2016 I created a zine written in Spanish that compiles some of the arguments and stories that also appear here. I distributed several dozen copies of the small, homemade, and staple-bound edition during my visit to Buenos Aires for the tenth anniversary of the FLIA-Capital, a trip facilitated by my appointment as faculty director of a short-term study abroad program. The resulting conversations with writers, presses, organizers, and friends have led me to rework some of the ideas in this book. In its current form, *The Book in Movement* is an object that is without a doubt an individual and bound academic book in all the usual ways. But it is also made of practices and relations that make it also—like any book could become—multiple.

The organic book, like autonomy, can only be defined by its practices: how it is made, what it does, and how it works. The organic book, as I have argued, is a *concept-practice*, wherein there is no division between materiality and ideas. In writing about it, I have endeavored to meld my descriptions of the practices with my analysis of the concepts they present. Moving through the life stages of any book, I have worked to make evident what this *concept-practice* looks like: from idea to page to print to reader. Through collective practices of reflection and theorization, the *horizontal* forms of organization of the movements are manifested in the arrangements of words and ideas on the pages. The book workshop, as a space where *experimentation* take precedence over efficiency and profitability, generates books that vary tremendously in weight, texture, aesthetic, and cost, as the conditions of each printing and binding process give shape to that object in that moment. As the books take flight and their digital alter-egos travel between presses, the definitions of property and authorship attached to them are transformed by the *transversal* networks of actors that make and remake the books. When they land again, touching ground in fairs, markets, social centers, libraries, and shops, they make physical spaces where other things can happen, where *encuentro*—face-to-face dialogue, exchange, and collaboration—takes place. And these *encuentros*, in turn, often multiply to other spaces and other moments.

As I have suggested throughout this work, the organic book presents the possibility for thinking about how objects travel: how they are at once the same and changing. Theory experiences a similar dynamic as it travels. My object of analysis—the organic book—and my empirical material provide a means of thinking conceptually about how local politics create networks of people and things but also of ideas, bringing different regions and societies into dialogical relations. The division between North and South may appear to be physically marked in our hemisphere by the US-Mexico border, but it pervades in the dynamics of knowledge production that continue to persist within Latin America, as well as the United States. In this networked ethnography—a book made in the North about books made in the South—I have endeavored to follow the materiality of what Holloway (2010b, xv) names "a turn in the flow of inspiration and of understanding." Conceptually and materially, the organic book shows us how the movements of people, ideas, and objects might reorient the flows that shape the continent.

NOTES

Introduction: The Organic Book in the Continent in Movement

1. All translations mine unless otherwise indicated.

2. For example, the Multiforo Alicia has maintained strong ties to Zapatismo since it opened, and for many years, in addition to concerts and cultural events, it hosted weekly Frente Zapatista de Liberación Nacional meetings. The Alicia is described as "un espacio para los jóvenes—los grandes olvidados de este país—y los no tan jóvenes pero con espíritu rebelde. Porque nos sentimos zapatistas de corazón y compartimos con nuestros hermanos el sueño por un México más justo, democrático y digno" (a space for young people—the forgotten of our country—and the not so young but who have a rebel spirit. Because we feel like we are Zapatistas at heart and we share with our brothers and sisters the dream of a more just, democratic, and dignified Mexico; Multiforo Alicia 2008). In an interview by the Colectivo Situaciones, Ignacio Pineda, the founder of the Alicia, stated, "El Alicia como espacio es parte del zapatismo aunque yo no me he afiliado, nunca me he ido a inscribir a nungún lado" (The Alicia as a space is part of Zapatismo even though I've never affiliated myself, I've never gone to register myself anywhere; Colectivo Situaciones 2005: 235).

3. The book's title is a combination of "imagination" and "marginalization." One of the poems in the book concludes with the statement: "Soy un producto de tu imaRginación" (I am a product of your imaRgination; Bocafloja 2008).

4. Functioning somewhat like an overture, "intros" are a stylistic convention in the structure of hip-hop albums. They are usually a very brief, somewhat abstract, montage of elements of the larger album, whether using themes or actual sound clips. Many albums, including Bocafloja's, also include "outros" as the final track.

5. Throughout the manuscript, I use the term "press" to refer to what would more commonly be called "publishing houses" in English. The Spanish term is *editorial*.

6. The subhead for this section translates as "We are the spokespeople of our own experiences" (Bocafloja 2008).

7. The alterglobalization movement (sometimes called the Global Justice Movement) is a "movement of movements," often dated as beginning either with the Zapatista uprising in Chiapas in 1994 or the World Trade Organization protests in Seattle in 1999 (Notes from Nowhere 2003). What connects the countless local and

translocal movements and moments of protest that make up the alterglobalization movement is the identification of a common enemy or target: neoliberalism and globalized capitalism, which activists and militants of the movements characterize as having destructive, consuming, and fragmenting effects.

8. See Azzellini and Sitrin 2014; Dixon 2014; Notes from Nowhere 2003; Rovira 2017; Sitrin 2005; Zibechi 2008b.

9. In the context of Zapatismo, Mariana Mora (2003) has discussed this in terms of a "politics of listening." Boaventura de Sousa Santos (2006) and others have similarly examined this in the alterglobalization movement and the World Social Forum.

10. The now well-rehearsed story of the Zapatistas begins not with their public appearance on January 1, 1994, but on November 17, 1983, when the EZLN was founded in the Lacandon Jungle of Chiapas through a collaboration between members of indigenous communities and a small group of urban mestizos, including the person who would come to be known as Subcomandante Marcos. The basic objectives of the movement have remained constant over the past thirty years: the construction of a more economically, socially, and culturally just world where all people, and especially indigenous peoples, can live in dignity. There have, however, been several watershed moments that mark new directions in the movement's orientation, reflecting an ongoing practice of *caminar preguntando* (walking by asking questions). Countless books and articles about Zapatismo have been published over the last twenty years. Since it would be impossible to attempt to list the most important analyses here, I want to highlight just two books. The first is *20 y 10: El fuego y la palabra*, by Gloria Muñoz, published in 2003. The second was published in 2011 and brings together seventeen chapters penned by the first and only generation of researchers who were granted access by the Zapatistas to conduct research in the autonomous communities of Chiapas: *Luchas muy otras: Zapatismo y autonomía en las comunidades indígenas de Chiapas*, edited by Bruno Baronnet, Mariana Mora Bayo, and Richard Stahler-Sholk.

11. Tapia's concept of the societal movement, which he develops drawing on René Zavaleta's earlier theorizations of Bolivia as a *sociedad abigarrada* (motley society), is based on a recognition of the existence of various societies within "society" and seeks to "nombrar y pensar el movimiento de una sociedad o sistema de relaciones sociales en su conjunto" (name and think about the movement of a society or system of social relations as a whole; Tapia 2002: 60).

12. The authors were also founding members of Comuna, a "grupo de acción social" (social action group; Prada 2012) based in La Paz that has included Luis Tapia, Oscar Vega Camacho, and Raúl Prada, among others. García Linera and Gutiérrez Aguilar separated in the late 1990s. Today, García Linera is the vice president of Bolivia alongside Evo Morales, the first indigenous president in South America. In 2001 Gutiérrez Aguilar returned to her home country, Mexico, where

she currently works as a professor and researcher at the Instituto de Ciencias Sociales y Humanidades de la Benemérita Universidad Autónoma de Puebla and is a cofounder of the Casa de Ondas, a social center in Mexico City.

13. In the introduction to the 2009 edition, the author describes how he came to have access to the primary materials that would become the object of his study. *Capital* was approved by the prison authorities as a "non-political" book:

> *El capital*, no cabe duda, literalmente no parecía nada riesgoso o político frente a los celosos guardianes de la cárcel. Al menos su título no hablaba ni de guerras, ni de sublevaciones y fácilmente podía ser entendido como un libro más de gestión empresarial, tan de moda en esos años de auge neoliberal. ¿*El capital*? por qué no. Talvez así el reo se dedique a hacer algunas empresas y deje de meterse tanto en política, comentó alguno de los guardias encargados de vigilarnos día y noche.

> To the jealous guards of the prison, *Capital*, without a doubt, literally seemed like a book that was neither risky nor political. At least its title didn't refer to wars or uprisings, and it could easily be interpreted as another one of those business books that were so popular in those years of neoliberal expansion. *Capital?* Why not. Maybe that way the prisoner will focus on creating some kind of business and will stop getting mixed up in politics, said one of the guards that was charged with watching us day and night. (García Linera 2009: 9)

The colonial chronicles, he explains, were smuggled into the prison during Alison Spedding's biweekly visits.

14. My approach to following the life of the organic book is, perhaps quite obviously, informed by Arjun Appadurai's notion of the "social life of things," and specifically his insistence that the meaning of things is inscribed in "their forms, their uses, their trajectories" (1986, 5). My study of the book in movement, is indeed, what Appadurai (1986, 5) calls an examination of a "thing-in-motion."

15. Cf. Ferguson 2014.

16. Cf. Rovira 2017 and Rovira 2009 for extensive studies of online activist networks.

17. Cf. López Winne and Malumián 2016, Griffin 2016, Epplin 2014, de Diego 2014, Subercaseaux 2000, and Salazar Embarcadero 2011 for extensive analyses of recent trends in Latin American publishing.

18. The concept of *autogestión* cannot be adequately translated to English. The rarely used cognate "autogestion" is not widely understood. The standard translation as "worker self-management" is too restrictive because it does not convey a key aspect of *autogestión* as a self-sustaining, autonomous practice. A foundational concept of anarchist praxis, it has been traced back to nineteenth-century anarchist Pierre-Joseph Proudhon (McKay 2011; Vieta 2014). While it has been in

circulation in Latin America for more than a hundred years, primarily in anarchist circles, today it appears as a common descriptor for the kinds of economic and political projects that ground the autonomous movements in Latin America. For these reasons, I use the Spanish term rather than attempt to translate it.

19. *La ciudad letrada* was published posthumously in 1984, shortly after Rama's death in a plane crash in Spain. For this reason, what I refer to here and elsewhere as the book's "final chapter" is in reality the last chapter that appears in the book, which was unfinished at the time of Rama's death.

20. I am grateful to Mary Murrell for her encouragement as I explored the new field of the anthropology of books and bookmaking. Her unpublished manuscript, *The Open Book*, is an excellent example of the ways that ethnography and science and technology studies can be deployed in the analysis of books as political and material objects.

21. Cf. Barry 2013; Gordillo 2014; Law 2004, 2007; Law and Singleton 2005; Latour 1996; Mol 2002; Knox, Savage, and Harvey 2006; and Riles 2001, 2006.

22. Tapia's 2008 book *Política Salvaje* is dedicated to Raquel Gutiérrez Aguilar.

23. My thinking about this kind of relational category is inspired by the ideas of members of the Subaltern Studies Group, who, following Gramsci, define "subalternity" in relational terms.

24. The most formal expression of this networking can be seen in the Zapatista's Otra Campaña. Announced in mid-2005 in the "Sexta declaración de la Selva Lacandona" (Sixth declaration of the Lacandon Jungle) and formally launched in January 2006, the Otra Campaña represented a new phase in the Zapatista struggle "against economic exploitation and for the radical recognition of ethnic-racial and gender differences in Mexico" (Mora 2007, 65). In anticipation of the 2006 presidential elections in Mexico, the EZLN organized the Otra Campaña—which included a tour of EZLN delegates through all thirty-two states of Mexico—in an effort to articulate nonpartisan, anticapitalist struggles across the country. In the first days of the tour, Subcomandante Marcos, now traveling as a civilian with the new title Subdelegado Zero, presented a speech to the *medio libres* who were accompanying the Otra Campaña, proclaiming that "el trabajo de los medios alternativos va a ser la columna vertebral en la primera parte de la Otra Campaña" (the work of the alternative media will be the spine of the first part of the Other Campaign; Subdelegado Zero 2006). The Otra Campaña marked my first formal introduction to what has come to be referred to as the Zapatista "politics of encuentro," as I traveled with the *karavana* through the states of Oaxaca and Guerrero as an international observer for the organization I was working with in Chiapas at the time. Since 2006 I have participated in several other major *encuentros* in Zapatista territory and in Mexico City, each of which included the presence of thousands of people from Zapatista communities around the state of Chiapas and from more than forty countries around the world.

25. Collectives and individuals were invited to register as "adherents" to the "Sexta declaración," and while that affiliation has little significance today, some groups still employ this language as a means of demonstrating that they are part of something bigger, a broader network of solidarity.

26. For an overview of the history of JRA and the Red de Resistencias Autónomas Anticapitalistas, see section 2.5 in Navarro Trujillo 2016.

27. Initially published online and in the newspaper *La Jornada*, the "Sexta Declaración" has been reprinted repeatedly in books and pamphlets published across the continent. While it is not, in itself, a book, the ways that it has taken flight in print form is an expression of the same dynamics of fluidity and accessibility that characterize the organic book.

28. On December 25, 2010, the vice president García Linera announced the passing of Supreme Decree 748, which removed the state subsidies of some fuels and raised taxes on gasoline, diesel, and aviation fuel. As a result, the cost of gasoline rose by 72 percent, diesel by 84 percent, and aviation fuel by 99 percent. The justification presented was that this was a necessary measure to halt the illegal traffic of fuels from Bolivia and to protect the country from foreign interests. Obviously, for the Bolivian people such a dramatic a hike in prices implied an economic disaster, as fuel prices affect the cost of all basic goods. See Zibechi 2011 for a discussion of the events and effects of the *gasolinazo*.

29. Cf. Oscar Olivera et al. 2010.

30. Many books have been published since 2001 documenting and analyzing the popular rebellion. See Caviasca et al. 2011; Sitrin 2005; Colectivo Situaciones 2002.

Chapter One: Becoming the Book

1. An English edition of *Dispersar el poder*, translated by Ramor Ryan, was published by AK Press in Oakland, California, in 2010. I refer to Ryan's translation for all citations.

2. John Holloway elaborates on this distinction in his now almost classic 2002 book about Zapatismo, *Change the World without Taking Power.*

3. In late 2016 JRA formally disbanded. A new collective project, Comunal, was created by some of the former JRA members in early 2017, and they continue to publish books as Bajo Tierra Ediciones. For a history of both JRA and Bajo Tierra, see Navarro Trujillo 2016.

4. With the exception of those conducted with public intellectuals, all of my interviews were group interviews or interviews with members of collective projects. For this reason, with a single exception in chapter 2, rather than assign pseudonyms, I have chosen not to cite personal names in quotes from interviews.

5. These terms appear as the titles of roundtable sessions at Zapatista *encuentros*, as well as in various communiqués and speeches.

6. Self-described as a "comunidad de aprendizaje, estudio, reflexión y acción" (community of learning, study, reflection, and action), Unitierra–Oaxaca is an autonomous project, founded by Gustavo Esteva, based in the capital city of Oaxaca dedicated to convivial, action oriented learning. While each operates autonomously, there are several other Unitierra projects, including in Chiapas, Puebla, and the San Francisco Bay Area.

7. Beginning in 2001 the Zapatistas abandoned all dialogue with the government and focused their efforts on building de facto autonomy locally. In 2003 they reemerged publicly with the announcement of the *caracoles*—the five new regional centers that house the Juntas de Buen Gobierno (Good Government Councils)—which reoriented the dynamics of interaction between the Zapatista communities and "national and international civil society." The "radically outward" gaze that I describe here refers to how the Zapatistas began to look explicitly past the government to what they call the "intergalactic" networks of autonomous and anticapitalist resistance that resonated with the struggle in Chiapas.

8. Cf. Shukaitis and Graeber 2007.

9. I borrow here from Dipesh Chakrabarty's (2000) idea of "asymmetric ignorance" that governs the production and flow of knowledge between North and South. With his call to "Provincialize Europe," he argues for a reorientation of history and theory that does not rely on "Europe."

10. *Dispersar el poder* appears again in each of the subsequent chapters in my analysis of the other stages in the life of an organic book.

11. This is the language used in Argentina to describe the occupation of public and private spaces. The distinction between recuperation and occupation is largely semantic, as similar practices to the Argentine recuperations are, in other contexts, called "occupations." Nevertheless, the choice of terminology is significant as recuperation implies that the group occupying the space is its rightful owner or steward. The term "recuperation" eludes the sorts of critique raised against the use of the term "occupy" in the United States in 2011, primarily in the context of Occupy Oakland, where indigenous groups rightfully insisted on recognizing the settler-colonial connotations of the concept of occupation (Gould et al. 2011).

Chapter Two: The Workshop Book

1. According to census data compiled by Centro Latinoamericano y Caribeño de Demografía, between 1991 and 2010, the Bolivian-born population in Argentina increased by 140 percent, from 143,735 in 1991 to 345,272 in 2010 (CELADE 2006).

2. La Cazona de Flores is located in Buenos Aires and is home to two small presses and a variety of other community organizations and projects.

3. *Cartoneros* are people who collect and recycle cardboard to make a living. *Cartoneras* are small presses born from this economy of recycling that use the

salvaged cardboard to make inexpensive books. Hundreds of small presses, such as Eloísa Cartonera (Argentina), have emerged in the past decade. In general, *cartoneras* mostly publish fiction, poetry, and classic political texts. For more on this phenomenon, see for example Bilbija and Celis Carbajal 2009.

As Ksenija Biblija (2009, 29) reminds us, however, "books made with cardboard covers are not new," and there is a long history of this method of bookbinding. What is new is the explicit economy of solidarity with the cardboard collectors and the common "surname" of *cartonera*.

4. The heading for this section translates as, "But here we have our idiosyncrasy in how we do things." Most of the books I discuss in this project have not been translated to English. Raúl Zibechi's work is an exception. As previously noted, in 2010, the English translation of *Dispersar el poder* was published by AK Press, and in 2012, *Autonomías y emancipaciones* was also translated by Ramor Ryan as *Territories in Resistance.* The epilogue addresses the few other exceptions.

5. This is a pseudonym.

6. See ¡A *desordenar! Por una historia abierta de la lucha social* by Raquel Gutiérrez (Textos Rebeldes, 2008) for more on the idea of *desordenar*.

7. The heading to this section translates as "a kind of school of publishing."

8. Cf. Schwartz 2016 for a discussion of reading and book culture in urban public transportation in Latin America.

9. In the popular Lunfardo dialect commonly used in Buenos Aires, *laburo* is a slang term for "work."

10. A great deal has been written on the phenomenon of recuperated and worker-run businesses in Argentina. See for example Lavaca 2007a and 2007b and Hudson 2011.

11. It is worth noting that members of this cooperative also make craft beer in another space in this occupied building.

12. The heading to this section translates as "until one day the union of anarcho-pacifist bookbinders brought an end to the monarchy." *Cultura libre,* or "free culture," refers to a loosely constituted movement that promotes the free sharing of creative works through the use of the internet and nonrestrictive licensing (like copyleft or some forms of Creative Commons). While this movement has had influence around the world, Buenos Aires has its own subculture, with close ties to alternative and independent publishing. See Busaniche 2010 for more on this. My next chapter focuses on the uses of these *cultura libre* practices in the circulation of organic books.

13. In the true spirit of copyleft, "Fábrica de Fallas" has been "copied"—their words—in Santiago de Chile since 2011.

14. Though no author is listed, I traced this poem to the blog Piedra Buena (piedrabuena.blogspot.com), maintained by one of the founders of Tinta China, a similar press and print shop run by two Uruguayans.

15. My next chapter focuses on the uses of copyright, copyleft, Creative Commons, and other alternative intellectual property practices by the presses.

16. The heading to this section translates as "Break away from the pattern to bring an end to this model."

17. For an extended discussion of the networks of migration and grassroots publishing in Argentina and Bolivia see Rabasa 2017.

18. The first part of the title of Rivera Cusicanqui's book is in Aymara, the rest in Spanish. Its title translates as "A Ch'ixi world also exists: A reflection on decolonizing practices and discourses" (Rivera Cusicanqui 2010a and 2010b).

19. *Potencia* is a term that resists simple translation. The translators of many works by Colectivo Situaciones, Nate Holdren and Sebastian Touza (2005) write: "Two Spanish words translate as the English word 'power': poder and potencia. Generally speaking, we could say that poder defines power as 'power over' (the sense it has, for instance, when it refers to state or sovereign power) and potencia defines 'power to,' the type of capacity expressed in the statement 'I can.'" John Holloway (2002), Raquel Gutiérrez (2006), and Raúl Zibechi (2006) all provide insightful analyses about the distinction between "power-over" and "power-to."

Chapter Three: The Unbounded Book

1. The *cartonera* presses mentioned in the previous chapter also engage in similar practices of republishing. A major difference, however, is that they do so in a much more conspicuous manner through their signature use of hand-painted cardboard covers.

2. See for example Clement and Oppenheim's (2002) discussion of IP in anarchist publishing or Barlow's (1996) discussion of the distinction between information as a verb versus as a noun.

3. Alternative book fairs held in parallel to official book fairs are often called "Other book fairs."

4. The Cospel edition of *Contra el copyright*, like some other organic books, doesn't exist online. There is no trace of it in cyberspace, and because the book itself bears no date of publication, it is difficult to know exactly when it first appeared, how many were printed, and when it made its way to the Buenos Aires bookstore where I bought it in 2016. Based on the trajectory of Cospel Ediciones that can be pieced together from the press's web presence, the press began around 2006, with an increasingly polished project developing over the years. Self-described as a "fábrica de lectores" (reader factory), Cospel has grown in parallel to the FLIA, though always maintaining its distinctly regional identity.

5. Here I follow Silvia Rivera Cusicanqui's (2010a, 65) call to shift away from the idea of a "geopolitics of knowledge" toward a more concrete notion of the "political economy of knowledge."

6. *Pachakuti* is an Aymara term that refers to a nonlinear cyclical time-space,

and with her analysis of the mobilizations that shook Bolivia from 2000 to 2005, Gutiérrez Aguilar asserts that a new era of Pachakuti has been opened.

7. I use "bibliography" here in the sense of "the systematic description and history of books, their authorship, printing, publication, editions, etc." (*Oxford English Dictionary Online*).

8. Until 2012 Sísifo Ediciones was the coeditor of all Bajo Tierra publications, though their role was minimal in the actual edition of the books. Sísifo is a press run by the owner of the print shop where Bajo Tierra's first seven titles were printed. The owner's son is a member of JRA, and this relationship greatly facilitated the economic and technical process of getting the first books published.

9. The idea of political, material, and cultural translation that I develop shares a great deal with the concept of translocality theorized by Alvarez et al. in their 2014 edited volume on feminist politics of translation.

Chapter Four: The Networking Book

1. Guadalajara and Buenos Aires compete for the title of biggest book fair in Latin America. As reported on their official websites, the 2016 Feria Internacional del Libro de Guadalajara received 800,821 visitors and included more than 2,000 presses, while the 2017 Feria Internacional del Libro de Buenos Aires received 1,200,000 visitors and included more than 4,000 presses.

2. For a study of reading practices in Latin America cities, see Schwartz 2018.

3. I borrow these phrases from Arturo Escobar's (2010) interpretation of J. K. Gibson-Graham's project.

4. I develop this idea borrowing from Luis Tapia's concept of wild politics. Wild networks, similarly, resist centralization and institutionalization and are made through practice, not design.

5. The heading to this section translates as "They're dignified books."

6. The PRD was the party of the former mayor Andrés Manuel López Obrador, whose 2006 run for president was defeated through electoral fraud that put Felipe Calderón in power. A particular brand of local populism grew out of López Obrador's subsequent protest movement.

7. The concept of the *tianguis* originated in Mexico as a hispanicization of the indigenous Nahuatl word for marketplace, *tianquiztli*, and today *tianguis* is a term used to refer to an informal, temporary, and mobile popular marketplace set up in a public space like a street or plaza.

8. The book being distributed my first day at the Feria Alternativa was *Zapatismo con vista al mar: El socialismo maya de Yucatán* (Zapatismo with an ocean view: The Mayan socialism of Yucatán) by sociologist Armando Bartra. The premise of the book is that the recent indigenous struggles for autonomy in Mexico, Bolivia, Ecuador, and elsewhere demand a reexamination of the role of indigenous socialisms in the Mexican Revolution. The text is an updated and expanded

version of an essay presented in 1979 and has an accessible narrative style that carries the reader easily through otherwise dense historical analysis. This small book could easily have been published as a pamphlet, but as the organizers of the *Brigada* insist, it is important that they have the form of books. The other book I received at the Feria was the first in a series of literary anthologies titled *De los cuates pa' la raza*, with nearly forty short essays, stories, and poems penned by some of Mexico's most well-known contemporary writers. In this heftier volume, just over two hundred pages, the narratives all center on the experience of being Mexican and, more specifically, the experience of living in Mexico City.

9. Marcy Schwartz (2014, 2016) has written extensively on the social uses of the book in urban space in Latin America, arguing that the encounters that books create "map new urban stories that challenge the hegemony of what Ángel Rama called the 'lettered city'" (2014, 419.)

10. The heading to this section translates as "We don't want to import the fair. . . . We want an alternative fair, from here."

11. This is a theme I discuss in chapter 2 in my analysis of networks connecting Argentina and Bolivia.

12. Beginning in 2006, an unprecedented publishing initiative emerged from the Office of Citizen Participation within the vice presidency of Bolivia. As one participant explained in an interview, the publishing initiative grew from a two-fold interest in disseminating information about the political agenda of the Morales administration while also theorizing the political process as it was unfolding. The books produced by this initiative are distributed for free through various venues and have included contributions from international figures such as Enrique Dussel, Gayatri Chakravorty Spivak, and Antonio Negri, as well as a range of Bolivian intellectuals.

13. The heading to this section translates as "our dignified rage."

14. Some of the most significant events in Mexico City have included Comandanta Ramona's participation in the Congreso Nacional Indígena in 1996; the caravan of 1,111 Zapatista delegates to the Congreso Nacional Indígena in 1997; the caravan of 23 *comandantes*, which was received by 100,000 people in the Zócalo, and Comandanta Esther's congressional address in 2001; the Otra Campaña tour in 2006 ("Chiapas" 2014).

15. The Digna Rabia was the fourth major Zapatista *encuentro* that I had participated in since 2005, though it was the first I attended outside of autonomous rebel territory in Chiapas.

16. The heading to this section translates as "We had to walk differently."

17. See Griffin 2016 and Subercaseaux 2000 for detailed analyses of the Editorial Quimantú during Allende's presidency.

18. I am grateful to Tamara Lea Spira for conversations that helped me to analyze this nuance with greater attention.

19. Concertación is the coalition of center-left parties founded in 1988.

20. Santiago de Chile seems to have more banks than any other city I've been to—and as a friend pointed out, drawing a parallel to the psychosomatic condition of Chile, for every bank there is also a pharmacy.

21. The heading to this section translates as "Identity gets constructed collectively."

On the name Proyección:

> Hay una editorial argentina de los años 60, quizás un poco antes o un poco después, anarquista. Que fue un proyecto muy interesante, de confluencia de distintos sectores del anarquismo argentino en esos años. . . . Ese nombre teníamos gran cariño por esa editorial, y ese proyecto. Y que ya no existe además, pensamos que podíamos ocuparlo sin ningún problema. . . . Creo que nos dimos cuenta después, o quizás lo teníamos en el inconsciente. . . . En términos metafóricos me gusta porque tiene una resonancia moderna en el fondo. Esos nombres así un poco clásicos, que además tienen resonancia metafórica interesante en avanzar desde hoy al futuro. Utópico en ese sentido, va desde hoy y llega a otro lugar. Y en ese sentido vemos que coincide con la perspectiva política de avanzar hacia lograr cosas en el tiempo de manera real. Y no lanzar ideales inalcanzables, sino trabajar por algo concreto.

> There's an anarchist Argentine press from the sixties, or maybe a bit earlier or later. It was an interesting project, a confluence of different sectors of Argentine anarchism at the time. . . . We felt a great fondness for that press, for the project. And since it doesn't exist anymore, we figured there'd be no problem, that we could use the name. . . . I think afterwards we realized it, or maybe we knew it subconsciously . . . metaphorically, I like it because it has a modern resonance deep down. It's one of those names that are sort of classic and that also have an interesting metaphorical resonance of moving toward the future from today. Utopic in a sense, from today we reach to another time and place. And in that sense we see that it coincides with the political perspective of working toward something in real time. And to not propose impossible ideals, but to work toward something concrete. (Interview, Santiago de Chile, 2011)

22. The heading to this section translates as "We launch in the street."

23. An intentional misspelling of "Latina"—América LeAtina Desde Abajo is a play on words that means "(Latin) America strikes from below."

24. The heading to this section translates as "the infinite fair."

25. Now the president of Argentina, then mayor of the city of Buenos Aires, Mauricio Macri is a right-wing businessman who many consider responsible for the rapid transformation of the spatial, economic, and social dynamics of the city, as evidenced in the fencing off of public plazas, the violent eviction of occupied social centers, and the growing housing crisis.

26. The Buenos Aires FLIA is called the FLIA-Capital, to refer spefically to the FLIA for the Ciudad Autónoma de Buenos Aires, as opposed to the province of Buenos Aires, home to the FLIA-Oeste, FLIA-Sur, FLIA-Norte, etc.

27. The name La Libre made me recall the Quimantú slogans that play with the idea of *libre/libertad* (being free/liberty/freedom) and *libros* (books).

28. University of Buenos Aires researcher Daniela Szpilbarg similarly asserts this connection to 2001 in her 2015 essay on presses associated with the FLIA.

29. The heading to this section translates as "The FLIA is like what I dreamed of, like what many dreamed of."

30. For example, alternative production and distribution strategies of the beats; writers that are editors that are publishers that are distributors; the urban experience of publishing; the use of public space, etc.

31. This recalls the Zapatistas' call to "share a dream" (EZLN 1996).

32. The heading to this section translates as "It cannot be destroyed because it doesn't exist."

33. The heading to this section translates as "You/We are the FLIA."

Epilogue

1. Series editors Arturo Escobar and Dianne Rocheleau are well-known theorists of alternative economies and ecologies of knowledge and politics, recognized for their critiques of the imperialism of the US academy. The author of the foreword, Sinclair Thomson, is a long-standing comrade of many of the protagonists of *The Rhythms of Pachakuti*, relations forged over many years of frequent travel to Bolivia. The reviewers listed on the back cover, Michael Hardt and Charles Hale, have, in different capacities, facilitated many transnational dialogues with organic intellectuals and activists, such as Gutiérrez Aguilar and Colectivo Situaciones, from the South.

2. I am grateful to my colleagues at the 2017 Tepoztlán Institute for the Transnational History of the Americas for our rich and challenging discussion of this essay.

REFERENCES

"Acerca." 2018. *La E del Coihue Infinito*. Accessed June 26, 2018. https://laeinfinita .wordpress.com.

"Agenda El Asunto." 2012. Agenda El Asunto. Accessed October 3, 2017. http:// agendaelasunto.blogspot.com.

Albertani, Claudio. 2011. "'Flores Salvajes': Reflexiones sobre el principio de autonomía." In *Pensar las autonomías: Alternativas de emancipación al capital y el estado*, edited by Jóvenes en Resistencia Alternativa, 53–70. Mexico City: Bajo Tierra Ediciones.

Alvarez, Sonia, Norma Klahn, Verónica Feliu, Rebecca Hester, and Claudia de Lima Costa, eds. 2014. *Translocalities/Translocalidades: Feminist Politics of Translation in the Latin/a Américas*. Durham: Duke University Press.

"América LeAtina la hizo otra vez." 2012. *El Ciudadano*, December 14. Accessed December 20, 2012. http://www.elciudadano.cl.

Anderson, Benedict. 1983. *Imagined Communities*. London: Verso.

Andrés. 2012. "Conversación con Retazos." Lo Sutil. Accessed January 10, 2013. http://losutil.blogspot.com.

Aparicio, Juan Ricardo, and Mario Blaser. 2008. "The 'Lettered City' and the Insurrection of Subjugated Knowledges in Latin America." *Anthropological Quarterly* 81, no. 1: 59–94. doi: 10.1353/anq.2008.0000.

Appadurai, Arjun. 1986. "Introduction: Commodities and the Politics of Value." In *The Social Life of Things*, edited by Arjun Appadurai, 3–63. Cambridge: Cambridge University Press.

Astutti, Adriana, and Sandra Contreras. 2001. "Editorials independientes, pequeñas. . . . Micropolíticas culturales en la literatura argentina actual." *Revista Iberoamericana* 67, no. 197: 767–80. https://dialnet.unirioja.es.

Atton, Chris. 1999. "A Reassessment of the Alternative Press." *Media Culture Society* 21, no. 1: 51–76. doi: 10.1177/016344399021001003.

Azzellini, Dario, and Marina Sitrin. 2014. *They Can't Represent Us! Reinventing Democracy from Greece to Occupy*. New York: Verso Books.

Barilaro, Javier. 2009. "And There Is Much More." In *Akademia Cartonera: A Primer of Latin American Cartonera Publishers*, edited by Ksenija Bilbija and Paloma Celis Carbajal, 28–34. Madison, WI: Parallel Press.

Barlow, J. P. 1996. "Selling Wine without Bottles: The Economy of the Mind on the Global Net." In *High Noon on the Electronic Frontier: Conceptual Issues in Cyberspace*, edited by Peter Ludlow, 9–34. Cambridge: MIT Press.

Baronnet, Bruno, Mariana Mora Bayo, and Richard Stahler-Sholk, eds. 2011. *Luchas muy otras: Zapatismo y autonomía en las comunidades indígenas de Chiapas*. Mexico City: UAM, UACH, CIESAS.

Barry, Andrew. 2013. *Material Politics: Disputes along the Pipeline*. West Sussex: Wiley-Blackwell.

Barthes, Roland. 1977. "Death of the Author." In *Image, Music, Text*, by Roland Barthes. Translated by Stephen Heath. New York: Hill and Wang.

Bell, Lucy. 2017. "'Las cosas se pueden hacer de modo distinto' (Aurelio Meza): Understanding Concepts of Locality, Resistance and Autonomy in the Cardboard Publishing Movement." *Journal of Latin American Cultural Studies* 26, no. 1: 51–72. doi: 10.1080/13569325.2016.1271313.

Benjamin, Walter. 1998. *Understanding Brecht*. Translated by Anna Bostock. London: Verso.

Benkler, Yochai. 2006. *The Wealth of Networks: How Social Production Transforms Markets and Freedom*. New Haven: Yale University Press.

Berardi, Franco Bifo. 2008. *Generación Post-alfa: Patologías e imaginarios en el semiocapitalismo*. Mexico: Bajo Tierra.

Bey, Hakim. 1991. *T.A.Z.: The Temporary Autonomous Zone, Ontological Anarchy, Poetic Terrorism*. Brooklyn: Autonomedia.

Bilbija, Ksenija. 2009. "The Nomadic Carto(nera)graphy of the Latin American *Cartonera* Publishing Houses." In *Akademia Cartonera: A Primer of Latin American Cartonera Publishers*, edited by Ksenija Bilbija and Paloma Celis Carbajal, 46–53. Madison, WI: Parallel Press.

Bilbija, Ksenija, and Paloma Celis Carbajal, eds. 2009. *Akademia Cartonera: A Primer of Latin American Cartonera Publishers*. Madison, WI: Parallel Press.

Bocafloja. 2007. *El manual de la otredad*. Quilombo Arte.

Bocafloja. 2008. *ImaRginación: La poética del hip hop como desmesura de los político*. Mexico City: Bajo Tierra Ediciones.

Bratich, Jack. 2007. "Fragments on Machinic Intellectuals." In *Constituent Imagination: Militant Investigations, Collective Theorization*, edited by Stevphen Shukaitis and David Graeber, 137–54. Oakland: AK Press.

Busaniche, Beatriz, ed. 2010. *Argentina Copyleft: la crisis del modelo de derecho de autor y las prácticas para democratizar la cultura*. Buenos Aires: Fundación Vía Libre.

Casas-Cortés, Maria Isabel. 2009. "Social Movements as Sites of Knowledge Production: Precarious Work, the Fate of Care and Activist Research in a Globalizing Spain." PhD diss., University of North Carolina, Chapel Hill.

Casas-Cortés, Maria Isabel, and Sebastián Cobarrubias. 2007. "Drifting through the Knowledge Machine." In *Constituent Imagination: Militant Investigations,*

Collective Theorization, edited by Stevphen Shukaitis and David Graeber, 112–26. Oakland: AK Press.

Caviasca, Guillermo, Roberto Perdía, Claudio Katz, Fernando Esteche, Vicente Zito Lema, Natalia Vinelli, Andrea D'Atri, Rubén "Pollo" Sobrero, Eduardo "Vasco" Murúa, Roberto Martino, and Martín Ogando. 2011. *¿Que se vayan todos? A 10 años del 19 y 20 de diciembre*. Buenos Aires: El Río Suena.

CELADE (Centro Latinoamericano y Caribeño de Demografía). 2006. *Migración Internacional—International Migration*. Santiago de Chile: CELADE-CEPAL/UNFPA.

Centro de Medios Libres. 2013. *Toma los medios, sé los medios, haz los medios*. Oaxaca: El Rebozo.

Cerrutti, Marcela, and Emilio Parrado. 2015. "Intraregional Migration in South America: Trends and a Research Agenda." *Annual Review of Sociology* 41: 399–421. doi:10.1146/annurev-soc-073014-112249.

Chakrabarty, Dipesh. 2000. *Provincializing Europe: Postcolonial Thought and Historical Difference*. Princeton: Princeton University Press.

Chartier, Roger. 1992. *The Cultural Origins of the French Revolution*. Durham: Duke University Press.

"Chiapas: Fechas claves." 2014. SIPAZ. Accessed December 10, 2015. www.sipaz.org.

Clement, Ellie, and Charles Oppenheim. 2002. "Anarchism, Alternative Publishers and Copyright." *Anarchist Studies* 11: 43–69.

Colectivo ¿Quién habla?. 2006. *¿Quién habla? Lucha contra la esclavitud del alma en los call centers*. Buenos Aires: Tinta Limón.

Colectivo Situaciones. 2002. *19 y 20: Apuntes para el nuevo protagonismo social*. Buenos Aires: Ediciones de Mano en Mano.

Colectivo Situaciones. 2005. *Bienvenidos a la Selva: Diálogos a partir de la Sexta declaración del EZLN*. Buenos Aires: Tinta Limón.

Colectivo Situaciones. 2006. Epilogue to *Dispersar el poder: los movimientos como poderes antiestatales*, by Raúl Zibechi, 221–32. La Paz: Textos Rebeldes.

Colectivo Situaciones. 2007. "Something More on Research Militancy: Footnotes on Procedures and (In)Decisions." In *Constituent Imagination: Militant Investigations, Collective Theorization*, edited by Stevphen Shukaitis and David Graeber, 73–93. Oakland: AK Press.

Colectivo Situaciones. 2010. "La Excusa Perfecta (un texto fundacional): Notas para pensar la casa de Flores." Cazona de Flores. Accessed November 1, 2010. http://Cazonadeflores.blogspot.com.

Colectivo Situaciones and Simbiosis Cultural. 2011. *De chuequistas y overlockas: Una discusión entorno a los talleres textiles*. Buenos Aires: Editorial Retazos.

Coleman, Gabriella. 2012. *Coding Freedom: The Ethics and Aesthetics of Hacking*. Princeton: Princeton University Press.

Composto, Claudia, and Magalí Rabasa. 2011. "Entrevista con David Harvey: Nuevo imperialismo y cambio social, entre el despojo y la recuperación de los bienes comunes." Translated by Isabel Harland de Benito. *Herramienta*. Accessed January 18, 2012. www.herramienta.com.ar.

Crawford, Matthew. 2009. *Shop Class as Soulcraft: An Inquiry into the Value of Work*. New York: Penguin.

Dangl, Benjamin. 2010. Foreword to the English edition. In *Dispersing Power: Social Movements as Anti-State Forces*, by Raúl Zibechi, ix–xiii. Oakland: AK Press.

de Diego, José Luis. 2014. *Editores y políticas editoriales en Argentina, 1880–2010*. Buenos Aires: Fondo de Cultura Económica.

de Laet, Marianne, and Annemarie Mol. 2000. "The Zimbabwe Bush Pump: Mechanics of a Fluid Technology." *Social Studies of Science* 30, no. 2: 225–63. http://www.jstor.org/stable/285835.

Deleuze, Gilles, and Félix Guattari. 1987. *A Thousand Plateaus: Capitalism and Schizophrenia*. Minneapolis: University of Minnesota Press.

De Pósfay, Guillermo. 2005. *La furia del libro (genérico)*. Buenos Aires: Onda Encantada de Latinoamérica.

Dinerstein, Ana Cecilia. 2015. *The Politics of Autonomy in Latin America: The Art of Organising Hope*. New York: Palgrave Macmillan.

Dixon, Chris. 2014. *Another Politics: Talking across Today's Transformative Movements*. Oakland: University of California Press.

Dusollier, Severine. 2002. "Open Source and Copyleft: Authorship Reconsidered?" *Columbia Journal of Law and the Arts* 26, no. 3/4: 281–96.

Eisenstein, Elizabeth. 1979. *The Printing Press as an Agent of Change: Communications and Cultural Transformations in Early-Modern Europe*. Cambridge: Cambridge University Press.

El Asunto. 2012. *El Asunto: Cultura Independiente*. http://elasunto.com.ar.

Elia, Anthony J. 2008. "Beyond Barthes and Chartier: The Theology of Books in the Digital Age." *ATLA Summary of Proceedings*: 105–16. doi: 10.7916/D8GT5XQ4.

El Kilombo Intergaláctico. 2007. *Beyond Resistance: Everything, An Interview with Subcomandante Insurgente Marcos*. Durham: PaperBoat Press.

Eloísa Cartonera. 2009. "Manifesto: Eloísa Cartonera." In *Akademia Cartonera: A Primer of Latin American Cartonera Publishers*, edited by Ksenija Bilbija and Paloma Celis Carbajal, 46–53. Madison, WI: Parallel Press.

El Surco. 2012. "1 de Septiembre: Si tu te libras, yo me libro!" *El Surco: Periódico Mensual Anarquista*, August 22. Accessed December 18, 2012. http://periodico elsurco.wordpress.com.

Epplin, Craig. 2014. *Late Book Culture in Argentina*. New York: Bloomsbury.

Escobar, Arturo. 2001. "Culture Sits in Places: Reflections on Globalism and Subaltern Strategies of Localization." *Political Geography* 20, no. 2: 139–74. doi: 10.1016/S0962-6298(00)00064-0.

Escobar, Arturo. 2010. "Latin America at a Crossroads." *Cultural Studies* 24, no. 1: 1–65. doi: 10.1080/09502380903424208.

Esteva, Gustavo. 2010. "The Oaxaca Commune and Mexico's Coming Insurrection." *Antipode* 42, no. 4: 978–93. doi: 10.1111/j.1467-8330.2010.00784.x.

Esteva, Gustavo. 2011. "Otra autonomía, otra democracia." In *Pensar las autonomías*, edited by Jóvenes en Resistencia Alternativa, 121–47. Mexico City: Bajo Tierra Ediciones.

Esteva, Gustavo. 2014. "Las nuevas respuestas." *La Jornada* (Mexico City), January 6.

Estrada Vázquez, Juan Carlos. 2010. *No olvidamos! A cuatro años de la tragedia en Caballito*. Buenos Aires: Editorial Retazos.

EZLN (Ejército Zapatista de Liberación Nacional). 1994. "Declaración de la Selva Lacandona." Accessed October 25, 2012. http://palabra.ezln.org.mx.

EZLN (Ejército Zapatista de Liberación Nacional). 1996. "Comunicado del EZLN: 9 febrero 1996." Accessed October 25, 2012. http://palabra.ezln.org.mx.

EZLN (Ejército Zapatista de Liberación Nacional). 2005. "Sexta Declaración de la Selva Lacandona." Accessed October 25, 2012. http://enlacezapatista.ezln .org.mx.

EZLN (Ejército Zapatista de Liberación Nacional). 2008. "Comunicado del CCRI-CG del EZLN: Comisión Sexta-Comisión Intergaláctica del EZLN." Accessed October 25, 2012. http://enlacezapatista.ezln.org.mx.

Febvre, Lucien, and Henri-Jean Martin. 1997. *The Coming of the Book: The Impact of Printing, 1450–1800*. New York: Verso.

Ferguson, Kathy. 2014. "Anarchist Printers and Presses: Material Circuits of Politics." *Political Theory* 42, no. 4: 391–414. doi: 10.1177/0090591714531420.

FLIA. 2006. *Feria del Libro Independiente*. Buenos Aires: FLIA.

"FLIA Buenos Aires." Feria del Libro Independiente y Alternativo. Accessed September 24, 2018. http://feriadellibroindependiente.blogspot.com.

Foucault, Michel. 1998. *Aesthetics, Method, and Epistemology*. Translated by Robert Hurley and others. New York: New Press.

Gago, Verónica. 2017a. "Intelectuales, experiencia e investigación militante: Avatares de un vínculo tenso." *Nueva Sociedad* 268: 65–76. http://nuso.org.

Gago, Verónica. 2017b. "Intellectuals, Experiences, and Militant Investigation: Avatars of a Tense Relation." Translated by Liz Mason-Deese. *Viewpoint Magazine*, June 6. Accessed August 2, 2017. www.viewpointmag.com.

García Linera, Alvaro. 2009. *Forma valor y forma comunidad*. La Paz: Muela del Diablo.

Genette, Gérard. 1997. *Paratexts: Thresholds of Interpretation*. Cambridge: Cambridge University Press.

Gibson-Graham, J. K. 1996. *The End of Capitalism (As We Knew It): A Feminist Critique of Political Economy*. Minneapolis: University of Minnesota Press.

Gibson-Graham, J. K. 2002. "Beyond Global Vs. Local: Economic Politics outside the Binary Frame." In *Geographies of Power: Placing Scale*, edited by Andrew Herod and Melissa Wright, 25–60. Oxford: Blackwell.

Gibson-Graham, J. K. 2006. *A Postcapitalist Politics*. Minneapolis: University of Minnesota Press.

Gibson-Graham, J. K. 2008. "Diverse Economies: Performative Practices for 'Other Worlds.'" *Progress in Human Geography* 32, no. 5: 613–32. doi: 10.1177/0309132508090821.

Giunta, Andrea. 2009. *Poscrisis: Arte argentino después de 2001*. Buenos Aires: Siglo XXI.

Gómez, Luis, and Raquel Gutiérrez Aguilar. 2006. "Los múltiples significados del libro de Zibechi." In *Dispersar el poder: los movimientos como poderes antiestatales*, by Raúl Zibechi, 7–24. La Paz: Textos Rebeldes.

Gómez, Nahuel. 2011. "DistriBULLA: 'Nuestra idea es reinventar las formas de distribuir un libro.'" *Revista NaN*, August 1. Accessed January 18, 2012. http://agencianan.blogspot.com.

Gordillo, Gastón. 2014. *Rubble: The Afterlife of Destruction*. Durham: Duke University Press.

Gould, Corrina, Morning Star Gali, Krea Gomez, and Anita DeAsis. 2011. "Decolonize Oakland: Creating a More Radical Movement." Occupy Oakland. Accessed June 12, 2018. https://occupyoakland.org.

Gramsci, Antonio. 1971. *Selections from the Prison Notebooks*. Edited by Quintin Hoare and Geoffrey Nowell Smith. New York: International Publishers.

Griffin, Jane. 2016. *The Labor of Literature: Democracy and Literary Culture in Modern Chile*. Amherst: University of Massachusetts Press.

Grossberg, Lawrence. 2006. "Does Cultural Studies Have Futures? Should It? (Or What's the Matter with New York?)." *Cultural Studies* 20, no. 1: 1–32. doi: 10.1080/09502380500492541.

Grosfoguel, Ramón. 2013. "The Structure of Knowledge in Westernized Universities: Epistemic Racism/Sexism and the Four Genocides/Epistemicides of the Long 16th Century." *Human Architecture* 11, no. 1: 73–90. https://scholarworks.umb.edu.

Guha, Ranajit. 1988. "The Prose of Counter-Insurgency." In *Selected Subaltern Studies*, edited by Ranajit Guha and Gayatri Chakravorty Spivak, 51–86. New York: Oxford University Press.

Gutiérrez Aguilar, Raquel. 2006. *¡A desordenar! Por una historia abierta de la lucha social*. México, DF: Casa Juan Pablos.

Gutiérrez Aguilar, Raquel. 2008a. *¡A desordenar! Por una historia abierta de la lucha social*. La Paz: Textos Rebeldes.

Gutiérrez Aguilar, Raquel. 2008b. *Los ritmos del Pachakuti: Levantamiento y movilización en Bolivia (2000–2005)*. Buenos Aires: Tinta Limón.

Gutiérrez Aguilar, Raquel. 2008c. "A manera de Prólogo." In *Generación Post-alfa: Patologías e imaginarios en el semiocapitalismo*, by Franco Berardi Bifo, xi–xvii. Mexico City: Bajo Tierra Ediciones.

Gutiérrez Aguilar, Raquel. 2009. *Los ritmos del Pachakuti: Levantamiento y movilización en Bolivia (2000–2005)*. Mexico City: Bajo Tierra Ediciones.

Gutiérrez Aguilar, Raquel. 2011. "Carta abierta a los hombres y mujeres sensibles de este mundo." *Narco News Bulletin*, July 22. Accessed October 5, 2011. www.narconews.com.

Gutiérrez Aguilar, Raquel. 2014. *The Rhythms of Pachakuti: Indigenous Uprising and State Power in Bolivia*. Translated by Stacey Alba D. Skar. Durham: Duke University Press.

Hall, Gary. 2013. "The Unbound Book: Academic Publishing in the Age of the Infinite Archive." *Journal of Visual Culture* 12, no. 3: 490–507. doi: 10.1177/1470412913502032.

Hall, Stuart. 1992. "Cultural Studies and Its Theoretical Legacies." In *Cultural Studies*, edited by Lawrence Grossberg, Cary Nelson, and Paula A. Treichler, 277–94. New York: Routledge.

Hall, Stuart. 1996b. "Gramsci's Relevance for the Study of Race and Ethnicity." In *Stuart Hall: Critical Dialogues in Cultural Studies*, edited by David Morley and Kuan-Hsing Chen, 411–41. New York: Routledge.

Hall, Stuart. 1996c. "On Postmodernism and Articulation: An Interview with Stuart Hall." In *Stuart Hall: Critical Dialogues in Cultural Studies*, edited by David Morley and Kuan-Hsing Chen, 131–50. London: Routledge.

Harvey, David. 2005. *A Brief History of Neoliberalism*. New York: Oxford University Press.

Hayek, Friederich. 1976. *Road to Serfdom*. Chicago: University of Chicago Press.

Holdren, Nate, and Sebastian Touza. 2005. "Introduction to Colectivo Situaciones." *Ephemera: Theory and Politics in Organization* 5, no. 4: 595–601.

Holloway, John. 2002. *Change the World without Taking Power: The Meaning of Revolution Today*. New York: Pluto Press.

Holloway, John. 2010a. *Crack Capitalism*. New York: Pluto Press.

Holloway, John. 2010b. Foreword to the German edition. In *Dispersing Power: Social Movements as Anti-State Forces*, by Raúl Zibechi, xv–xvii. Oakland: AK Press.

Howsam, Leslie. 2006. *Old Books and New Histories: An Orientation to Studies in Book and Print Culture*. Toronto: University of Toronto Press.

Hudson, Juan Pablo. 2011. *Acá no, acá no me manda nadie: Empresas recuperadas por obreros 2000–2010*. Buenos Aires: Tinta Limón.

Hull, Matthew. 2003. "The File: Agency, Authority, and Autography in an Islamabad Bureaucracy." *Language and Communication* 23: 287–314.

Hutchins, Edwin. 1995. *Cognition in the Wild*. Cambridge: MIT Press.

Identity Project. 2011. "Mexico-Barcelona Flight Barred from Overflying the US." *Papers Please*, July 25. Accessed July 29, 2011. http://papersplease.org.

Ingold, Tim. 2007. *Lines: A Brief History*. New York: Routledge.

Johns, Adrian. 1998. *The Nature of the Book: Print and Knowledge in the Making*. Chicago: University of Chicago Press.

Johns, Adrian. 2009. *Piracy: The Intellectual Property Wars from Gutenberg to Gates*. Chicago: University of Chicago Press.

JRA (Jóvenes en Resistencia Alternativa). 2008. "Nota de bajo tierra ediciones." In *Generación Post-alfa: Patologías e imaginarios en el semiocapitalismo*, by Franco Berardi Bifo, ix–x. Mexico: Bajo Tierra.

JRA (Jóvenes en Resistencia Alternativa). 2011. *Pensar las autonomías: Alternativas de emancipación al capital y el estado*. Mexico City: Bajo Tierra Ediciones.

Juris, Jeffrey S. 2008. *Networking Futures: The Movements against Corporate Globalization*. Durham: Duke University Press.

Kelty, Christopher M. 2008. *Two Bits: The Cultural Significance of Free Software*. Durham: Duke University Press.

Kirschenbaum, Matthew G. 2008. *Mechanisms: New Media and the Forensic Imagination*. Cambridge: MIT Press.

Knox, Hannah, Mike Savage, and Penny Harvey. 2006. "Social Networks and the Study of Relations: Networks as Method, Metaphor, and Form." *Economy and Society* 35, no. 1: 113–40. doi: 10.1080/03085140500465899.

Korol, Claudia. 2006. *Caleidoscopio de rebeldías*. Buenos Aires: América Libre.

"La potencia del trabajo multiforme." 2011. Lobo Suelto. Accessed September 20, 2018. http://anarquiacoronada.blogspot.com.

Larrinaga, Tomás. 2010. *Los subterráneos: Visiones e historias sobre la F.L.I.(A)*. YouTube video, 39:39. July 10, 2011. Accessed September 26, 2018. youtube.com/watch?v=GTYwK9eZ3Uk.

"La Toma Centro Cultural." Facebook. Accessed September 21, 2018. www.facebook.com.

Latour, Bruno. 1996. *Aramis, or the Love of Technology*. Cambridge: Harvard University Press.

Latour, Bruno. 2011. "From Multiculturalism to Multinaturalism: What Rules of Method for the New Socio-Scientific Experiments?" *Nature and Culture* 6, no. 1: 1–17. doi: 10.3167/nc.2011.060101.

Lavaca. 2007a. *Sin Patrón: Fábricas y empresas recuperadas de la Argentina*. Buenos Aires: Lavaca Editora.

Lavaca. 2007b. *Sin Patrón: Stories from Argentina's Worker-Run Factories*. Chicago: Haymarket Books.

Law, John. 2004. *After Method: Mess in Social Science Research*. New York: Routledge.

Law, John. 2007. "Actor Network Theory and Material Semiotics." *Heterogeneities*, April 5. Accessed July 18, 2012. www.heterogeneities.net.

Law, John. 2016. "Modes of Knowing: Resources from the Baroque." In *Modes of Knowing*, edited by John Law and Evelyn Ruppert, 17–56. Manchester: Mattering Press.

Law, John, and Vicky Singleton. 2005. "Object Lessons." *Organization* 12, no. 3: 331–55. doi: 10.1177/1350508405051270.

Lazzara, Michael. 2006. *Chile in Transition: The Poetics and Politics of Memory*. Gainesville: University Press of Florida.

Lefebvre, Henri. 1991. *The Production of Space*. Translated by Donald Nicholson-Smith. Malden: Blackwell.

López Bárcenas, Francisco. 2010. *Autonomías indígenas en América Latina*. Buenos Aires: Editorial Tierra del Sur.

López Winne, Hernán, and Víctor Malumián. 2016. *Independientes, ¿de qué?* Mexico City: Fondo de Cultura Económica.

Lorde, Audre. 2007. "The Master's Tools Will Never Dismantle the Master's House." *Sister Outsider*. Berkeley: Crossing Press.

Lugones, María. 2008. "Colonialidad y género." *Tabula Rasa* 9: 73–101. www.redalyc.org.

Malatesta, Errico. 2010. *En el café*. Buenos Aires: La E del Coihue Infinito.

Mamani Ramirez, Pablo. 2004. *El rugir de las multitudes: La fuerza de los levantamientos indígenas en Bolivia/Qullasuyu*. La Paz: Aruwiyiri-Yachaywasi.

Mamani Ramirez, Pablo. 2005. *Microgobiernos barriales: Levantamiento de la ciudad de El Alto (October 2003)*. El Alto: IDIA/UMSA-CADES.

Marcus, George E. 1995. "Ethnography in/of the World System: The Emergence of Multi-Sited Ethnography." *Annual Review of Anthropology* 24: 95–117. www.jstor.org/stable/2155931.

Marres, Noortje, and Javier Lezaun. 2011. "Materials and Devices of the Public: An Introduction." *Economy and Society* 40, no. 4: 489–509. doi: 10.1080/03085147.2011.602293.

Marx, Karl. 1993. *Grundrisse: Foundations of the Critique of Political Economy*. Translated by Martin Nicolaus. New York: Penguin Classics.

Mason-Deese, Liz. 2012. "The Neighborhood Is the New Factory." *Viewpoint Magazine* 2. http://viewpointmag.com.

Massey, Doreen. 2004. "Geographies of Responsibility." *Geografiska Annaler* 86, no. 1: 5–18. www.jstor.org/stable/3554456.

McKay, Iain, ed. 2011. *Property Is Theft! A Pierre-Joseph Proudhon Anthology*. Oakland: AK Press.

Mignolo, Walter. 1994. "Signs and Their Transmission: The Question of the Book in the New World." In *Writing without Words: Alternative Literacies in Meso-america and the Andes*, edited by Elizabeth Hill Boone and Walter Mignolo, 220–70. Durham: Duke University Press.

Mignolo, Walter. 2005. *The Idea of Latin America*. Malden: Blackwell.

Miller, Daniel. 1995. "Consumption and Commodities." *Annual Review of Anthropology* 24: 141–61. doi: 10.1146/annurev.an.24.100195.001041.

Miller, Laura. 2007. *Reluctant Capitalists: Bookselling and the Culture of Consumption*. Chicago: University of Chicago Press.

Mills, C. Wright. 1959. *The Sociological Imagination*. New York: Oxford University Press.

Mitchell, Timothy. 1998. "Fixing the Economy." *Cultural Studies* 12, no. 1: 82–101. doi: 10.1080/095023898335627.

Mol, Annemarie. 2002. *The Body Multiple: Ontology in Medical Practice*. Durham: Duke University Press.

Mora, Mariana. 2003. "The Imagination to Listen: Reflections on a Decade of Zapatista Struggle." *Social Justice* 30, no. 3: 17–31. www.jstor.org/stable/29768206.

Mora, Mariana. 2007. "Zapatista Anticapitalist Politics and the 'Other Campaign': Learning from the Struggle for Indigenous Rights and Autonomy." *Latin American Perspectives* 34, no. 2: 64–77. doi: 10.1177/0094582X06299086.

Morales Ayma, Evo. 2006. *Primer discurso como presidente del país*. Accessed January 18, 2011. http://ukhamawa.blogdiario.com.

Muñoz Ramírez, Gloria. 2003. *20 y 10: El fuego y la palabra*. Mexico City: La Jornada Ediciones.

Multiforo Alicia. 2008. "Multiforo Alicia: Laboratorio de culturas subterráneas y movimientos aleatarios." Accessed September 20, 2018. http://elchauhistle.blogspot.com.

Navarro Trujillo, Mina Lorena. 2016. *Hacer común contra la fragmentación en la ciudad: Experiencias de autonomía urbana*. Puebla: Instituto de Ciencias Sociales y Humanidades "Alfonso Vélez Pliego."

Notes from Nowhere, ed. 2003. *We Are Everywhere: The Irresistible Rise of Global Anticapitalism*. London: Verso.

Olivera, Oscar, Marcelo Rojas, Abraham Grandydier, Aniceto Hinojosa Vasquez, and Carlos Oropeza. 2010. "Carta pública a Evo Morales y Álvaro García, Contra el Gasolinazo y por el autogobierno de nuestro pueblo: Primero está la gente, no los números, ni las cifras." *Narco News Bulletin*. Accessed January 18, 2011. www.narconews.com.

Osterweil, Michal. 2005. "Place-Based Globalism: Theorizing the Global Justice Movement." *Development* 48, no. 2: 23–28. doi: 10.1057/palgrave.development.1100132.

Osterweil, Michal. 2010. "Italy's 'Movimento Dei Movimenti,' Theoretical-Practice and Re-making the Political." PhD diss., University of North Carolina, Chapel Hill.

Pacheco, Mariano. 2010. *De Cutral-Có a Puente Pueyrredón: Genealogía de los Movimientos de Trabajadores Desocupados*. Buenos Aires: El Colectivo/Desde El Subte.

Paul, Carlos. 2010. "La feria de libros confirmó 'que la gente lee si los libros son baratos.'" *La Jornada* (Mexico City), October 11.

Prada, Raúl. 2012. "Breve descripción de Comuna." *Bolpress*. Accessed September 20, 2013. www.bolpress.com.

"¿Qué es la FLIA?." 2015. Feria del Libro Independiente y Alternativa. Accessed October 15. http://feriadellibroindependiente.blogspot.com.

Quijano, Aníbal. 1999. "Colonialidad del poder, cultura y conocimiento en América Latina." *Dispositio/n* 24, no. 51: 137–48. www.jstor.org/stable/41491587.

Quijano, Aníbal. 2000. "Coloniality of Power, Eurocentrism, and Latin America." *Nepantla: Views from South* 1, no. 3: 533–77.

Rabasa, Magalí. 2011. "'Lo más importante es abrir espacios en común para expresarnos, intercambiar y crear algo. . . ': Entrevista con el pensador y activista uruguayo Raúl Zibechi." *Rebelión*. Accessed October 15, 2011. www.rebelion .org.

Rabasa, Magalí. 2017. "Movement in Print: Migrations and Political Articulations in Grassroots Publishing." *Journal of Latin American Cultural Studies* 26, no. 1: 31–50. doi: 10.1080/13569325.2016.1272445.

Rama, Ángel. 1984. *La ciudad letrada*. Hanover: Ediciones del Norte.

Rama, Ángel. 1996. *The Lettered City*. Translated by John Charles Chasteen. Durham: Duke University Press.

Restrepo, Eduardo. 2014. "Estudios culturales en América Latina." *Revista de Estudos Culturais* 1. www.revistas.usp.br.

Riles, Annelise. 2001. *The Network Inside Out*. Ann Arbor: University of Michigan Press.

Riles, Annelise, ed. 2006. *Documents: Artifacts of Modern Knowledge*. Ann Arbor: University of Michigan Press.

Rivera Cusicanqui, Silvia. 2010a. *Ch'ixinakax utxiwa: Una reflexión sobre prácticas y discursos descolonizadores*. Buenos Aires: Tinta Limón.

Rivera Cusicanqui, Silvia. 2010b. *Ch'ixinakax utxiwa: Una reflexión sobre prácticas y discursos descolonizadores*. Buenos Aires: Editorial Retazos.

Rivera Cusicanqui, Silvia. 2012. "Ch'ixinakax utxiwa: A Reflection on the Practices and Discourses of Decolonization." *South Atlantic Quarterly* 111, no. 1: 95–108. doi: 10.1215/00382876-1472612.

Rodgers, Dennis, Jo Beall, and Ravi Kanbur. 2012. "Re-Thinking the Latin American City." In *Latin American Urban Development into the Twenty First Century*, edited by Dennis Rodgers, Jo Beall, and Ravi Kanbur, 3–33. London: Palgrave Macmillan UK.

Rodríguez, Ana Mónica. 2010. "Propiciaremos una batalla contra la literatura chatarra." *La Jornada* (Mexico City), October 5.

Rose, Jonathan. 2003. "The Horizon of a New Discipline: Inventing Book Studies." *Publishing Research Quarterly* 19, no. 1: 11–19. doi: 10.1007/s12109-003-0019-1.

Rose, Mark. 1993. *Authors and Owners: The Invention of Copyright.* Cambridge: Harvard University Press.

Rovira, Guiomar. 2009. *Zapatistas sin fronteras: Las redes de solidaridad con Chiapas y el altermundismo.* Mexico City: Ediciones ERA.

Rovira, Guiomar. 2017. *Activismo en red y multitudes conectadas: Comunicación y acción en la era de internet.* Barcelona: Icaria.

Salazar Embarcadero, Juan José. 2011. *Leer o no leer: Libros, lectores y lectura en México.* Atlautla: CELTA Amaquemecan.

Santos, Boaventura de Sousa. 2006. *The Rise of the Global Left: The World Social Forums and Beyond.* New York: Zed Books.

Schwartz, Marcy. 2011. "The Right to Imagine: Reading in Community with People and Stories/Gente y cuentos." *PMLA* 126, no. 3: 746–52. www.jstor.org/stable/41414148.

Schwartz, Marcy. 2014. "Spaces for Reading: A Cartography of Used Books in Urban Latin America." *Journal of Urban Cultural Studies* 1, no. 3: 417–42. doi: 10.1386/jucs.1.3.417_1.

Schwartz, Marcy. 2016. "Reading on Wheels: Stories of *Convivencia* in the Latin American City." *Latin American Research Review* 51, no. 3: 181–201. doi: 10.1353/lar.2016.0040.

Schwartz, Marcy. 2018. *Public Pages: Reading along the Latin American Streetscape.* Austin: University of Texas Press.

Sennett, Richard. 2008. *The Craftsman.* New Haven: Yale University Press.

Shukaitis, Stevphen, and David Graeber. 2007. *Constituent Imagination: Militant Investigations, Collective Theorization.* Oakland: AK Press.

Sitrin, Marina. 2005. *Horizontalidad: Voces de poder popular en Argentina.* Buenos Aires: Cooperativa Chilavert Artes Gráficas.

Stallman, Richard. 2002. *Free Software, Free Society.* Boston: GNU Press.

Stallman, Richard, Wu Ming, César Ruendeles, and Kembrew McLeod. 2008. *Contra el copyright.* México: Tumbona.

Stallman, Richard, Wu Ming, César Ruendeles, and Kembrew McLeod. n.d. *Contra el copyright.* Resistencia: Cospel Ediciones.

Stern, Steve. 2010. *Reckoning with Pinochet: The Memory Question in Democratic Chile.* Durham: Duke University Press.

Strathern, Marilyn. 2004. *Partial Connections.* Walnut Creek: AltaMira Press.

Striphas, Ted. 2009. *The Late Age of Print: Everyday Book Culture from Consumerism to Control*. New York: Columbia University Press.

Subercaseaux, Bernardo. 2000. *Historia del libro en Chile*. Santiago: Editorial LOM.

Szpilbarg, Daniela. 2015. "Escrituras permeables: La autogestión editorial en la literatura." *Cuadernos LIRICO* 13. doi: 10.4000/lirico.2098.

Taller Hacer Ciudad. 2011. *Vecinocracia*. Buenos Aires: Editorial Retazos.

Tapia, Luis. 2002. "Movimientos sociales, movimiento societal y los no lugares de la política." In *Democratizaciones plebeyas*, edited by Raquel Gutiérrez et al., 25–72. La Paz: Muela del Diablo.

Tapia, Luis. 2008. *Política Salvaje*. La Paz: Muela del Diablo.

Thoburn, Nicholas. 2016. *Anti-Book: On the Art and Politics of Radical Publishing*. Minneapolis: University of Minnesota Press.

Thomson, Sinclair. 2014. "Foreword: Beyond the Old Order of Things." In *The Rhythms of Pachakuti: Indigenous Uprising and State Power in Bolivia*, by Raquel Gutiérrez Aguilar, ix–xiii. Durham: Duke University Press.

Thwaites Rey, Mabel. 2010. "La autonomía: entre el mito y la potencia emancipadora." In *Pensar las autonomías: Alternativas de emancipación al capital y el estado*, edited by Jóvenes en Resistencia Alternativa, 151–214. Mexico City: Bajo Tierra Ediciones.

Tinta Limón Ediciones. Accessed September 21, 2018. http://tintalimon.com.ar.

Vanoli, Hernán. 2010. "Sobre editoriales literarias y la reconfiguración de una cultura." *Nueva Sociedad* 230: 129–51. http://nuso.org.

Vázquez, Sebastián. 2010. "Traficando Futuro: cultura libre y comunicación alternativa." In *Argentina Copyleft: la crisis del modelo de derecho de autor y las prácticas para democratizar la cultura*, edited by Beatriz Busaniche, 159–64. Buenos Aires: Fundación Vía Libre.

Vega Camacho, Oscar. 2011. *Errancias: Aperturas para vivir bien*. La Paz: Muela del Diablo.

Vieta, Marcelo. 2010. "The New Cooperativism." *Affinities: A Journal of Radical Theory, Culture, and Action* 4, no. 1: 1–11. https://ojs.library.queensu.ca.

Vieta, Marcelo. 2014. "The Stream of Self-Determination and *Autogestión*: Prefiguring Alternative Economic Realities." *Ephemera: Theory and Politics in Organization* 14, no. 4: 781–809. www.ephemerajournal.org.

Viveiros de Castro, Eduardo. 2008. *La mirada del jaguar: Introducción al perspectivismo amerindio*. Buenos Aires: Tinta Limón.

Williams, Raymond. 1983. *Keywords*. Oxford: Oxford University Press.

Winik, Marilina. 2010. "Ediciones copyleft." In *Argentina Copyleft: la crisis del modelo de derecho de autor y las prácticas para democratizar la cultura*, edited by Beatriz Busaniche, 143–50. Buenos Aires: Fundación Vía Libre.

Zibechi, Raúl. 2000. *La mirada horizontal*. Quito: Ediciones Abya-Yala.

Zibechi, Raúl. 2006. *Dispersar el poder: Los movimientos como poderes antiestatales*. La Paz: Textos Rebeldes.

Zibechi, Raúl. 2007a. *Autonomías y emancipaciones: América Latina en movimiento*. Lima: Programa Democracia y Transformación Global.

Zibechi, Raúl. 2007b. *Dispersar el poder*. Guadalajara: Casa del Mago.

Zibechi, Raúl. 2008a. *América Latina: Periferias urbanas, territorios en resistencia*. Bogotá: Ediciones Desde Abajo.

Zibechi, Raúl. 2008b. *Autonomías y emancipaciones: América Latina en movimiento*. Mexico, DF: Bajo Tierra Ediciones.

Zibechi, Raúl. 2009. *Territorios en Resistencia*. La Paz: Textos Rebeldes.

Zibechi, Raúl. 2010. *Dispersing Power: Social Movements as Anti-State Forces*. Translated by Ramor Ryan. Oakland: AK Press.

Zibechi, Raúl. 2011a. "Bolivia: Después de la tormenta." Americas Program. Accessed January 25, 2012. www.cipamericas.org.

Zibechi, Raúl. 2011b. *Dispersar el poder: Los movimientos como poderes antiestatales*. 2nd ed. Santiago: Quimantú.

Zibechi, Raúl. 2012. *Territories in Resistance: A Cartography of Latin American Social Movements*. Translated by Ramor Ryan. Oakland: AK Press.

INDEX

anarchism: and Argentina, 159, 187n21; and *autogestión*, 179n19; and autonomy, 42; and book fairs, 169–70; and the FLIA, 160; and Latin America, 15, 159; and the organic book, 15; and the United States, 170

anticapitalist: approaches to book production, 62; and autonomous politics, 24, 57; ethic, 75; organizing, 122; practices, 14; wild politics as, 71

Argentina, 28, 50–55, 72–97, 102–9; and "2001," 28, 65, 77, 91, 111, 123, 158–59, 165; and the Kirchner government, 28

articulation: as de-centering, 124; grassroots forms of, 16; medium of, 15; spaces and forms of, 15; and Stuart Hall, 8; transversal, 28, 99

artisan, 63, 71; bookbinding, 84, 85; press, 93. *See also* craft

assembly, 28–29, 89, 105, 150, 158, 165–66

authorship: and the author, 36, 101, 120; and the division of labor, 36, 63; and intellectual production, 36; and the modern book, 14; and property relations, 88, 101. *See also* intellectual property; organic book

autogestión, 16, 42, 65, 83 179n18; and student protests, 27; mentioned, 122, 152

autonomy, 23, 25, 34, 40–43, 57, 62,

64, 77, 175; and alterity, 43; editorial, 120–21, 129, 149; as experimentation, 42; urban, 145

Bell, Lucy, 65, 133
Benjamin, Walter, 13, 36
Berardi, Franco "Bifo," 121–23
Bolivia, 26, 45–48, 61, 66–71, 117, 129, 184n6; and migration, 61, 90–91, 95, 182n1

book: as double, 10; and the editor, 124–25; as fluid object 7, 89, 97, 125; "generic," 60, 71, 99; independent, 161–62; modern, 13–14; as "mutable mobile," 89; as network, 124–25; "proper," 13; as relations 8–9, 13, 32, 39, 100, 116; and technological determinism, 63; as tool of autonomous political-economic praxis, 16, 56; as "unbound," 99; and "worlds of work," 42. *See also* organic book

book fair(s), 133–34; alternative, 137–38, 140, 141, 143; Feria del Libro Independiente de Oaxaca (FILO, Oaxaca Independent Book Fair), 110; Feria de Libro Independiente y Alternativa (FLIA, Independent and Alternative Book Fair), 82, 102–5, 156–68, 175; Feria del Libro de El Alto, 141; Feria del Libro Popular Latinoamericano (América LeAtina Desde Abajo), 154–55;

ethnography: multi-sited, 21; as networked, 28; object-oriented, 9, 20,
24, 29
experimentation, 62, 66, 68–69, 80, 89,
95, 149, 175; versus model, 71; and
"new cooperativism," 76, 79; and
provisoriedad continua (continuous
provisionality), 63–64, 95; *trabajo
multiforme* (multiform work) as,
95. *See also* autonomy; craft
Epplin, Craig, 16, 19, 20
Escobar, Arturo, 135–36, 185n3, 188n1
Esteva, Gustavo, 23, 34, 43
Estrada Vazquez, Juan Carlos, 91, 94
Ejército Zapatista de Liberación
Nacional (EZLN), 6, 23, 25, 26, 29,
133, 145, 188n31

feminist: ethics, 52; political economists, 63; politics of translation,
185n9; spatiality, 135; theorists, 13
Foucault, Michel, 14, 36, 101
free software, 81, 86, 98, 112

García Linera, Álvaro, 10–11, 178n12
Gibson-Graham, J.K., 64, 135–36, 150
Gramsci, Antonio, 12–13, 55, 61; traditional versus organic intellectuals,
12, 55–56, 61, 172; and organic ideology, 13; and philosophy of praxis,
13; and Subaltern Studies, 180n23
Guadalajara, 133, 185n1
Gutiérrez Aguilar, Raquel, 10–12, 34,
48, 109, 117, 120, 122, 171, 178n12

Hall, Stuart, 8, 13, 20, 22
Holloway, John, 34, 37, 64, 170, 181n2
horizontality, 29, 37, 58, 73, 99, 150;
and Chilean social movements, 27;
and dialogical relations, 44; and
Zapatistas, 12

imperialism: intellectual, 5–6; of US
academy, 188n1
Industrias Metalúrgicas y Plásticas
Argentina (IMPA), 52–54
informal: commerce, 139; distribution
networks, 100; markets, 136, 145;
networks, 124; sector, 165; and
tianguis, 185n7
Ingold, Tim, 63
intellectual labor, 56
intellectual property: and the book as
commodity, 88; and bureaucracy,
118; and copyleft, 80, 87, 106, 109,
116; and copyright, 69–70, 73, 86,
88, 101, 106, 109–13, 117, 120, 131;
Creative Commons, 106, 116, 118,
119, 131; and *cultura libre* (free culture), 80, 108, 112, 183n12; *depósito
legal* (legal deposit), 70, 107; and
disorder, 109, 120; and "fake" copyright, 107–8; versus functionality,
70; and information, 107, 184n2;
and organic IP, 101, 108, 112–13, 120,
132; and piracy, 70, 101–2, 116; and
"productive freedom," 112

Johns, Adrian, 7, 9, 20, 79, 100–102
Jóvenes en Resistencia Alternativa
(JRA), 25, 40, 57, 121–30, 181n26,
181n3; and Bajo Tierra Ediciones,
40; and the university, 41, 44; and
Zapatista solidarity, 40–41

knowledge: and academic institutions,
44, 171–73; antistate, 58; autonomous, 52, 55; and *autonomous
knowledge practices*, 38, 41, 50,
55, 58; and the circulation of, 61,
112, 170; and collective knowledge
practices, 55, 57, 95, 122, 134;

knowledge (*cont.*): and "common sense," 55; and "epistemological earthquake," 45; Eurocentric, 47; and the isolated intellectual, 55; as *knowledge-as-doing*, 38, 57; and "negation and other-doing," 37; and South-North flows, 170–73; political economy of, 115, 173–74; and the production of history, 49; and subject-object dichotomy, 47; and the thought/action binary, 38

Korol, Claudia, 50–56

La Paz, 61, 66, 141–44

Librería Proyección, 151–53, 187n21

Lima, 130

Madres de la Plaza de Mayo, 53; and the Fundación Madres de la Plaza de Mayo, 53, 54

Mamani Ramírez, Pablo, 67, 143

map(s): of books, 4; as description and articulation, 15; library as, 67; as made of relations, 53, 116; as multidimensional connections, 8, 20; and a topography of print, 20

Marx, Karl, 10, 38, 62, 64

marxism, 42, 51

Mason-Deese, Liz, 167

materiality, 127–28; of autonomous politics, 18; of books, 66, 93, 95; and book studies, 20; and Gramsci, 12–13; and knowledge practices, 17–18; of networks, 4, 136; and politics, 87; variations in, 113; mentioned, 66, 87, 93, 95, 97, 116, 144, 176

media: digital vs. face-to-face communication, 6–7; Indymedia, 6; and Zapatismo 6

medios libres (independent or free media), 6

Mexico, 10, 24–25, 111, 121, 139–40; and the Partido Revolucionario Democrático (PRD), 137, 185n6

Mexico City, 22, 41, 42, 144–46

migration. *See* Bolivia: migration

movement(s): alterglobalization, 121, 177n7; autonomous, 4, 5; *cartonero*, 65, 182n3; indigenous, 22–23; and intellectuals, 55; "old," 33; and political theory, 4, 45; La Revolución de los Pingüinos (Penguin Revolution), 150, 153; social vs. societal, 7–8, 119. *See also medios libres*

Movimento Sem Terra, 52–54; and the Florestán Fernández Popular Education Center, 53–54

Movimiento Popular La Dignidad, 53, 165, 167

Movimiento de Trabajadores Desocupados (MTD), 167

Mol, Annemarie, 38

Mora, Mariana, 177n9

Morales, Evo, 26–27, 129

Multiforo Alicia, 3; and Zapatismo, 177n2

mutual aid, 5, 75, 76, 78

Navarro Trujillo, Mina, 145, 181n26, 181n3

neoliberalism, 32, 66; and Chile, 147–49; and the state, 34–35; challenges to, 46; mentioned, 128, 134, 147, 156

networks, 123–24; created through *encuentro*, 135, 166; and the "dispersing social machine," 69, 71; and ethnography, 28; grassroots, 25, 180n24; materiality of, 4, 136–37, 166; and *medios libres* 6, 180n24; online activist, 99, 179n16; and place-based politics, 135;

transnational and transversal, 99, 124, 175; and the unbounded book, 100, 124; "wild," 136, 153, 185n4

organic, 12–13; and ideology, 13
organic book, 10, 13, 88, 98,100, 170, 174, 175; and anarchist ethic, 15; and authorship, 36, 48, 55; and authorial intent, 36; and autonomous knowledge practices, 39, 56, 58; as autonomous object, 14; and autonomous politics, 46, 57; and the "book workshop," 62, 66, 76, 82, 93; and digital technology, 99, 118–19; and distributive production, 98, 128, 132; and the division of labor, 63, 72, 74–75, 96; and *encuentro*, 135–39; as experiment, 45, 86, 89, 97, 101; and horizontality, 58, 72, 99, 150; and intellectual property practices, 100–102; as "machine," 14, 39; and marketing, 136–37, 146; vs. the modern and colonial book, 14; as multiple, 50, 95, 99, 129, 131–32, 167; as *networking book*, 135; and networks of distribution, 133–34; and "new economic imaginaries," 64; as organic object 14, 32, 46, 49, 57, 61, 128; and popular education, 52; and production relations, 13, 74–75, 79; and space-making, 134–35, 140, 146; as "thing-in-motion," 179n14; as unbounded, 100, 102, 119–20, 131–32; as *underground*, 18; and use-value, 61, 71, 80, 96
Osterweil, Michal, 135

Pañuelos en Rebeldía, 53–54
paratexts, 49–50, 102, 129

patriarchal: and antipatriarchal practices, 14; dynamics, 36; order, 102; structure of the state, 35
piracy, 68, 70, 76, 101–2; and the tools of, 76
place-based, 135, 166
politics: anticapitalist, 57; autonomous, 5, 15, 23, 59, 140; and the division of political labor, 54; of encuentro, 136, 180n24; and "inquietud de hacer algo," 92; and place, 140; prefigurative, 5, 23, 52, 177n9; and the reclamation of public space, 153–55, 158, 165–68; state, 24; wild, 23–24, 57, 71, 98
popular education, 52–54, 56, 121; and anarchism, 15; and emancipatory pedagogy, 52, 54–55, 58; and solidarity, 50, 52–53, 55, 58. *See also* solidarity
power: "anti-state," 34–35; dispersion of, 46, 50, 119; multiform, 95; *poder sobre* (power-over) vs *poder hacer* (power-to), 34, 184n19; and social cooperation, 119; state conception of, 47, 50
practice(s): autonomous, 23, 42; of autonomous movements, 5; and the analysis of concepts,10, 29; book marketing and distribution as space-making, 134; cooperate vs. cooperative, 76; and Gramsci, 12; material, 4; and the practical book, 71; of *política salvaje* (wild politics), 71. *See also* knowledge; organic book
press(es): AK Press, 170, 171; América Libre, 50–51, 54; Asociación de Representantes de Editoriales de El Alto (AREA), 141; El Asunto, 164;

talleres textiles (textile workshops), 90–91

Tapia, Luis, 8, 23, 35, 57, 71, 98 178n11

Thoburn, Nicholas, 63

Thomson, Sinclair, 172, 188n1

Thwaites Rey, Mabel, 65

tianguis, 138, 139, 145–46; and *encuentro*, 145–46, 168

translation, 113, 128, 171, 185n9; between traditions, 12; material and aesthetic, 127–28, 132; political, 49, 129. *See also* feminist

Universidad de la Tierra-Oaxaca, 43, 182n6

urban spatiality: and El Alto, 46–47

Villegas, Aldo (Bocafloja), 4

wild politics (*política salvaje*). *See* anticapitalist: wild politics as; practice(s): of *política salvaje*

Williams, Raymond, 12–13, 63

Winik, Marilina, 166, 168

Zapatistas, 23, 33–34, 52, 144–46, 168, 178n10, 188n31; and digital technologies, 5; and Mexico City, 186n14; and the Other Campaign, 121, 144; and the Primer Festival Global de la Digna Rabia, 144–46; and Sexta declaración de la Selva Lacandona, 25–26, 144, 146, 181n27; and the San Andrés Accords, 43; and solidarity campaigns, 40–41. *See also* Ejército Zapatista de Liberación Nacional

Zapatismo, 26, 105, 121; and *encuentro*, 136; and the principle of autonomy, 42–43; mentioned, 185n8

Zibechi, Raúl, 7–8, 33–35, 39, 45–50, 66, 69, 119, 130–31, 170

zine(s), 9, 106, 151, 169, 175